Riding CENTRAL OREGON *Horse Trails*

Expanded and Updated

By Kim McCarrel

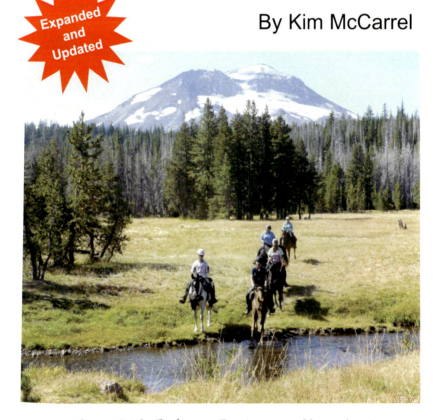

Over 150 Trails to Explore on Horseback
14 Horse Camps
Over 1,800 Miles of Trails

Ponderosa Press
Bend, Oregon

Riding Central Oregon Horse Trails
1st Edition 2005
2nd Edition 2012

ON THE COVER:
South Sister from Park Meadow

AT RIGHT:
Indian Prairie Trail, Ochoco Mountains

Published by

Ponderosa Press

64495 Old Bend Redmond Hwy., Bend, OR 97701
www.OregonHorseTrails.com
Copyright 2012
ISBN 978-0-9826770-2-5

Safety Notice: Every effort has been made to ensure that the information in this guidebook is as accurate as possible at press time. However, horseback riding is an inherently dangerous activity, and you are responsible for your own safety on the trails. Ponderosa Press and the author are not responsible for any loss, damage, or injury that may occur to anyone using this book. The information contained in this guidebook cannot replace good judgment. The fact that a trail is described in this book does not mean it will be safe for you. Trail conditions can change from day to day, so always check local conditions and know your own limitations.

Do not go where the path may lead; go instead where there is no path, and leave a trail.

Ralph Waldo Emerson

4

Contents

Contents **4**
  Area Map 10
  Saddlebag Savvy 13
  Certified Feed Required 15
  Leave No Trace Principles 16
  Wilderness Riding 18
  Best Maps 19

Bandit Springs **21**
  Corral Flat Primitive Camping 23
  Coyle Butte Loop 24
  Indian Prairie 26
  Old Stock Road Loop 28
  Walton Lake 30

Bend Area **33**
  Deschutes River 36
  Horse Ridge East 38
  Horse Ridge West 40
  Juniper Woodlands 42
  Mayfield Pond Recreation Area 44
  Rickard Road Area 46

Black Butte **49**
  Graham Corral .51
  Fourmile Butte .52
  Glaze Meadow .54
  Gobblers Knob .56
  Green Ridge 58
  Metolius River .60
  Sisters 62
  Sisters Cow Camp 64
  Skylight Cave 66
  Upper Butte Loop 68

6

8

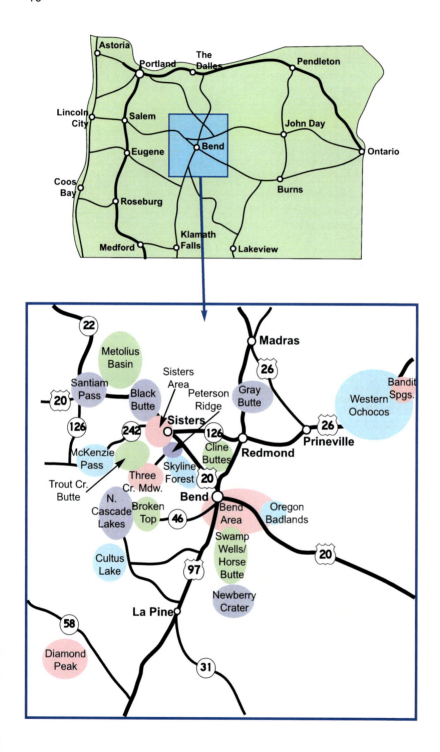

Foreword

So much has changed for Central Oregon equestrians since *Riding Central Oregon Horse Trails* was first published in 2005. We have new trails to enjoy at Peterson Ridge, the Oregon Badlands, Horse Ridge, Skyline Forest, and Swamp Wells/Horse Butte. The Cline Buttes recreation plan is beginning to be implemented. And the trails burned by the B&B fire look very different today than they did in 2005. The time has definitely come for a second edition.

Like the other Oregon Horse Trails books, the purpose of this book is to provide the information you need to decide whether a particular trail is right for you: what the terrain is like, how difficult the ride is, how to find the trailhead, and what facilities you will find when you get there. We hope this book encourages you to try out some trails you haven't ridden yet.

The information provided here is as accurate as possible as of our publication date. But of course, conditions change over time so we've also included information on how to contact local land managers for updated conditions.

See you on the trails!

Acknowledgements

This book could not have been written without the help and support of many others.

My wonderful husband, Steve, never complained once about how often I went riding and camping or how many hours I spent in front of my computer screen while dinner went uncooked.

Many people at the Forest Service and BLM reviewed the book and gave me excellent feedback. Special thanks are owed to Marv Lang, John Schubert, Kirk Flannigan, Kit Dickey, Cathy Lund, and Robert Gentry at the Forest Service, and Gavin Hoban and Greg Currie at the BLM.

Linda Nolte provided valuable editing and proofreading assistance, and kept me from using the same superlatives over and over to describe the beautiful places we ride in Central Oregon

My riding buddies provided companionship on the trails, ideas and feedback on the book, and corrections every time I said "left" when I should have said "right" (which unfortunately happened quite a lot). They are: Lydia Hemsley, Debbie Withrow, Whitney Rhetts, Linda Nolte, Connie Thornton, Diana Pyle, and Teresa Healer. You couldn't ask for friends who are more fun to ride with.

While researching this book I had the pleasure of riding with a number of delightful people that I don't get to ride with very often, including Dottie Ashley, Eli Ashley, Michal Bailey, Donita Elbert, Mark Freedlun, Janice Hade, Lee Haverland, Suzanne Heskett, Kenna Hoyser, Veronica Hudson, Don Jimerson, Gerry Jimerson, Suzi Lewis, Rhonda Marquis, Ann Maudlin, Pat Melchiori, Gillian Ochner, Nancy Ring, Mona Steinberg, Ray Thornton, and Donna Timmerman. Their presence added immensely to the fun of researching all these trails.

Finally, my mares, Jane and Tex, carried me literally thousands of miles over the wonderful trails of Central Oregon. Without their tireless efforts, this book could not have been written.

Kim McCarrel

Saddlebag Savvy

The difference between a great ride and a lousy one, or between a mild misadventure and a disaster, may hinge upon whether you brought along the proper gear. Even on a short ride, it's a good idea to carry the "Ten Essentials" for survival, and know how to use them.

1. Navigation: Always carry a map of the area you'll be riding, even if you know the trail. Carry a compass and/or GPS and know how to use it. And of course, extra batteries for the GPS are a must. The best maps for the Central Oregon area are the Central Oregon Hiking-Trail Map produced by Adventure Maps (www.adventuremaps.net), the wilderness maps for the Three Sisters, Mt. Washington, Mt. Jefferson, and Diamond Peak Wildernesses, and the fire maps for the Bend-Ft. Rock, Sisters, and Prineville Ranger Districts. These maps are all available from REI and Bend Mapping and Blueprint, and all but the Adventure Maps are available from any Forest Service office. See the "Best Maps" discussion later in this chapter.

2. Water: You can live for weeks without food, but only a few days without water. Carry extra water, along with water purification tablets just in case.

3. Extra Clothing: Always bring one more layer of clothing than you think you'll need. Rain gear, a hat, and gloves are the most important items, and an extra fleece jacket is a good idea. Extra packets of hand and toe warmers are easy to carry, and an emergency space blanket takes up little room but you'll be glad you have it if you have to spend a night on the trail.

4. Food: Bring along food for one more meal than you think you'll need. Trail mix, energy bars, dried fruit, and other snacks are good items to have on hand. A neat trick is to keep a can of tuna in your saddle bag. You won't be tempted to snack on it during a normal ride and it will keep forever, so if an emergency occurs and you need it, it will be there.

5. Light: If you have to spend the night on the trail, you'll be glad to have a flashlight and extra batteries on hand. A flashlight also comes in handy for signaling. Don't store the flashlight with the batteries inside, in case the flashlight gets accidentally switched on and drains the batteries. A headlamp is nice for keeping your hands free.

6. **Fire:** Waterproof matches and a fire starter like a candle stub can make a night stranded on the mountain a lot more comfortable.

7. **Sun Protection:** Sunglasses and extra sunscreen may not seem like survival essentials, but the lack of them can sure make your trip less enjoyable. Sunscreen needs to be reapplied occasionally for optimal effectiveness, so bring some extra along.

8. **First Aid:** Any Scout worth his or her salt knows you should carry a first aid kit. Equestrians should carry first aid items for people (bandaids, insect repellent, insect bite cream, antibiotic ointment, gauze pads, adhesive tape, a needle for removing splinters, ace bandage, small scissors, personal prescriptions, etc.) as well as first aid items for horses (vet wrap, equine thermometer, antiseptic scrub, Banamine, etc.) Be sure someone in your party has had training in first aid.

9. **Knife:** A good knife is essential, since it can help with fire building, first aid, and food preparation. A Leatherman-type tool will include other helpful gadgets in addition to a knife, like saws, tweezers, screwdrivers, scissors, can opener, etc.

10. **Signal:** With a cell phone and a fully-charged battery you may be able to summon help in an emergency. However, cell coverage is not reliable, especially in the wilderness. A loud whistle and a metal signaling mirror can help rescuers find you faster. Three blasts or flashes mean "help needed." A Spot emergency locator beacon is a good idea, and walkie-talkies can help keep a group in contact if you get separated.

Bonus Ideas: It goes without saying that wearing a helmet may save your life. Other things that can come in very handy in a trail emergency include a large plastic garbage bag (can be used as a poncho, a tent, a ground cloth, or to carry water) and twine or a shoelace for tack repairs. Put your contact information in your saddle bag in case your horse gets loose and runs off. And be sure to carry your important medical information on your person (in your pocket, or tucked inside the inner rim of your helmet) in case you get hurt and are unconscious when paramedics arrive.

It's also important to consider which items should be on your person instead of in your saddlebag. Waterproof matches, your cell phone, and a knife are probably the bare minimum. If you and your horse get separated, all that great emergency equipment in your saddlebag won't do you any good. If your riding clothes are short on pockets, use a fanny pack or a Cashel Ankle Safe trail pouch to carry critical items.

Finally, always tell someone where you are going and when you'll be returning, then stick with your plan. That way if something goes wrong, they'll know where to start looking for you.

Ride safely, be prepared, and have fun!

Certified Feed Required

To help control the spread of invasive species in our forests, the Forest Service now requires that any horse feed brought into a National Forest in Oregon or Washington must be certified to be free of weed seeds. The Bureau of Land Management is planning to implement a similar requirement for BLM land in the near future.

The Forest Service's catchy name for this special horse feed is "Weed Seed Free Feed." (Say that three times fast!) Most folks call it "certified feed" instead.

There are two types of certified feed: hay that a state agricultural inspector has deemed to be free of weed seeds, or heat-processed feed pellets. (The heat treatment kills the seeds and prevents them from germinating.)

The bottom line for horseback riders is that if you go on public land, you are allowed to have only certified feed in your trailer or at your campsite. If you violate this requirement, you can be ticketed and fined.

You can purchase certified hay or pellets from most feed stores, or go to www.oregon.gov/ODA/CID/weed_free_forage.shtml for a list of certified hay producers.

Leave No Trace Principles

Leave No Trace is a nationally-recognized outdoor skills and ethics education program. Its seven Leave No Trace Principles outline the ways that recreational users can minimize the impact we have on the land. The principles are listed below, followed by specific things we equestrians can do to ensure that the beautiful places we enjoy today will be preserved for generations to come.

Plan Ahead and Prepare
-- Educate yourself about the area you plan to visit. Talk with local land managers to find out about trail conditions. Know before you go.
-- Carry and use a map and take responsibility for knowing your route and staying on it.
-- Tell someone where you are going, and stick with your itinerary.

Travel and Camp on Durable Surfaces
-- Water your horse directly from a stream or lake only at trail crossings or if there is a rocky or sandy bank. Otherwise, bring water to your horse using a collapsible bucket to protect fragile shoreline vegetation.
-- Above the tree line, please stay on the trails to avoid damaging fragile alpine environments.
-- Use trails designated for horse use.
-- When traveling cross-country, don't ride single file. Each rider should pick his own route to disperse hoofprints, staying on durable surfaces.
-- Avoid steep slopes and soft ground. Ride across slopes rather than straight up or down to reduce erosion.
-- To minimize damage, don't ride trails that are wet and muddy.

Dispose of Waste Properly
-- Pack out all garbage.
-- Disburse any manure piles after rest breaks on the trail.
-- When you stop for a bathroom break, make sure you're at least 200 feet (that's 70 steps) away from any streams, lakes, or springs. Bury all waste, and carry out your used toilet paper.

Leave What You Find
-- Use certified feed to help prevent the spread of invasive species. Start feeding your animals 3 or more days before entering the forest so their digestive systems are clear of weed seeds.
-- Fill in pawed ground to help the vegetation regrow.
-- Do not allow horses to paw or chew vegetation.

Minimize Campfire Impacts
-- Build fires only if the weather is safe, and use only dead and downed wood that is smaller than your wrist. Make sure your campfire is dead out before leaving it.

Respect Wildlife
-- Control your dog. Electronic collars work well on the trail.

Be Considerate of Other Visitors
-- Please keep horses out of lakes in the wilderness, as these lakes are used for drinking water by backpackers.
-- Keep horses off of designated bike trails. Horse hooves break up the firm trail tread that bicyclists enjoy.
-- If you encounter hikers that are not familiar with horse traffic, greet them and ask them to move off to the downhill side of the trail and coach them as needed.
-- A friendly equestrian makes a lasting impression on hikers.

For more information about Leave No Trace principles, go to www.lnt.org/programs/principles.php.

A late fall ride at Green Ridge.

Wilderness Riding

Central Oregon has five designated wilderness areas: Three Sisters, Mt. Jefferson, Mt. Washington, Diamond Peak, and Oregon Badlands. These areas are permanently protected by Congresss in order to preserve their special characteristics and protect fish and wildlife habitat, water quality, and vegetation.

Wilderness areas are managed differently than other federal land, with emphasis on environmental protection, solitude and primitive recreation. As a result, wilderness riding is a different experience than front-country riding. The terrain is typically more rugged, the trails are more challenging, and you'll see fewer signs along the way.

In the Deschutes National Forest, wilderness trail junction signs have historically shown trail names and/or destinations. But as these signs reach the end of their useful lives, they are being replaced with signs that show only the trail numbers. This means you will need to carry a map and know how to use it. Wilderness maps are available from any forest service office.

Special regulations apply to designated wilderness areas, including:

-- Wilderness Permits are required. These free, self-issued permits (one per group) are available at all wilderness trailheads. They are important in locating injured visitors, and they provide the Forest Service with valuable information about trail usage patterns over time.

-- Groups must be no larger than 12 people and 12 stock animals in order to reduce impacts.

-- All wheeled devices (bicycles, carts, strollers) are prohibited to protect traditional wilderness values.

-- Horses must be secured more than 200 feet from water and main trails to protect fragile plants and keep water clean.

-- Bury human waste 6 inches deep and at least 200 feet (70 steps) from water and trails to prevent disease. Carry out toilet paper.

-- No entry is allowed in any site, area, or trail marked "Closed for Restoration."

-- Campfires, where allowed, must be at least 100 feet (35 steps) from all water and main trails. They must be out cold before you leave them.

The Best Maps

One of the most important items in your saddlebag is your map. You should always carry a map of the area you're riding, even if you know the trail. While the Deschutes and Ochoco National Forest maps cover most of the trails included in this book, the scale on these maps is so small that they are useful only for things like finding trailheads. They're not detailed enough to be useful on the trail. The best maps for each of the areas covered by this book are shown in the table below. The maps labeled "RD" are Forest Service Ranger District Maps (also known as "fire maps"). The maps labeled "W" are Wilderness maps produced by Geo-Graphics. The map referred to as the "Adventure Map" is the Central Oregon Hiking-Trail Map produced by Adventure Maps, Inc. You can also find on-line maps for some riding areas on BLM land.

Area	Maps
Bandit Springs	Prineville RD
Bend Area	Bend RD, Ft. Rock RD
Black Butte	Sisters RD
Broken Top	Three Sisters W, Bend RD, Adventure Map
Cline Buttes	Sisters RD
Cultus Lake	Three Sisters W, Bend RD, Adventure Map
Diamond Peak	Diamond Peak W, Crescent RD
Gray Butte	Adventure Map
McKenzie Pass	Three Sisters W, Mt. Washington W, Sisters RD, Adventure Map
Metolius Basin	Mt. Jefferson W, Sisters RD, Adventure Map
Newberry Crater	Ft. Rock RD, Adventure Map
N. Cascade Lks.	Three Sisters W, Adventure Map
Oregon Badlands	Adventure Map
Peterson Ridge	Sisters RD
Santiam Pass	Three Sisters W, Mt. Jefferson W, Mt. Washington W Sisters RD, Adventure Map
Sisters Area	Sisters RD
Skyline Forest	Sisters RD, Bend RD
Swamp Wells/ Horse Butte	Ft. Rock RD
Three Creek	Three Sisters W, Sisters RD, Bend RD, Adventure Map
Trout Creek Butte	Three Sisters W, Sisters RD, Adventure Map
Western Ochocos	Prineville RD

There is nothing so good for the inside of a man as the outside of a horse.

Winston Churchill

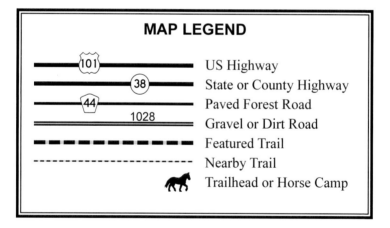

MAP LEGEND

═══(101)═══	US Highway
═══(38)═══	State or County Highway
═══(44)═══	Paved Forest Road
═══1028═══	Gravel or Dirt Road
━ ━ ━ ━ ━ ━	Featured Trail
- - - - - - -	Nearby Trail
🐎	Trailhead or Horse Camp

Bandit Springs
Corral Flat Primitive Camping Area
Ochoco National Forest

Each year the Pacific Northwest Endurance Rides (PNER) group organizes an endurance race in the Bandit Springs area. Riders camp at Corral Flat and ride the surrounding forest roads and trails. The routes go through one of the prettiest sections of the Ochocos, with ponderosa forests, open meadows, gently rolling terrain, and beautiful wild flowers in season. These are not official forest service trails, though, so the routes are not marked and some of the trail junctions are easy to miss. We've done our best to describe the various routes, and even though the roads typically are not physically signed we show the forest road numbers in our text and maps. Please keep a spirit of adventure and realize that you are truly exploring when you ride in this beautiful area. Oh, yes, and please bring along a map and your GPS or compass. You'll need them.

*Whitney rides Dixie through a flower-filled meadow
along the Indian Prairie Trail.*

Getting to Bandit Springs

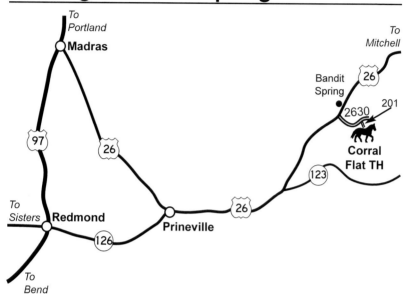

Bandit Springs Trails

Trail	Difficulty	Elevation	Round Trip
Coyle Butte Loop	Moderate	4,600-5,500	10 miles
Indian Prairie	Moderate	4,800-6,000	18 miles
Old Stock Road Loop	Moderate	4,400-5,500	13 miles
Walton Lake	Moderate	4,800-5,500	12.5 miles

Corral Flat Primitive Camping

Directions: To reach the Corral Flat primitive camping area, take Hwy. 26 east from Prineville for 29 miles. Just after the 48-mile post turn right on Road 2630 toward Marks Creek Sno-Park. Drive 1.9 miles and turn right on Road 201, an unmarked dirt road that runs beside a large meadow bordered by a rail fence. Continue 0.1 mile to the parking/camping area.

Elevation: 4,750 feet

Campsites: Primitive camping only

Facilities: None -- no toilets, no water

Permits: None

Season: Late spring through fall

Contact: Ochoco National Forest, 541-416-6500

*At Corral Flat you can set up a primitive camp
outside the log fence that marks the perimeter of the meadow.*

Coyle Butte Loop

Trailhead: Start at Corral Flat primitive camping area

Length: 10 miles round trip

Elevation: 4,600 to 5,500 feet

Difficulty: Moderate -- the riding is easy but the route is unsigned, so a Prineville Ranger District map and a GPS will come in handy

Footing: Suitable for barefoot horses

Season: Late spring through fall

Permits: None

Facilities: Plenty of trailer parking at Corral Flat. Stock water is available on the trail.

Highlights: This trail is the 10-mile fun ride that is held each year in conjunction with the PNER Bandit Springs endurance race. The trail runs on a combination of single-track trails and forest roads that wind through beautiful forest and grassy meadows filled with wildflowers in season. Watch the turns, though, because if you miss one you could get a longer ride than you planned.

The Ride: Start on the south side of the Corral Flat camping area, next to the forest service kiosk. The trail goes over a low knoll and

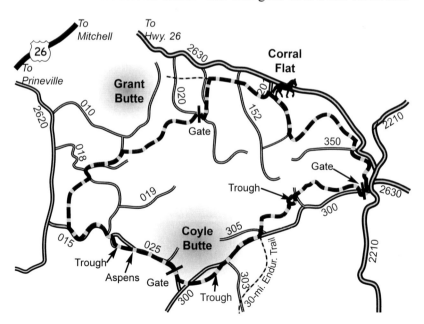

veers to the right, runs for 0.7 mile, then forks in a meadow. Turn left, and in 0.3 mile the trail reaches Road 020. Turn right on Road 020, go through the gate in the fence a few feet away, and pick up the trail on the left. The route winds across several meadows on trails and old dirt roads, and in another 2.3 miles it reaches lightly-graveled Road 015. Go left, and in 0.5 mile when the road forks, go to the right on Road 025. In 100 feet the road forks again. Go right, and in 0.1 mile you'll pass a water trough, then the trail returns to Road 025. About 0.2 mile later you'll pass an exclosure fence around an aspen thicket. In another 0.4 mile the road forks. Stay to the right and in 0.2 mile you'll go through a gate in a fence. A nice view of Round Mountain is straight ahead. Go downhill on the eroded dirt road, and about halfway down veer left on a single track trail. It crosses Road 300 and continues, and in 0.3 mile you'll pass another water trough. About 0.2 mile later you'll reach Road 300 again. Turn right on Road 300 and follow it 0.5 mile, then turn left onto the endurance trail. In 0.5 mile the trail forks at another exclosure fence. The right fork takes you to a water trough and then rejoins the left fork. In another mile the trail crosses Road 300 again, goes through a gate, then recrosses Road 300 and continues 1.5 miles to a junction with a wide ATV track. Turn right here and in 0.3 mile you'll be back at Corral Flat.

*Lydia and Connie ride Shadow and Diamond
through a sunlit meadow on the Coyle Butte Loop.*

Indian Prairie

Trailhead:	Start at Corral Flat primitive camping area
Length:	18 miles round trip
Elevation:	4,800 to 6,000 feet
Difficulty:	Moderate -- the riding is easy but the route is unsigned, so a Prineville Ranger District map and a GPS will come in handy
Footing:	Hoof protection recommended
Season:	Late spring through fall
Permits:	None
Facilities:	Plenty of trailer parking at Corral Flat. Stock water is available on the trail.

Highlights: This is a rather long ride, but it goes through easy terrain and the scenery is great -- lush meadows, beautiful forest, and nice views from several spots. Seeing the vast Indian Prairie nestled between Slide Mountain and Mt. Pisgah is worth riding the entire 18 miles.

The Ride: From Corral Flat, ride east on Road 201 (the road through the camping area), which soon becomes a trail. In 0.3 mile, turn left on the trail where a wide ATV track goes off to the right. Continue 1.4

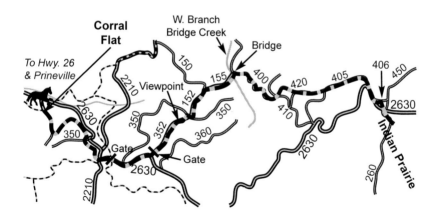

Lydia and Shadow stroll across Indian Prairie.

miles, and when you can see the junction of gravel Roads 2630 and 2210, veer left and ride cross country to the road junction. Ride Road 2630 for 0.2 mile, go through the gate at the cattle guard, and continue along Road 2630 for another 0.7 mile. Turn left on Road 352, go through the wire gate, and ride about 0.9 mile. Look left for a nice view through a clearcut. In another 0.1 mile you'll reach a spot where a dirt road comes in on the left and in about 100 feet Road 352 ends at gravel Road 350. Veer right on Road 350 and in 50 feet take a hard left down the embankment onto dirt Road 152. In 0.6 mile you'll reach another junction, with Road 150 going to the left and Road 155 going to the right. Turn right on Road 155, and in 0.6 mile you'll reach the bridge over the West Branch of Bridge Creek. Cross the bridge and turn right on Road 400. In 1.2 miles a single-track trail goes off to the left. Follow it uphill, and it soon becomes Road 420. Stay on it for a total of 1.1 miles and you'll see another single-track trail depart on the left. Follow it for 1 mile, and when the trail forks go left again. In 0.7 mile you'll reach the beautiful Indian Prairie. The aspen grove in the upper meadow and the forest shelter are both worth exploring.

Old Stock Road Loop

Trailhead: Start at Corral Flat primitive camping area

Length: 13 miles round trip

Elevation: 4,400 to 5,500 feet

Difficulty: Moderate -- the riding is easy but the route is unsigned, so a Prineville Ranger District map and a GPS will come in handy

Footing: Hoof protection recommended

Season: Late spring through fall

Permits: None

Facilities: Plenty of trailer parking at Corral Flat. Stock water is available on the trail.

Highlights: This loop mostly follows gravel and dirt forest roads up and down over low, forested ridges and through lush meadows. From several vantage points it offers panoramic views to the north.

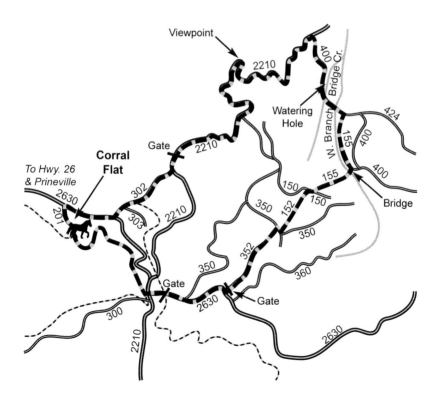

Whitney and Dixie at the viewpoint on Road 2210.

The Ride: From Corral Flat, ride Road 201 back to Road 2630 (the road you drove in on) and turn right. Follow Road 2630 for 0.5 mile and turn left on Road 302. Follow Road 302 for 1.2 mile, passing Road 303 and a wide trail on the right, to gravel Road 2210. Turn left on Road 2210 and in about 0.1 mile go through the gate next to the cattle guard. Continue on Road 2210 for 2.1 miles as it winds down the ridge to a splendid viewpoint where the road makes a hairpin turn. Continue 1.7 miles farther and turn right on unmarked dirt Road 400. (There will be a barbed-wire fence on your right for a short distance.) You'll start gaining elevation now, and after 0.8 mile there is a short spur trail on the left that leads to a watering hole along the creek. About 0.8 mile beyond that, the road forks. Go the right on Road 155, which runs beside the West Branch of Bridge Creek. In 0.7 mile, turn right and cross the bridge over the creek. In 0.6 mile you'll reach Road 150. Turn right on it, and almost immediately veer left on Road 152. About 0.6 mile later you'll come to Road 350. Jog to the right and immediately turn left on Road 352. Follow it for 0.7 mile to a gate at gravel Road 2630. Go through the gate and turn right on Road 2630, following it for 0.8 mile to a cattle guard. Go through the gate next to the cattle guard and continue down Road 2630 for 0.2 mile. When you reach gravel Road 2210, cross it and ride cross-country straight ahead for a short distance. When you come to a trail, turn right and follow it 1.9 miles back to Corral Flat.

Walton Lake

Trailhead: Start at Corral Flat primitive camping area

Length: 12.5 miles round trip

Elevation: 4,800 to 5,500 feet

Difficulty: Moderate -- the riding is easy but the route is unsigned, so a Prineville Ranger District map and a GPS will come in handy

Footing: Hoof protection recommended

Season: Late spring through fall

Permits: None

Facilities: Plenty of trailer parking at Corral Flat. Stock water is available on the trail.

Highlights: This is a delightful ride that follows single-track trails and dirt roads to Walton Lake. It travels through ponderosa forest, fir groves, and lush flower-filled meadows. It's easy to make a wrong turn on these unmarked trails, so be sure to carry a map and a GPS or compass.

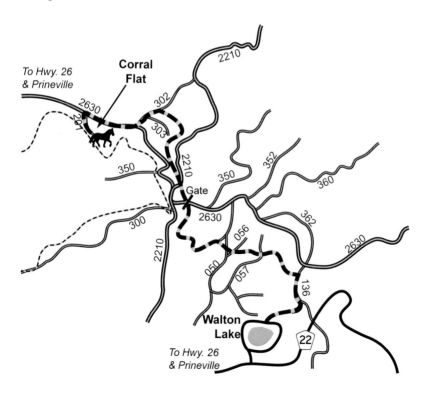

*Diana rides Mo and Whitney rides Dixie
through a meadow filled with wild asters.*

The Ride: From Corral Flat, ride Road 201 to Road 2630 and turn right. Follow Road 2630 for 0.5 mile and turn left on Road 302. Follow Road 302 for 0.5 mile, passing Road 303 on the way. Turn right on a wide trail that is occasionally marked with white diamonds on the trees. Continue 1.3 miles and cross gravel Road 2210, then in 0.2 mile cross gravel Road 2630 next to the cattle guard. Go through the wire gate and ride 0.9 mile. At the junction with an unnumbered dirt road, stay to the right on the trail. In another 0.2 mile you'll cross dirt Road 050, then 200 feet later you'll cross dirt Road 056. In this stretch, blue diamonds (ski trail markers) begin to appear on the trees. In 0.6 mile the trail crosses a ski trail -- continue straight ahead. In 0.2 mile after that, veer right on a wide trail marked by a white diamond. About 0.5 mile later, veer right onto dirt Road 136. In another 0.2 mile, turn right on an indistinct dirt road that leads downhill into a meadow filled with corn lilies. Follow it for 0.7 mile, then turn left on a wide trail and continue 0.2 mile to Walton Lake. Note that horses are not permitted in the campground that surrounds Walton Lake, so if you want to go down to the lake you'll need to tie your horse outside the campground and walk to the lake on foot.

Riding: the art of keeping a horse between you and the ground.

Anonymous

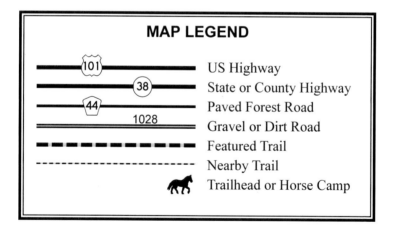

Bend Area

Various Locations Near Bend

Several trails and large tracts of public land near Bend offer very nice riding opportunities, and some are accessible year round.

On the west side of Bend, the Deschutes River Trail is a fabulous low-elevation trail along the Deschutes. It's a spectacular ride in the autumn when the brilliant fall foliage contrasts with the blue sky and water and the nearby black lava flows.

Northeast of Bend you'll find Mayfield Pond Recreation Area, a 19,500-acre site with very nice fall, winter, and spring riding on dirt roads and trails.

The Horse Ridge Recreation Area is 40 square miles located southeast of the Oregon Badlands. It includes Horse Ridge itself as well as a large tract of land northwest of the Ridge. It can be accessed via the Rickard, Horse Ridge, and Big Sagebrush trailheads.

Along the Deschutes River Trail, near the Slough trailhead.

33

You can see forever from the Horse Ridge West Trail.

Whitney and Debbie ride Dixie and Cowboy along the Deschutes River Trail.

Mayfield Pond reflects the snowcapped mountains in early spring.

Getting to Bend Area Trailheads

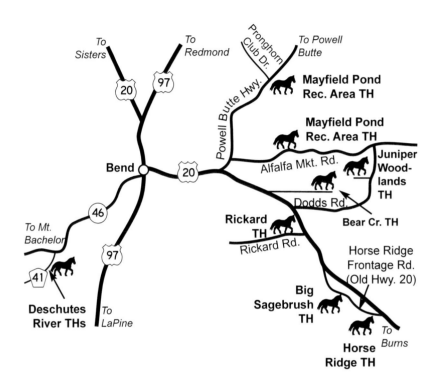

Bend Area Trails

Trail	Difficulty	Elevation	Round Trip
Deschutes River	Easy	3,950-4,100	7.5-13.5 miles
Horse Ridge East	Challenging	3,650-4,900	10 miles
Horse Ridge West	Moderate	3,750-4,650	6.5-10 miles
Juniper Woodlands	Easy	3,350-3,450	Varies
Mayfield Pond Rec. Area	Easy	3,200-3,500	Varies
Rickard Road Area	Moderate	3,600-3,900	Varies

Deschutes River

Trailhead: Start at the Lava Island, Big Eddy, Aspen, Dillon Falls, or Slough trailheads

Length: 7.5 miles round trip from Lava Island trailhead to Dillon Falls, or 13.5 miles round trip to Benham Falls

Elevation: 3,950 to 4,100 feet

Difficulty: Easy

Footing: Suitable for barefoot horses

Season: Early spring through late fall

Permits: Northwest Forest Pass required.

Facilities: Toilets at each trailhead. Parking for 2-4 trailers each at Lava Island and Dillon Falls. Additional parking possible at Big Eddy, Aspen, and Slough trailheads. Stock water is available on the trail.

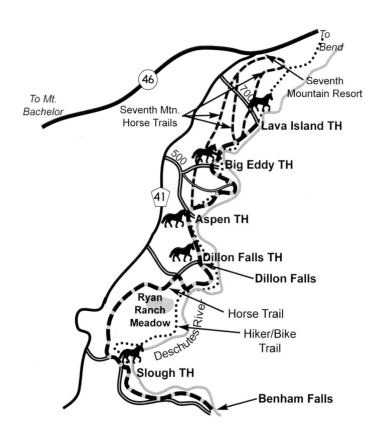

Highlights: This trail along the Deschutes River offers excellent views of the river, the lush vegetation it supports, and the rapids created by the ancient lava flows on the east side of the river. In mid-October the fall colors along this trail are spectacular. You can start from any trailhead along the river except Benham Falls, which is too small for trailer parking. Dogs are required to be on leash on this trail from May 15th to September 15th.

Finding the Trailheads: From Hwy. 97 in Bend, take Exit 138 (Colorado Ave.) and head west on Hwy. 46 (the Cascade Lakes Hwy.) Follow the signs toward Mt. Bachelor for 7.5 miles and turn left on Road 41, the first road on the left after passing the Seventh Mountain Resort. Follow the signs about 0.5 mile to the Lava Island trailhead. To reach the other trailheads, continue along Road 41 and follow the signs.

The Ride: The trail roughly parallels the river, with entry/exit opportunities at every trailhead but Benham Falls. The horse trails are well marked and the footing is good. From Lava Island to Dillon Falls there are separate trails for horses, hikers, and bicyclists. From Dillon Falls to Slough the horse trail skirts around Ryan Ranch Meadow to the west on a closed forest road that has gates at both ends. From Slough to Benham Falls, all users share the same trail.

You'll enjoy excellent views along the Deschutes River Trail.

Horse Ridge East

Trailhead: Start at the Horse Ridge trailhead

Length: 10 miles round trip to make a loop to the top of the ridge. Shorter rides are possible.

Elevation: 3,650 to 4,900 feet

Difficulty: Challenging -- steep hills, extremely rocky, many mountain bikes, limited room to get off the trail in some places

Footing: Hoof protection recommended

Season: Nearly year-round, but trail is very dusty in summer

Permits: None

Facilities: Parking for 2-3 trailers, depending on how many bicyclist cars are in the lot. No stock water on the trail.

Highlights: Even though the views from the top of Horse Ridge are panoramic and this BLM trail is open to horses, we recommend that equestrians steer clear, for several reasons. First, the trail is very popular with mountain bike riders. Second, the trail from the trailhead to the summit goes through a narrow ravine that offers limited space to

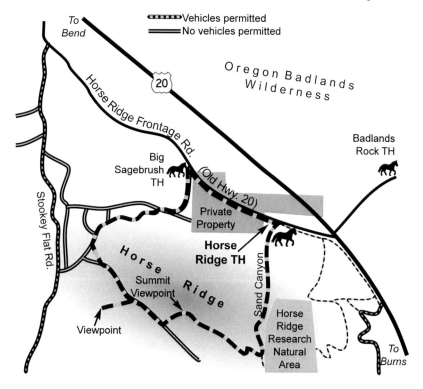

Coming down the back side of Horse Ridge, Whitney leads Dixie over some nasty rocks.

get off the trail to avoid bicyclists speeding downhill. And third, the trail down from the summit on the back side of the ridge is steep and extremely rocky, with dozens of large boulders to clamber over. For horseback riders, the Horse Ridge West trail is a much better bet. If you are determined to ride this trail, do it on a weekday morning in mid-summer or early fall, when the downhill mountain bike traffic is likely to be lighter.

Finding the Horse Ridge Trailhead: From Bend, drive east on Hwy. 20. Just before the 18-mile marker, make a hard right on the paved Horse Ridge Frontage Road. Drive 0.7 mile to the trailhead on the left side of the road.

The Ride: From the Horse Ridge trailhead, take the trail on the right and stay to the right at the next trail junction. The first 0.5 mile is a gentle grade, then you'll climb very steeply for 1.2 miles. The next 2 miles have a more moderate elevation gain, and offer expansive views to the north. About 3.7 miles from the trailhead you'll reach the summit and a nice viewpoint. Then the trail steeply descends the back side of the ridge, where huge rocks in the trail are a nightmare for horses. The trail finally levels out when it reaches a dirt road on a lower ridge, where you can ride to the viewpoint that is the highlight of the Horse Ridge West trail. Follow the dirt road down off the ridge and veer left on an unmarked dirt road (if you reach a fence, you've gone too far) and ride it to the Horse Ridge Frontage Road. Ride on the wide shoulder beside the road for 1.5 miles to return to the trailhead.

Horse Ridge West

Trailhead:	Start at Big Sagebrush trailhead, an unimproved parking area on the Horse Ridge Frontage Road (old Hwy. 20)
Length:	6.5 to 10 miles round trip
Elevation:	3,750 to 4,650 feet
Difficulty:	Moderate -- steep hills to climb
Footing:	Suitable for barefoot horses
Season:	Nearly year-round -- trail is dusty in summer but offers good footing in spring, fall, and early winter
Permits:	None
Facilities:	Parking for 3 trailers. No stock water on the trail.

Highlights: Horse Ridge is actually 3 ridges that run parallel to one another. This route takes you up onto the middle ridge. The views are fabulous. From several vantage points you can see Bend, Redmond,

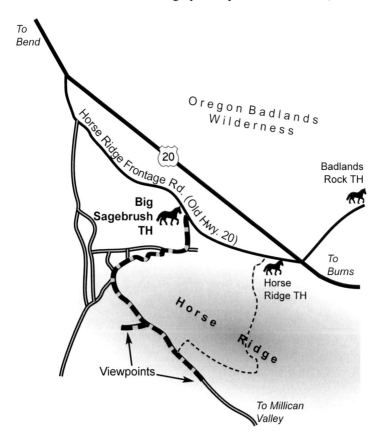

Whitney, Debbie, and Diana ride up Horse Ridge, with
Mt. Washington, Black Butte, and Mt. Jefferson behind them.

the Three Sisters, Mt. Jefferson, Mt. Hood, Pine Mountain, and Millican Valley. Some of the oldest junipers known to science are located
on this ridge.

Finding the Big Sagebrush Trailhead: From Bend, drive east on
Hwy. 20 for 12.5 miles and turn right on the Horse Ridge Frontage
Road, a paved but unsigned road that goes off to the right between
mileposts 12 and 13. Drive 3.2 miles and turn right on an unsigned
dirt road that runs between two rock cribs toward a gate on the far end
of the trailhead parking area.

The Ride: Go through the gate and ride 0.5 mile, then when you come
to a dirt road, turn right. Follow this road for several miles, keeping to
the left at each junction. The road will take you up a steep hill, level
out, and then climb again for a total elevation gain of 800 feet in 2
miles. When the road levels out for the second time, you'll be on the
middle Horse Ridge. You are now about 3 miles from your trailer. Detour to the right on the next dirt road to reach an excellent viewpoint.
Return to the road you rode up on, and continue straight for another 1.5
miles to look down into the Millican Valley. After exploring the ridge
top area and enjoying the views, retrace your steps to return to your
trailer.

Juniper Woodlands

Trailhead: Start at the Juniper Woodlands trailhead off Alfalfa Market Road, or possibly at the Bear Creek trailhead* off Hwy. 20

Length: Varies -- multiple routes on about 12 miles of dirt roads

Elevation: 3,350 to 3,450 feet

Difficulty: Easy, but a GPS may come in handy

Footing: Some rocky spots, but overall fine for barefoot horses

Season: Year-round -- trails are dusty in summer but excellent in winter, spring, and fall

Permits: None

Facilities: Parking for 4-5 trailers at Juniper Woodlands trailhead, or 1-2 trailers at Bear Creek trailhead. Stock water is available on the trail during irrigation season.

Highlights: As of our publication date the signs on the Juniper Woodlands trails show only trail numbers, but at some point the signs may also show the trail names. Trail 1, the Bobcat Trail, isn't the most interesting riding, since it's a long straight stretch that runs mostly along a power line. But it connects you to other trails and dirt roads to explore in the area. The terrain is fairly flat, punctuated by occasional

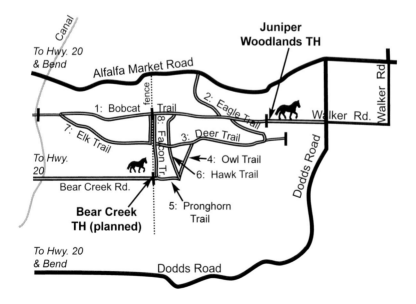

*Teresa rides Kodie and Whitney rides Dixie
along Trail 1 at the Juniper Woodlands.*

rock outcroppings and covered with old-growth juniper. You'll even
have some nice views of the Cascades.

Finding the Trailheads: <u>Juniper Woodlands trailhead</u>: drive east
from Bend on Hwy. 20 for 4.7 miles. Turn left on Powell Butte Highway, and in 0.9 mile turn right on Alfalfa Market Road. Follow it 8.5
miles and turn right on Dodds Road. In another mile, turn right on
Walker Road. Continue 1.1 mile to the trailhead at the end of the road.
<u>Bear Creek trailhead*</u>: take Hwy. 20 east from Bend for 6.9 miles and
turn left on Bear Creek Road. In 2.2 miles the road turns to gravel, and
the trailhead is 2.5 miles beyond that.

The Ride: Trail 1 starts at the Walker Road trailhead and runs nearly
straight for 2.5 miles. While the official trail ends where Trails 1 and
7 meet, you can continue straight ahead on a dirt road for another 0.4
mile to reach an irrigation ditch where you can water your horse (in
season). In addition to the official trails shown, there are several other
dirt roads you can investigate. You'll also find cow/game trails winding through the old growth juniper, so there are plenty of opportunities
to explore the area.

* As of our publication date, BLM planners had not yet determined whether im-
provements planned for this trailhead will accommodate horse trailers. We've included it here just in case, but please scout it in a car before taking your trailer there.

Mayfield Pond Recreation Area

Trailhead: Start at the Alfalfa Market Road trailhead or the Powell Butte Highway trailhead

Length: Varies -- multiple routes possible

Elevation: 3,200 to 3,500 feet

Difficulty: Easy, but a GPS may come in handy on these unsigned roads

Footing: Suitable for barefoot horses

Season: Year-round -- trails are dusty in summer but excellent in winter, spring, and fall

Permits: None

Facilities: Parking for 4-6 trailers at either trailhead. No stock water on the trail.

Highlights: Mayfield Pond Recreation Area is located a little north of the Oregon Badlands, in an area bounded by Alfalfa Market Road to

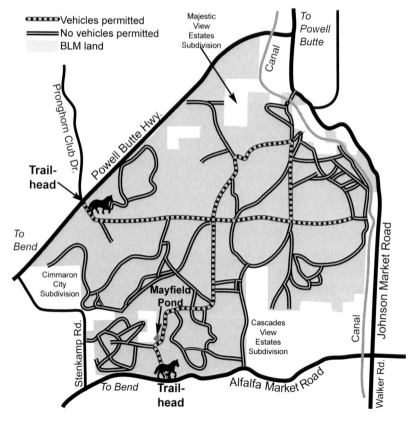

Debbie and Split explore the trails at Mayfield Pond
Recreation Area on a sunny winter day.

the south, Powell Butte Highway to the west, and Johnson Market Road to the east. This 19,500-acre BLM area has a few roads where motor vehicle use is allowed, but most of the riding is on old dirt roads where motorized vehicles are not permitted. The terrain is fairly flat sagebrush and juniper country, with a few interesting rock outcroppings thrown in--good riding for green horses or inexperienced riders, and a nice place to ride to keep your horse conditioned in winter.

Finding the Trailheads: Alfalfa Market Road Trailhead: From Bend, drive east on Hwy. 20 for 4.7 miles. Turn left on Powell Butte Highway, and in 0.9 mile turn right on Alfalfa Market Road. Follow it 4.5 miles to the trailhead on the left side of the road. Powell Butte Highway Trailhead: From Bend, drive east on Hwy. 20 for 4.7 miles. Turn left on Powell Butte Highway and continue 6.3 miles to the trailhead on the right side of the road, directly across from the entrance to the Pronghorn resort. From Redmond, take Hwy. 26 east 6.5 miles to Powell Butte Hwy., turn right, and drive 12 miles to the trailhead on the left side of the road.

The Ride: The riding is easy and relaxed at the Mayfield Pond Recreation area. You can have fun exploring the old dirt roads in the area, or you can ride cross-country. It's a good idea to use a GPS here, because none of the dirt roads are signed and it's easy to get disoriented.

Rickard Road Area

Trailhead: Start at the Rickard trailhead

Length: The closest southern loop is about 6.5 miles round trip, but several other loops of varying lengths are possible

Elevation: 3,600 to 3,900 feet

Difficulty: Moderate -- the riding is easy, but a GPS and BLM's on-line map of the Horse Butte area will come in handy on these unsigned roads

Footing: Suitable for barefoot horses

Season: Year-round -- trails are dusty in summer but have good footing in winter, spring, and fall

Permits: None

Facilities: Parking for 4 trailers. No stock water on the trail.

Highlights: This trailhead provides access to the northern part of the Horse Ridge area and offers several loop trails of varying lengths. Just north of the trailhead are trails with a combined length of about 2 miles

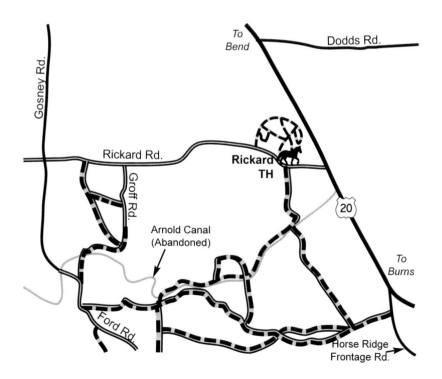

*Connie, Lydia, Debbie, and Whitney take a winter ride
near the Rickard Road trailhead.*

-- better suited to dog walking than horseback riding. Heading south from the trailhead, though, you can use the area's dirt roads and a few single-track trails to create some nice equestrian loops. The footing is great for barefoot horses, and the trails are easy. Much of the area is covered with juniper and sagebrush, but as you travel west you'll reach the area burned by the 1996 Skeleton Fire. This area has few trees so it offers good views of the Cascades. None of the roads are numbered and there isn't much variation in the terrain, so it can be easy to get lost. Be sure to carry a map and a GPS or compass.

Finding the Rickard Trailhead: From Bend, take Hwy. 20 eastbound and turn right on Rickard Road, next to the 11-mile marker. Drive 0.5 mile and turn right into the trailhead parking lot.

The Ride: You can ride several good loops from the parking area. To reach the trails south of the trailhead, ride east on Rickard Road for 200 feet and turn right to go through a gate that is partially blocked by large boulders (to exclude motor vehicles). Explore the area's roads and trails, but note that the trail beside the abandoned canal (really, a small ditch) is faint in places and can be easy to miss.

There is something about riding down the street on a prancing horse that makes you feel like something even when you ain't a thing.

Will Rogers

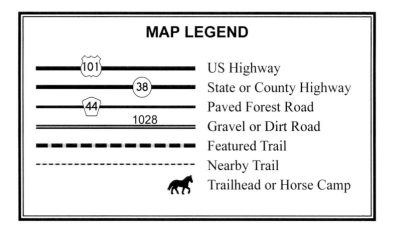

Black Butte
Graham Corral
Deschutes National Forest

Black Butte is a 6,000-foot cinder cone located about 7 miles north-west of Sisters. The riding in this area features open ponderosa pine forest and occasional impressive mountain views. Most of the trails have little elevation change. The snow is typically gone from the area by April, so you can enjoy riding here for several months before the trails of the high Cascades are accessible. Graham Corral doubles as an overnight camping facility and the primary trailhead in the area. It's only 18 miles east of Santiam Pass (or about 100 miles from Salem), so it's easily accessible for riders from the Willamette Valley who want a chance to ride in the sunshine. And because the riding is both easy and scenic, the Black Butte area is popular with local riders.

Debbie and Cowboy on the Metolius-Windigo Trail,
enjoying the views of the Cascades across Glaze Meadow.

49

Getting to Black Butte

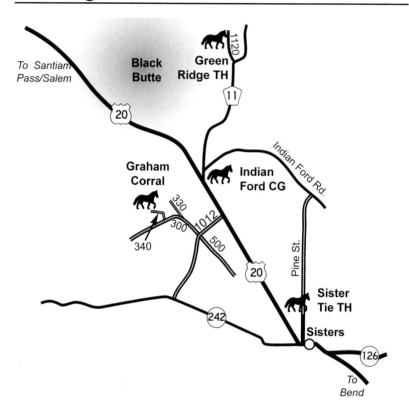

Black Butte Trails

Trail	Difficulty	Elevation	Round Trip
Fourmile Butte	Moderate	3,300-4,050	10 miles
Glaze Meadow	Easy	3,300-3,350	4-12 miles
Gobbler's Knob	Moderate	3,300-3,450	6.5 miles
Green Ridge	Moderate	3,800-4,800	18 miles
Metolius River	Moderate	3,000-4,000	17 miles
Sisters	Moderate	3,200-3,350	20 miles
Sisters Cow Camp	Easy	3,250-3,550	13.5 miles
Skylight Cave	Moderate	3,300-4,100	12.5 miles
Upper Butte Loop	Moderate	3,250-4,000	16-20 miles

Graham Corral

Directions: From Sisters, drive northwest on Hwy. 20 for 4.4 miles and turn left on Road 1012. Continue 0.9 mile, turn right on Road 300 and drive 1.2 miles, then turn right on Road 340 and go 0.6 mile to the horse camp. The route is clearly signed.

Elevation: 3,300 feet

Campsites: 11 sites, 4 of which have 4-horse corrals, plus 4 large central corrals to be shared

Facilities: Toilet, potable water, manure dump. Picnic tables, fire pits, and easy parking for 2+ rigs at each campsite.

Permits: Fees for camping; no fee for day use

Season: Early spring through fall

Contact: Sisters Ranger District: 541-549-7700, www.fs.usda.gov/centraloregon, then click on "Recreation," "Horse Riding and Camping." Concessionaire: 541-338-7869, www.hoodoo.com, then click on "Campgrounds," "Horse Camping," "Graham Corral."

In addition to the four large central corrals, four campsites at Graham Corral have individual 4-horse corrals.

Fourmile Butte

Trailhead: Start at Graham Corral Horse Camp

Length: 10 miles round trip

Elevation: 3,300 to 4,050 feet

Difficulty: Moderate -- easy riding, but navigation skills, a Sisters Ranger District map, and a GPS will come in handy

Footing: Suitable for barefoot horses

Season: Early spring through late fall

Permits: Camping fee; no fee for day use

Facilities: Toilets, potable water and corrals at the horse camp. No stock water on the trail.

Highlights: At one time the summit of Fourmile Butte was excavated as a source of road cinders. Its excavated summit is treeless now, providing panoramic 360-degree views. Getting to the butte is a fun, easy

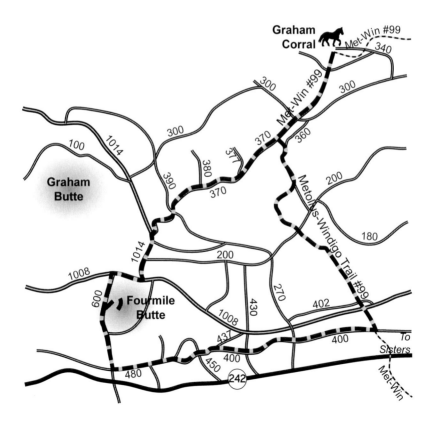

ride on the Metolius-Windigo Trail and several forest roads. Many of the roads in this area are signed, but bring along a map and GPS in case you need them.

The Ride: On the west side of Graham Corral, pick up the southbound Metolius-Windigo Trail #99 (heading toward Sisters Cow Camp/Three Creek Meadow). After 0.7 mile it crosses the red-cinder Road 300 and begins to run along Road 370. In 0.3 mile the Met-Win veers left off Road 370, but you'll continue straight on Road 370 for 1.5 mile more. When you reach red-cinder Road 1014, turn left on it and ride 0.4 mile to the junction with Road 1008. Turn right on Road 1008, and in 0.4 mile turn left on Road 600, which will take you to up on the shoulder of Fourmile Butte. In 0.4 mile, take a hard left onto an unmarked dirt road that will take you to the top of the butte. After enjoying the view, come back down to Road 600 and turn left to ride down off the butte. After 0.5 mile, turn left on Road 480, which soon becomes Road 400. Ride 2.3 miles, then turn left on the Metolius-Windigo Trail and follow it 3 miles back to Graham Corral.

On top of Fourmile Butte, Pat and Tucker take in the view toward Sisters.

And if you look the other direction, Mt. Washington is close enough to reach out and touch.

Glaze Meadow

Trailhead: Start at Graham Corral Horse Camp
Length: 4 to 12 miles round trip, depending on trails taken
Elevation: 3,300 to 3,350 feet
Difficulty: Easy
Footing: Suitable for barefoot horses
Season: Early spring through late fall
Permits: Camping fee; no fee for day use
Facilities: Toilets, potable water and corrals at the horse camp. Stock water is available on the trail.

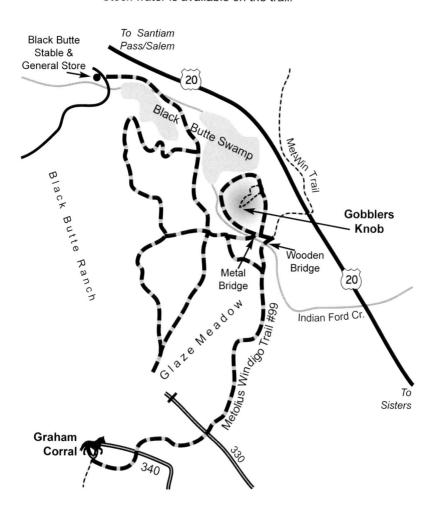

Highlights: If you like to explore new trails, you'll enjoy riding in the Glaze Meadow area. You'll start on the Metolius-Windigo Trail, but when you reach Indian Ford Creek you'll veer off onto the trail network used by Black Butte Ranch for their rental horse rides. Depending on which trails you ride, you could see a beaver dam, pass through groves of aspen, or even ride to the Black Butte General Store for a soda or an ice cream bar. We recommend that you ride these trails primarily in the spring and fall, since in summer they have significant rental-horse traffic and get quite dusty.   If you encounter a string of rental-horse riders, please move off the trail and allow them to pass safely.

The Ride: From Graham Corral, pick up the Metolius-Windigo Trail #99 on the east side of the campground and head toward the Metolius River/Sheep Springs. The Met-Win Trail is marked with yellow diamonds. After 1.3 miles the trail runs along the edge of Glaze Meadow. If you ride out into the meadow you'll have splendid views of Black Butte and the Three Sisters. The Met-Win continues along the meadow for another 0.5 mile, then crosses Indian Ford Creek on a wooden bridge. If you stay to the right here, the Met-Win will take you to Hwy. 20. If you turn left, you'll be on the Black Butte rental horse trail network. All of the trails are easy, with no significant elevation change. Have fun exploring!

Whitney and Dixie stroll across Glaze Meadow,
with Gobblers Knob and Black Butte in the background.

Gobblers Knob

Trailhead: Start at Graham Corral Horse Camp
Length: 6.5 miles round trip
Elevation: 3,300 to 3,450 feet
Difficulty: Moderate
Footing: Suitable for barefoot horses
Season: Early spring through late fall
Permits: Camping fee; no fee for day use
Facilities: Toilets, potable water and corrals at the horse camp. Stock water is available on the trail.

Highlights: On a clear day this trail offers glorious views of the Three Sisters, with Glaze Meadow immediately below. Part of the ride is on

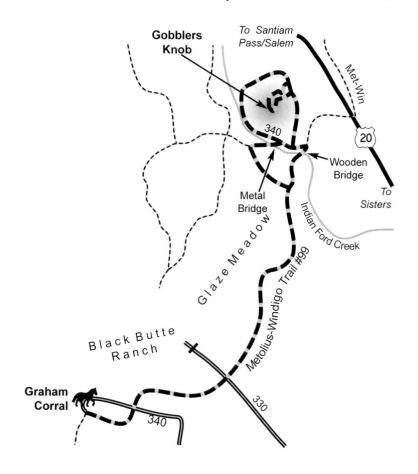

*Debbie and Split enjoy the fabulous view of
the Three Sisters from atop Gobblers Knob.*

the Black Butte Ranch rental-horse trail network, so please yield to the rental-string riders if you encounter them.

The Ride: From Graham Corral, pick up the Metolius-Windigo Trail #99 on the east side of the campground and head toward the Metolius River/Sheep Springs. The Met-Win Trail is marked with yellow diamonds. After about 1.3 miles the trail runs along the edge of Glaze Meadow, then about 1.8 miles from camp it crosses a wooden bridge over Indian Ford Creek. After crossing the creek veer left, leaving the Met-Win Trail. Ride through the old corral and along the creek as it circles the west side of Gobblers Knob. When you reach the metal bridge, don't cross it, but instead veer right on Road 340. As you ride around Gobblers Knob, watch for evidence of beaver activity in the creek. On the north side of Gobblers Knob, about 0.7 mile after leaving the Met-Win Trail, veer right at a trail junction and make your way to the top of Gobblers Knob. You can return the way you came, or go part way down from the summit and veer right to take a different trail down, then circle around the east side of the butte and back to the Met-Win for the return to camp. If you want to detour to Glaze Meadow, ride back to the metal bridge and this time cross it. Continue straight ahead, and when you reach the meadow turn left and ride along the trail beside it to an unobstructed view of the Sisters. Continue along the meadow to reconnect with the Met-Win Trail.

Green Ridge

Trailhead: Start at the Green Ridge trailhead
Length: 18 miles round trip
Elevation: 3,800 to 4,800 feet
Difficulty: Moderate
Footing: Suitable for barefoot horses
Season: Early spring through late fall
Permits: None
Facilities: Parking for 3-4 horse trailers. No facilities at the trailhead. No stock water on the trail.

Highlights: Green Ridge is a fault-block ridge that runs north from Black Butte nearly to the Warm Springs Indian Reservation. The trail follows the crest of the ridge and offers amazing views of the Cascade

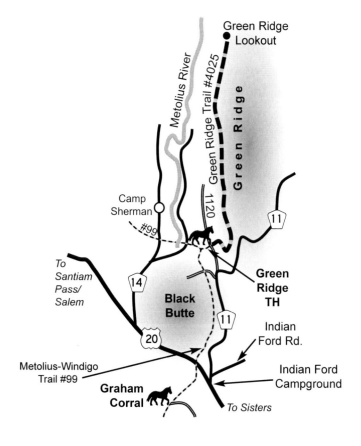

*The Green Ridge Lookout at the end of the Green Ridge Trail
has a spectacular view of Mt. Jefferson.*

peaks and the Metolius Basin. The trail ends at the Green Ridge Lookout, which is available for overnight rental through the Forest Service.
(Sorry, no horse facilities there.) Please respect the privacy of the
guests who have rented the lookout.

Finding the Green Ridge Trailhead: From Sisters, take Hwy. 20
northwest for 6 miles. Turn right on Forest Road 11 near Indian Ford
Campground. Drive north 4.2 miles and turn left on Road 1120 (about
0.5 mile past the turnoff to the Black Butte hiker trailhead), then go 0.9
mile to the parking area, which is little more than a dirt loop on your
left. There is normally a sign on a post on the right side of the road
that indicates where the trail begins, but last time we were there the
post was standing but the sign was lying on the ground.

The Ride: The Green Ridge Trail #4025 climbs to the top of the ridge
via several switchbacks and then follows the crest of the ridge for almost the entire distance. After the initial climb there is not much elevation change. The views of the Cascades are impressive, and on hot
summer days cool breezes waft up from the Metolius Basin below.

Metolius River

Trailhead: Start at Graham Corral Horse Camp
Length: 17 miles round trip
Elevation: 3,000 to 4,000 feet
Difficulty: Moderate
Footing: Suitable for barefoot horses
Season: Early spring through late fall
Permits: Camping fee; no fee for day use
Facilities: Toilets, potable water and corrals at the horse camp. Stock water is available at the Metolius River.

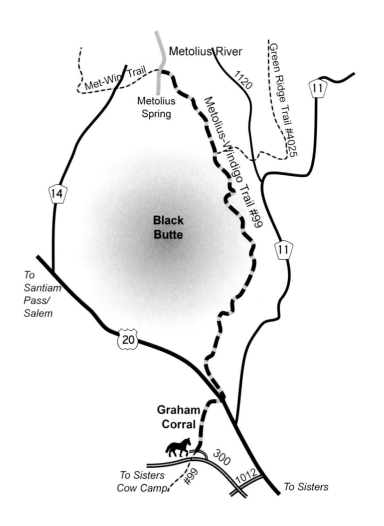

*Michal rides Tex and Whitney rides Dixie through
the forest on the east flank of Black Butte.*

Highlights: This section of the Metolius-Windigo Trail travels through a pleasant forest of ponderosa pines and incense cedars. Some previously-logged stretches offer filtered views from the lower flank of Black Butte. You'll reach the Metolius River about 0.4 mile below its headwaters.

The Ride: Pick up the Metolius-Windigo Trail #99 on the east side of Graham Corral and head toward Metolius River/Sheep Springs. Follow the trail northeast for 2 miles to a wooden bridge over Indian Ford Creek. Stay on the Met-Win and it will take you across Hwy. 20 and continue northward around the east side of Black Butte. The trail, which is clearly marked with yellow diamonds, eventually turns northwest and crosses the Metolius River not far from its headwaters, where the river springs out of the base of Black Butte at the astonishing rate of 50,000 gallons a minute. The Metolius is easy to ford here because it is fairly wide but not very deep, so if you like you can cross it and continue exploring the Met-Win Trail.

Sisters

Trailhead: Start at Graham Corral Horse Camp

Length: 20 miles round trip

Elevation: 3,200 to 3,350 feet

Difficulty: Moderate

Footing: Suitable for barefoot horses

Season: Early spring through late fall

Permits: Camping fee; no fee for day use

Facilities: Toilets, potable water and corrals at the horse camp. Stock water is available on the trail.

Highlights: If you're camping at Graham Corral and want to pick up supplies or get a restaurant meal, head on into Sisters. It's a rather long jaunt but it's easy riding. The route begins on the Metolius-

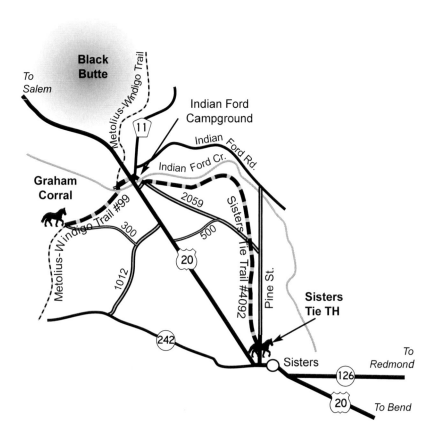

Lydia and Shadow on the Sisters Tie Trail, headed to Sisters.

Windigo Trail, then takes dirt roads to Hwy. 20, skirts Indian Ford Campground, and follows the Sisters Tie Trail into town.

The Ride: Pick up the Metolius-Windigo Trail #99 on the east side of Graham Corral and head toward Metolius River/Sheep Springs. Follow the trail northeast for 2 miles to the bridge over Indian Ford Creek. (The "No Trespassing" signs you may see in this section refer to the private property the trail crosses, not to the trail itself.) About 200 feet after crossing the creek, leave the Met-Win Trail and turn hard right on a dirt road marked with Sisters Trails Alliance signs. Follow the Sisters Trails signs 0.6 mile to the intersection of Hwy. 20 and Road 11. Cross Hwy. 20 and ride beside Road 11 for a short distance to the entrance to Indian Ford Campground. Bushwhack around the western edge of Indian Ford Campground, using the campground bridge to cross Indian Ford Creek. Continue skirting the campground and pick up the Sisters Tie Trail #4092, marked by a small sign next to campsite #11. For the next 2 miles the Sisters Tie Trail (marked by Sisters Trails signs) runs along Indian Ford Creek. Watch for evidence of beaver activity in this area. It's 6.5 miles from Indian Ford Campground to the Sisters Tie trailhead on Pine St. From this trailhead, ride south along the lightly-traveled Pine St. for 0.5 mile to reach town.

Sisters Cow Camp

Trailhead: Start at Graham Corral Horse Camp
Length: 13.5 miles round trip
Elevation: 3,250 to 3,550 feet
Difficulty: Easy
Footing: Suitable for barefoot horses
Season: Early spring through late fall
Permits: Camping fee; no fee for day use
Facilities: Toilets, potable water and corrals at Graham Corral. Stock water in season at Sisters Cow Camp.

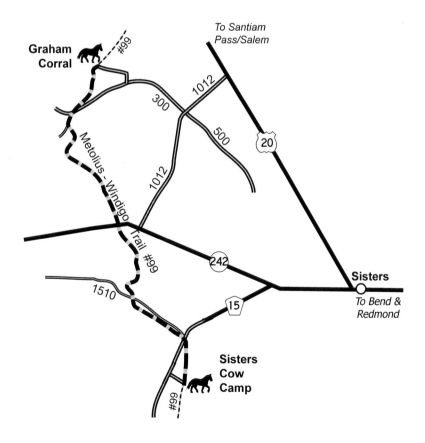

Lydia, Debbie, and Connie let their horses graze in the little grotto midway between Graham Corral and Sisters Cow Camp.

Highlights: This is a nice forested ride on the segment of the Metolius-Windigo Trail that runs between Graham Corral and Sisters Cow Camp. The trail goes over a small ridge that offers nice mountain views through the trees.

The Ride: Pick up the Metolius-Windigo Trail #99 on the west side of Graham Corral and head toward Sisters Cow Camp/Three Creek Meadow. Part of the route is on single-track trail and part is on old forest roads. The way is clearly marked with yellow diamonds. In 0.7 mile the trail crosses Road 300, then it gradually gains elevation for 1.5 miles to go over a low ridge. Near the top of the ridge, look to the north and west to see the mountain views. About 1.9 miles beyond the ridge top, the trail runs down into an interesting little grotto with rock outcroppings, old growth ponderosas, and plentiful grass. A short distance beyond the grotto the trail crosses the paved Hwy. 242. In another 1.8 miles it crosses Road 1510 and runs beside it for 1.1 miles, then it crosses gravel Road 15 and continues 0.6 mile to Sisters Cow Camp.

Skylight Cave

Trailhead:	Start at Graham Corral Horse Camp
Length:	12.5 miles round trip
Elevation:	3,300 to 4,100 feet
Difficulty:	Moderate -- easy riding, but navigation skills, a Sisters Ranger District map, and a GPS will come in handy
Footing:	Hoof protection recommended
Season:	Early spring through late fall
Permits:	Camping fee; no fee for day use
Facilities:	Toilets, potable water and corrals at the horse camp. No stock water on the trail.

Highlights: Skylight Cave doesn't look all that impressive from above -- it's just a hole in the ground with a ladder leading into it. However, if you visit Skylight Cave at the right time of year you'll be treated to an amazing sight. Arrive on a May or June morning between 9:00 and 11:00, tie your horse, and go inside to see the sun streaming through the holes in the roof of the cave. You won't see this later in the day, or at any other time of year. Wow! Be sure to bring a warm jacket, sturdy shoes, and extra flashlights. The cave is

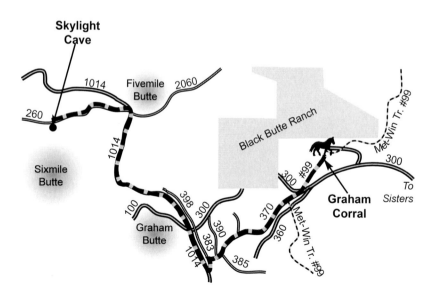

*Go into Skylight
Cave on a May
or June morning
and be treated to
an amazing light
show.*

closed from November 1 to April 15th to protect hibernating big-eared
bats, but that's OK because the sunbeams don't enter the cave then
anyway.

The Ride: On the west side of Graham Corral, pick up the southbound
Metolius-Windigo Trail #99 (heading toward Cow Camp and Three
Creek Meadow). After 0.7 mile, it crosses the red-cinder 300 Road
and runs along Road 370. In 0.3 mile the Met-Win veers left off Road
370, but you'll continue straight on Road 370 for 1.5 mile more. When
you reach red-cinder Road 1014, turn right and ride along it for 2.5
miles. (Or you can ride on dirt Roads 383 and 398 for part of this distance.) At the base of Five Mile Butte (which has antennas on top),
turn left on dirt Road 260 and ride 1.4 miles to Skylight Cave. The
cave is located at the junction of Road 260 and an unmarked dirt road.
Watch for a wooden Forest Service "Events" sign on the left, next to
the cave entrance. Climb down the ladder into the cave. With your
back to the ladder, turn left and walk 200 feet on the boulder-strewn
floor to reach the skylights.

Upper Butte Loop

Trailhead: Start at Graham Corral Horse Camp, or at the entrance to Indian Ford Campground

Length: 20 miles round trip from Graham Corral, or 16 miles round trip from Indian Ford Campground

Elevation: 3,250 to 4,000 feet

Difficulty: Moderate

Footing: Hoof protection recommended

Season: Early spring through late fall

Permits: Camping fee; no fee for day use at Graham Corral or outside Indian Ford campground.

Facilities: Toilets, potable water and corrals at Graham Corral. Parking for 2 trailers outside Indian Ford Campground. Stock water at Indian Ford Creek, next to Indian Ford Campground.

Highlights: The trail makes a loop completely around Black Butte and offers impressive mountain views through breaks in the trees.

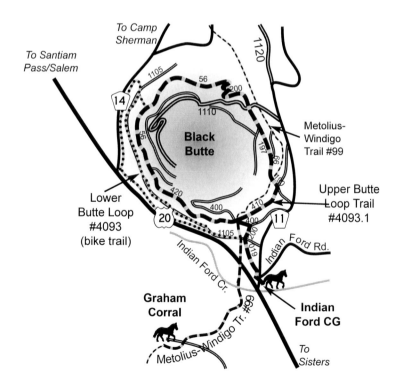

View of Mt. Jefferson from the Upper Butte Loop Trail.

Finding Indian Ford Campground: From Sisters, drive northwest on Hwy. 20 for 6 miles. Turn right on Road 11, then turn right into Indian Ford Campground and park next to the kiosk outside the entrance.

The Ride: From Graham Corral, on the east side of the campground, pick up the northbound Metolius-Windigo Trail #99 (toward Metolius River/Sheep Springs). You'll cross Hwy. 20 in about 2.4 miles. Continue on the Met-Win for 0.7 mile to the junction of Roads 400, 410, and 420. Turn right on Road 410, following the sign indicating the Upper Butte Loop. From Indian Ford Campground, cross Road 11 and pick up the trail immediately across the street. The trail veers to the right, and in 0.1 mile it turns left on Road 019 and heads toward Black Butte. After 1.1 miles, veer left next to a 4x4 post and follow the trail 0.1 mile to the intersection of Roads 1105 and 200. Follow the sign to the right on Road 200, then in 0.1 mile turn left on Road 400, and in another 0.1 mile you'll see a sign indicating you've reached the loop part of the trail. Turn right on Road 410. All, follow the Upper Butte Loop trail signs, as the trail is better signed in this direction. In several places the trail is somewhat overgrown, but it is discernable. The mountain views through the trees are impressive.

The world is best viewed through the ears of a horse.

Anonymous

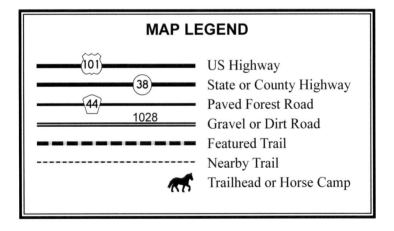

Broken Top
Todd Creek Horse Camp
Deschutes National Forest

Located less than 25 miles west of Bend, the trails that lie between Broken Top and Mt. Bachelor feature close-up mountain views, dense forests, alpine lakes, and beautiful wildflowers in season. Todd Creek Horse Camp doubles as a trailhead and overnight horse camp, and provides access to excellent high country riding in the Three Sisters Wilderness. You can also ride from several other trailheads that are a short distance west of Todd Creek. Be aware that the Broken Top, Todd, and Green Lakes Trails are very popular with hikers. Dogs are required to be on leash on these trails. In addition, the Metolius-Windigo Trail in this area is frequently used by mountain bike riders.

Whitney on Dixie and Debbie on Cowboy, enjoying the view of Mt. Bachelor along the Broken Top Trail.

Getting to Broken Top Area

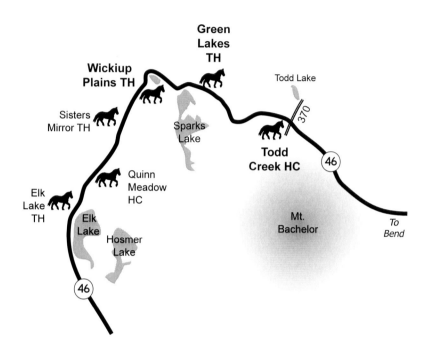

For more trails a short distance away, see the South Sister chapter.

Broken Top Area Trails

Trail	Difficulty	Elevation	Round Trip
Broken Top Loop	Moderate	6,100-7,200	13 miles
Green Lakes from Todd Cr.	Moderate	6,100-6,800	15 miles
Green Lakes Loop	Moderate	5,450-6,500	9-12.5 miles
Moraine Lake	Moderate	5,400-6,700	7.5-10 miles
Sparks Lake & Quinn Mdw.	Moderate	6,100-5,000	8-13 miles
Sparks & Hosmer Lakes	Moderate	6,100-5,450	8-14 miles
Wickiup Plain	Moderate	5,500-6,300	9-11 miles

Todd Creek Horse Camp

Directions: From Hwy. 97 in Bend, take Exit 138 (Colorado Ave.) and head west. Follow the signs toward Mt. Bachelor, which will put you on Hwy. 46 (Century Drive/Cascade Lakes Hwy.) Continue for 23 miles and turn left into the horse camp. The entrance is directly across the highway from the sign for Todd Lake.

Elevation: 6,200 feet

Campsites: 7 sites, each with a 2- or 4-horse metal corral. Easy parking for multiple rigs at each site. There is also day-use parking for 5-6 trailers.

Facilities: Toilet, fire pits, picnic tables. Stock water is available from nearby Todd Creek.

Permits: Northwest Forest Pass required for camping or day use. Camping fees may be imposed in the future.

Season: June through October

Contact: Bend/Ft. Rock Ranger District, 541-383-4000, www.fs.usda.gov/centraloregon, then click on "Recreation," "Horse Riding and Camping"

Campers hang out with their horses at Todd Creek Horse Camp.

Broken Top Loop

Trailhead:	Start at Todd Creek Horse Camp
Length:	13 miles round trip
Elevation:	6,100 to 7,200 feet
Difficulty:	Moderate -- several stream crossings
Footing:	Hoof protection recommended
Season:	Summer through fall
Permits:	Northwest Forest Pass required
Facilities:	Toilets, stock water, and manure bins at the horse camp. Stock water is available on the trail.

Highlights: The trail goes through beautiful forest, along sunlit meadows, and across a broad pumice plain. It offers a close-up look at craggy Broken Top, plus views of Mt. Bachelor and Sparks Lake. You'll pass Todd Lake, but horses are not permitted at the lake. About a month after the snow melts, the creekside wildflowers are dazzling.

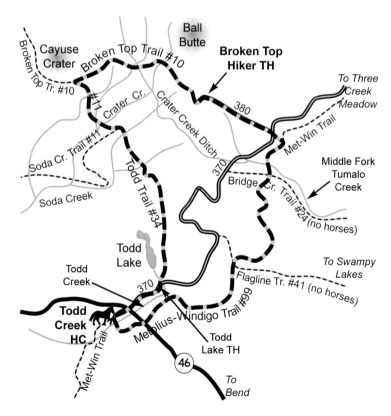

Please keep your horse on the trail in this fragile alpine environment. Dogs must be on leash on this trail. This stretch of the Met-Win is frequently used by mountain bike riders.

The Ride: From Todd Creek Horse Camp, cross Todd Creek and pick up the northbound Metolius-Windigo Trail #99, which crosses Hwy. 46 in 0.7 mile. The trail is marked with 4x4 posts, and is shared with mountain bikes. About 1.8 miles after crossing the road, the Flagline Trail #41 to Swampy Lakes goes off to the right and in 0.1 mile it goes off to the left to Road 370. In another 1.7 miles, the Bridge Creek Trail #24 crosses the Met-Win Trail. (There's a sign for the Bend Watershed on the right.) Continue straight for 0.6 mile and turn left at the next junction. In 0.2 mile you'll come to Road 370. Cross Road 370 and ride up Road 380 for 1.3 miles to the Broken Top hiker trailhead. Continue on the Broken Top Trail #10 for 2.2 miles, during which you'll have wonderful views of Broken Top and Mt. Bachelor, and you'll cross the man-made Crater Creek Ditch. When you reach the junction with the Soda Creek Trail #11, turn left. In 0.9 mile veer left on the Todd Trail #34, and in 2.2 miles you'll reach the hiker trailhead at Todd Lake. Turn right and ride beside Road 370 to return to the horse camp.

Joan on Bug, Whitney on Dixie, and Debbie on Cowboy,
riding at the foot of Broken Top.

Green Lakes from Todd Creek

Trailhead: Start at Todd Creek Horse Camp
Length: 15 miles round trip
Elevation: 6,100 to 6,800 feet
Difficulty: Moderate
Footing: Hoof protection recommended
Season: Summer through fall
Permits: Northwest Forest Pass required
Facilities: Toilets, stock water, and manure bins at the horse camp. Stock water is available on the trail.

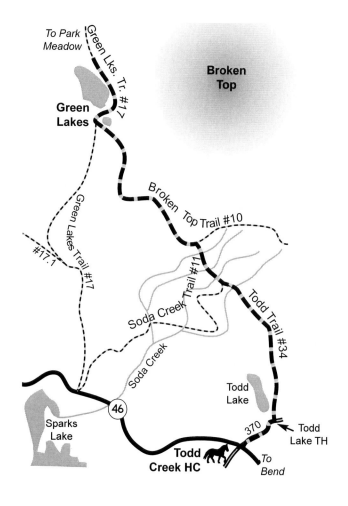

Highlights: Although this trail is a little less scenic than the Green Lakes Trail along Fall Creek, the Green Lakes themselves are just as impressive. And there are some good reasons to take this route: if you are camping at Todd Creek you can ride to Green Lakes without having to trailer out, Todd Creek has more parking for day riders than the Green Lakes trailhead, and you'll encounter fewer hikers on this route than on the Green Lakes Trail. Dogs must be on leash on this trail. Please keep your horse out of the lakes, as they are used for drinking water by backpackers.

The Ride: From Todd Creek Horse Camp, ride out the campground road to Hwy. 46, cross it, and continue for 0.6 mile along the side of Road 370 to Todd Lake. Pick up the Todd Trail #34 and follow it 2.2 miles to the junction with the Soda Creek Trail #11. Veer right on the Soda Creek Trail. In late July/early August you'll see beautiful wild-flower displays along the banks of the Soda Creek tributaries. After 0.9 mile, turn left on the Broken Top Trail #10 and follow it 3 miles to the southern-most Green Lake. Veer right on the Green Lakes Trail #17 to reach the larger Green Lake. The views of Broken Top and South Sister are impressive.

South Sister reflected in the largest of the Green Lakes.

Green Lakes Loop

Trailhead: Start at the Green Lakes trailhead

Length: 12.5 miles round trip for the loop, or 9 miles up and back to Green Lakes on the Green Lake Trail

Elevation: 5,450 to 6,500 feet

Difficulty: Moderate

Footing: Hoof protection recommended

Season: Summer through fall

Permits: Northwest Forest Pass required

Facilities: Toilet, hitching post, and parking for several trailers at the trailhead. Stock water is available on the trail.

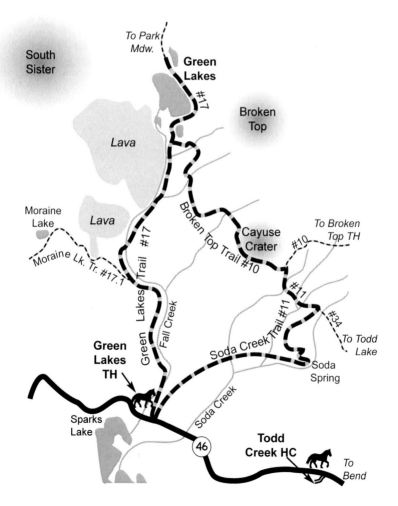

Nancy and Mesa take a break along the Green Lakes Trail. That's a waterfall behind them.

Highlights: This trail has it all. The Green Lakes are nestled between South Sister and Broken Top, with the mountains looming so close you can almost reach out and touch them. Add to this the waterfalls along Fall Creek and the enormous lava mesa on the flank of South Sister, and you have the makings of an unforgettable ride. The downside is that the Green Lakes Trail is one of the most popular hiking trails in Central Oregon. Plan to ride it on a weekday after Labor Day, as it can be very crowded in summer and on weekends. Dogs must be on leash on this trail. Please keep your horse out of the lakes, as they are used for drinking water by backpackers.

Finding the Green Lakes Trailhead: Take Highway 46 west from Bend about 26 miles. The Green Lakes trailhead is on the right side of the road.

The Ride: From the Green Lakes trailhead, ride north on the Green Lakes Trail #17. It goes through fairly dense forest and along the bank of the lovely Fall Creek (aptly named, as it has many small waterfalls). In 2.1 miles you'll reach the junction with the Moraine Lake Trail #17.1. Stay to the right, and in 2.3 more miles you'll reach the Green Lakes, passing a massive lava flow from South Sister along the way. After visiting the lakes, return to the south end of the Green Lakes basin, turn right on the Broken Top Trail #10 and follow it 3 miles, then veer right on the Soda Creek Trail #11. In 0.9 mile stay to the right at the junction with the Todd Trail #34, and follow the Soda Creek Trail 3.9 miles back to the trailhead. The return part of the loop is less heavily forested (and less heavily used) than the Fall Creek Trail, and offers some nice views to the south.

Moraine Lake

Trailhead: Start at either the Green Lakes trailhead or the Wickiup Plains trailhead

Length: 10 miles round trip from Wickiup Plains trailhead, or 7.5 miles round trip from Green Lakes trailhead

Elevation: 5,400 to 6,700 feet

Difficulty: Moderate

Footing: Hoof protection recommended

Season: Summer through fall

Permits: Northwest Forest Pass required

Facilities: Toilets and parking for several trailers at either trailhead. Stock water is available on the trail.

Highlights: As its name would suggest, Moraine Lake is located at the foot of a glacial moraine, a pile of unconsolidated dirt and rock deposited by a long-ago glacier. The sparse vegetation on the hills around the lake contrasts sharply with the beautiful alpine forest you ride

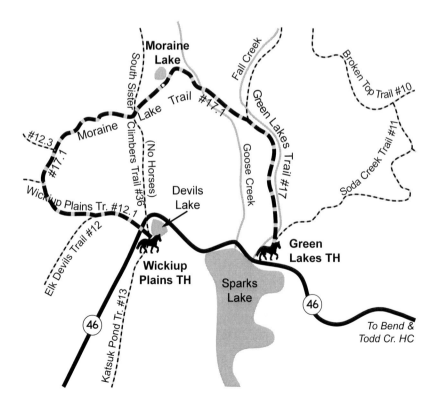

through to get there. Please keep your horse out of the lake, as it is a source of drinking water for many backpackers. Dogs must be on leash on this trail.

Finding the Green Lakes and Wickiup Plains Trailheads: From Bend, take Hwy. 46 west toward Mt. Bachelor for 26 miles to reach Green Lakes trailhead or 28 miles to reach Wickiup Plains trailhead.

The Ride: From the Green Lakes trailhead, pick up the Green Lakes Trail #17 and follow it along the beautiful Fall Creek for 2.1 miles. At the junction with the Moraine Lake Trail #17.1, turn left and ride about 1.5 mile farther to reach Moraine Lake. From the Wickiup Plains trailhead, pick up the Wickiup Plains Trail #12.1 and ride it 0.9 mile. At the junction with the Elk-Devils Trail #12, stay to the right. Continue another mile and turn right on the Moraine Lake Trail #17.1. In 1.4 miles more you'll cross the South Sister Climbers Trail and a mile after that you'll reach the lake. For a fun 9-mile variation on this ride, you can drop a trailer at the Green Lakes trailhead, drive another trailer the 2 miles to the Wickiup Plains trailhead, then ride the Wickiup Plains/Moraine Lake Trails up and the Green Lakes trail down to retrieve the dropped trailer.

Whitney on Luke, Mona on Eclipse, and Lydia on Shadow,
on a beautiful day at Moraine Lake.

Sparks Lake & Quinn Meadow

Trailhead: Start at Todd Creek Horse Camp

Length: 8 miles round trip to Sparks Lake, or 13 miles round trip to Quinn Meadow

Elevation: 6,100 to 5,000 feet

Difficulty: Moderate

Footing: Hoof protection recommended

Season: Summer through fall

Permits: Northwest Forest Pass required

Facilities: Plenty of parking for horse trailers. Toilets and stock water at Todd Creek and Quinn Meadow Horse Camps. Stock water is available on the trail.

Highlights: This is a mostly-forested ride that connects Sparks Lake with the two horse camps in the area.

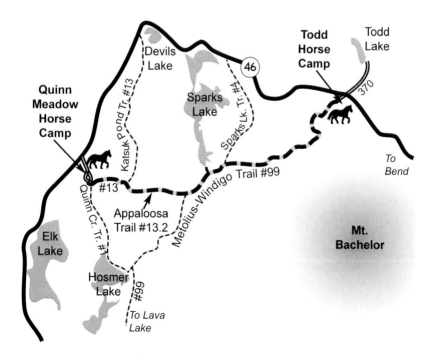

The Ride: Start by riding south from Todd Horse Camp on the Metolius-Windigo Trail #99, which begins along the dirt road on the west side of Todd Creek.   The road leads through an old quarry and crosses the creek, where it becomes a single-track trail that winds through the forest to a ridge that skirts the base of Mt. Bachelor.   You'll have good close-up views of the mountain, and on the other side of the ridge you can catch glimpses of Sparks Lake through the trees. After 3.5 miles you'll come to the junction with the Sparks Lake/Soda Creek Trail #4.   Stay to the left on the Met-Win Trail, and in 0.5 mile you'll come to a spur trail on the right that leads to Sparks Lake in a couple hundred yards.   The shore of Sparks Lake is a nice spot for a picnic.   About 0.5 mile past Sparks Lake the Met-Win Trail goes left toward Hosmer Lake, and the Appaloosa Trail #13.2 goes right toward Quinn Meadow.   Turn right on the Appaloosa Trail.   In 1.6 miles you'll reach another junction.   Veer left on the Katsuk Pond Trail #13, and in 0.8 mile you'll reach Quinn Meadow Horse Camp.

Ray and Connie ride through a meadow
not far from Quinn Meadow Horse Camp.

Sparks & Hosmer Lakes

Trailhead: Start at Todd Creek Horse Camp

Length: 8 miles round trip to Sparks Lake, or 14 miles round trip to Hosmer Lake

Elevation: 6,100 to 5,450 feet to Sparks Lake, or 6,100 to 5,100 feet to Hosmer Lake

Difficulty: Moderate

Footing: Hoof protection recommended

Season: Summer through fall

Permits: Northwest Forest Pass required for camping or day use

Facilities: Plenty of parking for horse trailers. Toilet, stock water, and manure bin at the horse camp. Stock water is available on the trail.

Highlights: This trail runs from Todd Creek Horse Camp to Sparks Lake and Hosmer Lake. Most of the trail is forested but there are filtered views of Mt. Bachelor and South Sister at several points along the trail. While at Sparks Lake, be sure to walk to your right along the

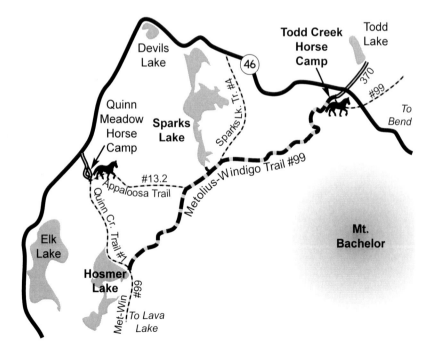

Lydia, Whitney, and Debbie ride the Metolius-Windigo Trail near Hosmer Lake. Mt. Bachelor is in the background.

lake shore to get a marvelous view of South Sister. This stretch of the Met-Win is often used by mountain bike riders.

The Ride: Pick up the southbound Metolius-Windigo Trail #99, which initially runs along a dirt road on the west side of Todd Creek. For the first 0.7 mile, the trail follows the dirt road as it runs through a cinder quarry. Then it crosses Todd Creek and becomes a single-track trail through the forest. After 3.5 miles you'll come to a junction with the Sparks Lake/Soda Creek Trail #4. Stay to the left on the Met-Win Trail and 0.5 mile later you'll reach the spur trail that leads to the right a few hundred yards to the shore of Sparks Lake and a very nice picnic spot. Return to the Met-Win Trail, and in 0.5 mile the Appaloosa Trail #13.2 to Quinn Meadow goes off to the right. Continue left toward Lava Lake for 3 miles, to the junction with the Quinn Creek Trail #1. If you turn right on the Quinn Creek Trail and ride a short distance you can leave the trail, ride to the edge of the ridge you're on, and see Hosmer Lake below you. There are only filtered views of the lake from either the Quinn Creek or Met-Win Trails, and you can't get close enough to Hosmer Lake to water your horse. Retrace your steps to return to Todd Creek.

Wickiup Plain

Trailhead: Start at Wickiup Plains trailhead

Length: 9 miles round trip to the end of Wickiup Plain, or 11 miles round trip out and back to Mesa Creek

Elevation: 5,500 to 6,300 feet

Difficulty: Moderate

Footing: Hoof protection recommended

Season: Summer through fall

Permits: Northwest Forest Pass required

Facilities: Toilets, hitching posts, plenty of parking for trailers. No water is available on the trail unless you continue to Mesa Creek.

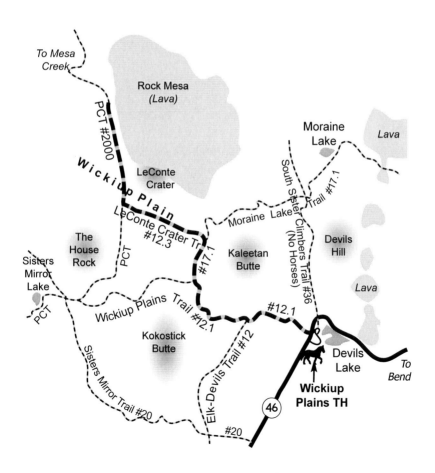

Connie and Lydia ride Jane and Shadow across
Wickiup Plain, with South Sister in the background.

Highlights: Wickiup Plain is an ancient ash flow that lies at the base of Rock Mesa and LeConte Crater, south and a little west of South Sister. Its gravelly surface and sparse vegetation contrast sharply with the surrounding forest, plus it offers spectacular views of South Sister. The trail includes stands of beautiful old-growth forest. Above the tree line, please stay on the trail to protect the plain's fragile ecosystem.

Finding the Wickiup Plains Trailhead: Take Highway 46 west from Bend toward Mt. Bachelor for 28 miles. The Wickiup Plains trailhead is on the left side of the road just past Devils Lake.

The Ride: Pick up the Wickup Plains Trail #12.1 from the horse trailer parking area. After 0.9 mile, stay to the right at the junction with the Elk-Devils Trail, and in another mile veer right on the Moraine Lake Trail #17.1. Follow it 0.5 mile, then turn left toward Wickiup Plain on the LeConte Crater Trail #12.3. Ride across the plain, and after 1.4 miles the trail intersects with the Pacific Crest Trail #2000. Turn right on the PCT and continue another 1.3 miles across the plain. Once you reach the forest at the north end of Wickiup Plain, you can continue on the PCT another mile to Mesa Creek to water your horses before returning to the trailhead.

No hour of life is wasted that is spent in the saddle

Winston Churchill

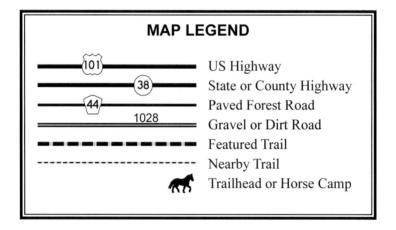

Cline Buttes Recreation Area

Bureau of Land Management

The Cline Buttes Recreation Area's year-round accessibility and proximity to Bend, Redmond, and Sisters make this a very popular equestrian riding area. The Bureau of Land Management (BLM) has completed a lengthy public planning process for the Cline Buttes area, and as this book went to press they were just beginning to implement the plan, which will take several years to accomplish.

The intent of the Cline Buttes plan is to balance the public's desire for recreation opportunities with the need to protect habitat for wildlife and plants. (The area is home to nesting golden eagles and prairie falcons, plus deer and elk and a rare plant called Peck's milkvetch.) To accomplish this balance, some trails and roads will be decommissioned and seasonal trail closures will be implemented to protect wildlife. BLM will also try to decrease user conflicts by separating non-motorized and motorized users to the extent possible. The result is that current use patterns at Cline Buttes will change as OHV use is limited to specific areas, some of the existing trails and *(continued on next page)*

The Three Sisters from the Cline Buttes Recreation Area.

89

Cline Buttes Recreation Area

(continued from previous page) roads are closed, and other new trails are developed. These changes are necessary in order to keep humans from loving the area to death.

It's also important to note that there is some privately-owned land within the Cline Buttes area and cattle are still grazed on the BLM land. If you encounter a fence, please respect it, and if you come to a closed gate, please shut it again after you go through it.

As of this writing, there are 4 trailheads in the Cline Buttes area that can accommodate horses: Fryrear, Dusty Loop, Tumalo Canal, and Maston. (The latter 3 are dirt turnouts on the side of the road.) The long-term plan calls for three more equestrian trailheads to be built and for the existing trailheads to be improved, including moving the Fryrear trailhead to a location with safer highway access.

The maps in this chapter are based upon the plan for the Cline Buttes Recreation area, rather than reflecting the current network of trails and roads. For the next few years equestrians will likely find that conditions on the ground don't match the plan. Over time, however, the changes will be implemented. The trails may eventually be signed with names and numbers so users can more easily find their way. Until then, half the fun of riding in the Cline Buttes area is exploring the vast network of trails and roads and getting to know your way around through trial and error. So head to a trailhead, pick a trail or dirt road to ride, and go exploring!

Ann rides Brass through Dry Canyon, not far from the Fryrear trailhead.

Getting to Cline Buttes Trailheads

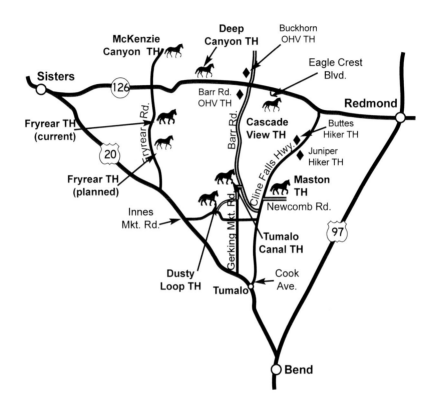

Cline Buttes Area Trails

Trail Area	Difficulty	Elevation	Round Trip
Buttes	Easy	3,100-3,900	8-12 miles
Cascade View	Easy	Varies	8-12 miles
Deep Canyon	Easy	2,700-3,100	Varies
Dusty Loop	Easy	3,150-3,300	Varies
Endurance Loop	Challenging	3,000-3,900	25-30 miles
Fryrear	Easy	2,900-3,300	Varies
Maston	Easy	Varies	Varies
Tumalo Canal	Easy	3,100-3,450	Varies

Buttes

Trailhead: Start at either the Cascade View or Maston trailheads
Length: Currently, 8 miles round trip from the Cascade View turnout, or 12 miles round trip from the Maston trailhead
Elevation: 3,100 to 3,900 feet
Difficulty: Easy
Footing: Hoof protection is recommended
Season: Year-round
Permits: None
Facilities: Until the trailheads are built you'll find parking for 2 trailers at the Cascade View turnout and 3 trailers at the Maston trailhead. No stock water on the trail.

Highlights: The views from the top of the middle Cline Butte are panoramic, and well worth the exertion of getting there. You can ride from either the Maston or the Cascade View trailheads, although currently from Cascade View you can only reach the buttes by riding cross country around the north and east sides of Eagle Crest Resort.

Finding Cascade View and Maston Trailheads: See the Cascade View and Maston ride pages for directions to the two trailheads.

The Ride: From the Maston trailhead you can ride across the Maston area, cross Cline Falls Hwy., and make your way to the buttes. From

Connie and Teresa want to take in the view from the middle butte, but Diamond and Kodie only want to eat the bunchgrass.

the Cascade View trailhead, you will ultimately be able to make a loop by riding between Eagle Crest and the planned Thornburgh resort, climbing over the buttes, and circling Eagle Crest on the east and north. For now, though, this route is blocked by a fence that stretches from Eagle Crest to Barr Road, so you'll have to do an out-and-back ride around Eagle Crest to the north and east. See the Cascade View ride pages for more information.

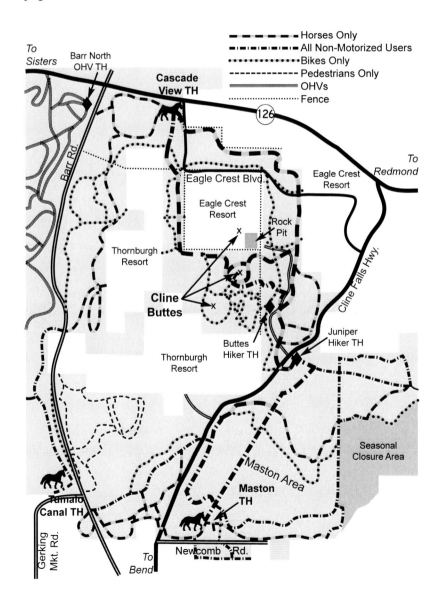

Cascade View

Trailhead: Start at Cascade View trailhead

Length: 8 miles round trip to the summit of middle Cline Butte by riding around Eagle Crest Resort to the north and east. In the future, there will be an approximately 9 mile loop through the buttes, and an approximately 12 mile round trip out-and-back trail to Tumalo Canal trailhead

Elevation: 3,100 to 3,900 feet to the top of the middle butte, or 3,050 to 3,200 to Tumalo Canal trailhead

Difficulty: Easy, but a GPS and a Sisters Ranger District map will come in handy

Footing: Lower-elevation trails are suitable for barefoot horses. Hoof protection recommended for the trail up the butte.

Season: Year-round

Permits: None

Facilities: Until the trailhead is built there is parking for 2 rigs at a small roadside turnout. No stock water on the trail.

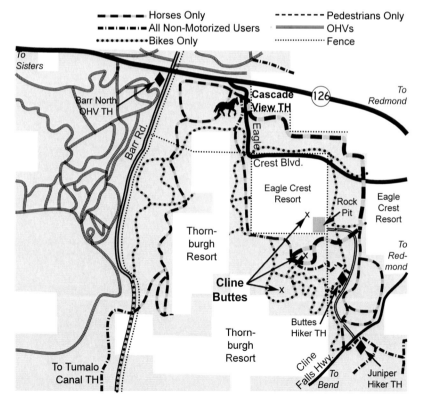

Teresa on Kodie and Connie on Diamond, riding near the Cascade View trailhead.

Highlights: From this trailhead you will eventually be able to ride to the Tumalo Canal trailhead or ride between the Eagle Crest and Thornburgh Resorts and make a loop over the Cline Buttes. For now, though, you'll have to content yourself with an out-and-back ride that skirts Eagle Crest Resort to reach the summit of the middle Cline Butte, because there isn't yet a gate through the fence that runs from Eagle Crest to Barr Road. And since the official trail hasn't been built yet you'll have to ride cross country a good bit of the way. The south butte is designated for bike trails, the middle butte has horse trails, and the north butte is private property. The views from the summit of the middle butte are panoramic.

Finding Cascade View Trailhead: From Redmond, drive west on Hwy. 126 for 7 miles and turn left on Eagle Crest Blvd. From Sisters, take Hwy. 126 east toward Redmond. In 12 miles, turn right on Eagle Crest Blvd. All, continue 0.5 mile on Eagle Crest Blvd. to the small dirt parking turnout on the right.

The Ride: From the trailhead, cross Eagle Crest Blvd. and ride south along the fence line (there is no trail), following it as it curves to the southeast. After awhile you'll hit a dirt road that will take you south, past the rock pit, and to the dirt road that runs to the top of the middle butte, where you'll enjoy a marvelous 360-degree view.

Deep Canyon

Trailhead: Start at the Deep Canyon or McKenzie Canyon trailheads

Length: Varies by route taken

Elevation: 2,700 to 3,100 feet

Difficulty: Easy

Footing: Suitable for barefoot horses

Season: Year-round

Permits: None

Facilities: Trailheads are not yet developed. No stock water on the trail.

Highlights: As of our publication date, the Deep Canyon and McKenzie Canyon trailheads do not yet exist. When they are developed, they will provide access to rimrock-walled Deep Canyon. The trails down into the canyon will be closed seasonally to protect wildlife, but there will be trails around the canyon that are open year-round. The area

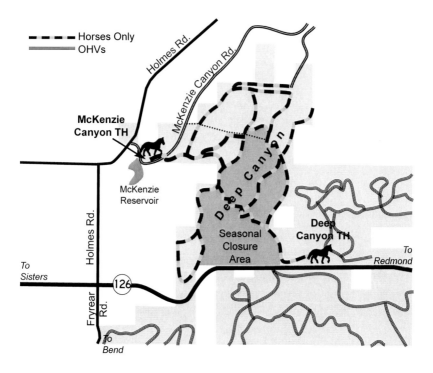

northwest of the canyon is relatively flat and offers nice views down into the canyon from several vantage points.

Finding Deep Canyon Trailhead: This trailhead will be located on the north side of Highway 126 about 9 miles east of Sisters and 11 miles west of Redmond, just west of the 102-mile marker. There is currently a dirt road here, but nowhere for trailers to park or turn around.

Finding McKenzie Canyon Trailhead: This trailhead will eventually be located along McKenzie Canyon Road about 0.5 mile east of Holmes Road.

The Ride: From the McKenzie Canyon trailhead you will be able to explore the juniper- and sage-covered flat above Deep Canyon, ride the western rim of the canyon, or make your way down into the canyon itself.   From the Deep Canyon trailhead, the trails will go along the eastern rim and down into the canyon.

Linda and Beamer on the rim above Deep Canyon.

Dusty Loop

Trailhead: Start at the Dusty Loop trailhead

Length: Varies by route taken

Elevation: 3,150 to 3,300 feet

Difficulty: Easy, but a GPS and a Sisters Ranger District map will come in handy

Footing: Suitable for barefoot horses

Season: Year-round

Permits: None

Facilities: Parking for 2-3 trailers. No stock water on the trail.

Highlights: From the unimproved parking area on Dusty Loop, you can easily ride to the Tumalo Canal trailhead on Barr Road or create your own loops using the dirt roads in the area. You may even be able

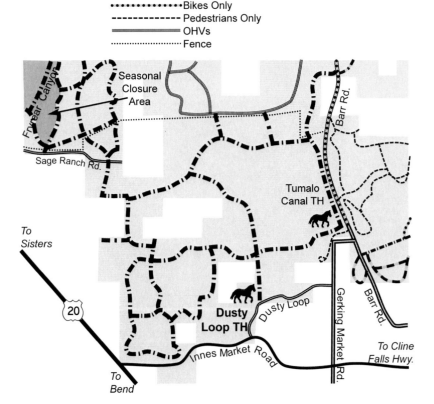

Debbie rides Mel down a dirt road near Dusty Loop, with North Sister in the background.

to find your way to the south ends of Dry Canyon and Fryrear Canyon. All of this riding is easy, and most of it is on dirt roads. However, none of the roads are signed, so you will truly be exploring.

Finding Dusty Loop Trailhead: <u>From Bend</u>, drive northwest on Hwy. 20 for 11 miles, turn right on Innes Market Road and follow it 1.8 miles.   <u>From Redmond</u>, take Hwy. 126 west for 4.5 miles, turn south on Cline Falls Hwy. and continue 6.5 miles. Turn right on Innes Market Road and follow it 2.5 miles. <u>From Sisters</u>, drive southeast on Hwy. 20 for 10 miles, turn left on Innes Market Road and follow it 1.8 miles.   <u>All</u>, turn north on Dusty Loop and go 0.4 mile to the trailhead on the left.

The Ride: From the parking area, pick up one of the trails or dirt roads that leads northward. Skirt the private property in the area (shown on the map in white) and after about a mile you can head east toward the Tumalo Canal trailhead or west to the loops between Highway 20 and Innes Market Road. Or if you continue northward about 2 more miles you can veer left and make your way toward Dry and Fryrear Canyons. It's almost guaranteed that on the first try to you won't end up where you intended to go, but isn't that the challenge of going exploring?

Endurance Loop

Trailhead: Start at the Tumalo Canal, Cascade View, or Maston trail-heads

Length: 25 to 30 miles round trip, depending on route taken

Elevation: 3,000 to 3,900 feet

Difficulty: Trails are easy, distance is challenging; a GPS and a Sisters Ranger District map will come in handy

Footing: Suitable for barefoot horses (except the rocky trail to the summit of the middle butte)

Season: Year-round

Permits: None

Facilities: As of this writing, the Tumalo Canal trailhead can accommodate many trailers, the Cascade View trailhead can hold 2 trailers, and the Maston trailhead can hold 2-3 trailers. No stock water on the trail.

Highlights: You can easily create your own long-distance route by linking the various trails that run between the Cascade View, Tumalo Canal, and Maston trailheads, including climbing to the top of the middle Cline Butte if you're so inclined.

Finding The Trailheads: See the directions to the Tumalo Canal, Cascade View, or Maston trailheads on their respective ride pages in this chapter.

The Ride: The plan is to eventually have a loop trail that goes around the Cline Buttes, Eagle Crest Resort, the proposed Thornburgh Resort,

Linda and Beamer move out along one of the trails in the Maston area.

the Tumalo Canal area, and Maston Plateau. As of this writing, it isn't possible to complete this loop because of the fence that runs from Barr Road to Eagle Crest. However, most of the dirt roads that comprise the route are open and rideable, so with a bit of creativity you can make your own long-distance ride. Until the Maston and Cascade View trailheads are built, the best parking is at the Tumalo Canal parking area on the south end of Barr Road.

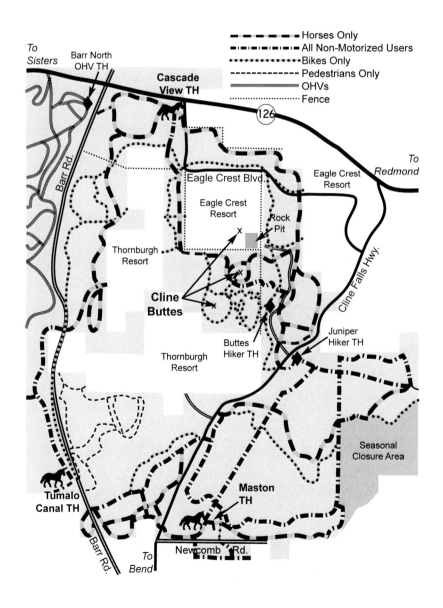

Fryrear

Trailhead: Start at the Fryrear Trailhead

Length: Varies depending on route taken

Elevation: 2,900 to 3,300 feet

Difficulty: Easy, but a GPS and a Sisters Ranger District map will come in handy

Footing: Suitable for barefoot horses

Season: Year round

Permits: None

Facilities: Parking for 4-5 trailers at the current Fryrear Trailhead, but a larger parking area is planned when the trailhead is moved. No stock water on the trail.

Highlights: Equestrians who have ridden here for years know that the most delightful features of the Cline Buttes area, with the possi-

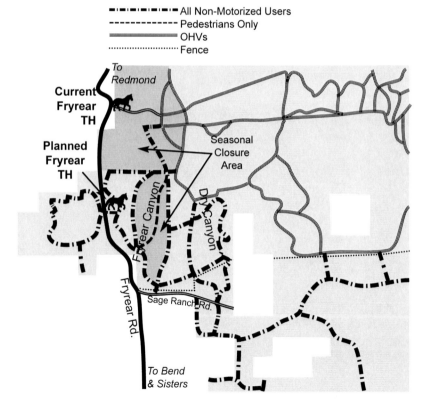

ble exception of the buttes themselves, are Fryrear Canyon and Dry Canyon. The basalt walls of the canyons tower impressively above the trail, and if you look carefully you can even find pictographs in Fryrear Canyon. The seasonal trail closure of Fryrear Canyon for wildlife protection extends from February 1 to August 1. You can ride around Fryrear Canyon during the closure period, but not through it. Dry Canyon is open year-round.

Finding Fryrear Trailhead: In the future, the Fryrear trailhead will be moved about 2.5 miles south of the current trailhead. To reach the current Fryrear trailhead <u>from Bend</u>, drive northwest on Hwy. 20 for 13 miles, turn right on Fryrear Road, and continue 4 miles to the trailhead. <u>From Redmond</u>, drive west on Hwy. 126 for 13.5 miles, turn left on Fryrear Road, and continue 1.8 miles to the trailhead. <u>From Sisters</u>, drive east on Hwy. 126 for 5 miles, turn right on Fryrear Road, and continue 1.8 miles to the trailhead.

The Ride: To explore the canyons, head south from the current trailhead. It's important to note that while OHVs will not be permitted on the non-motorized trails, horses and other non-motorized users may, at their own risk, use the motorized trails.

Lydia on Shadow and Whitney on Dixie,
traveling through Dry Canyon.

Maston

Trailhead: Start at the Maston trailhead

Length: Varies by route taken in the Maston area. 12 miles round trip to the summit of the middle Cline Butte

Elevation: 3,050 to 3,300 feet for the Maston area only, or 3,100 to 3,900 feet to ride to the summit of the middle Cline Butte

Difficulty: Easy, but a GPS and a Sisters Ranger District map will come in handy

Footing: The Maston area is suitable for barefoot horses, but hoof protection is recommended if you ride to the top of the buttes

Season: Year-round

Permits: None

Facilities: Until the trailhead is built the turnout has parking for 2-3 rigs. No stock water on the trail.

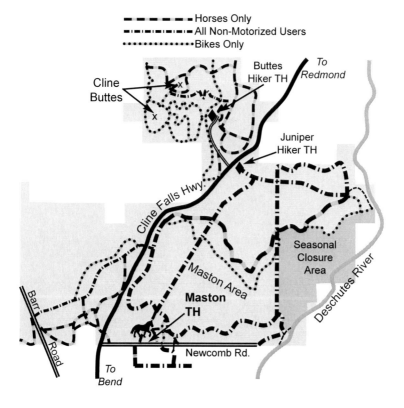

Highlights: The first place you'll see evidence of the implementation of the Cline Buttes Recreation Plan will be in the Maston area, east of Cline Falls Hwy. A large gravel trailhead on Newcomb Road is planned for this non-motorized area, along with trails for horses and mountain bikes. If you ride to the rim of the Deschutes River, you'll have nice views overlooking the river and the canyon it flows through.

Finding Maston Trailhead: <u>From Bend</u>, take Hwy. 20 northwest for 6 miles. In Tumalo, turn right on Cook Ave., which soon becomes Cline Falls Hwy., and drive 13 miles. <u>From Redmond</u>, drive east on Hwy. 126 for 4.5 miles, turn south on Cline Falls Hwy. and continue 5.5 miles. <u>From Sisters</u>, drive east on Hwy. 126 for 15 miles, turn south on Cline Falls Hwy. and continue 5.5 miles. <u>All</u>, turn east on Newcomb Road and drive 0.9 mile to the trailhead.

The Ride: The terrain is fairly flat in the Maston area, and the footing is sandy. This is a popular mountain biking destination in the winter. The horse trails will be partially separated from the mountain bike trails, though the two types of trails will run next to one another in some areas in order to minimize the disruption to native wildlife. You can also ride to the summit of the middle Cline Butte from this trailhead. See the Buttes ride pages in this chapter for more information.

You can't ride down to the Deschutes River, but you can tie your horse and walk to the canyon rim to see the river below.

Tumalo Canal

Trailhead: Start at the Tumalo Canal trailhead

Length: Varies depending on route taken

Elevation: 3,100 to 3,450 feet

Difficulty: Easy, but a GPS and a Sisters Ranger District map will come in handy

Footing: Suitable for barefoot horses

Season: Year round

Permits: None

Facilities: Parking for many trailers. No stock water on the trail.

Highlights: The Tumalo Canal trailhead provides access to miles of easy riding on old dirt roads. You'll encounter several of the historic

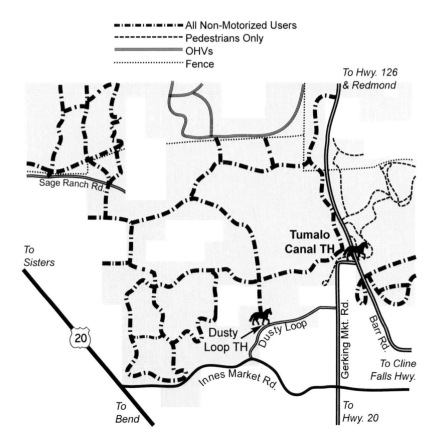

Lydia and Shadow ride past a rock outcropping
east of the Tumalo Canal trailhead.

canals that lace the area. These canals were built in the very early 1900's but were never used because Tumalo Reservoir failed to hold water.

Finding Tumalo Canal Trailhead: From Redmond, take Hwy. 126 west for 4.5 miles, turn south on Cline Falls Hwy. and drive 6.5 miles, then turn right on Barr Road. Follow it for 1.5 miles to the trailhead. From Bend, take Hwy. 20 northwest for 5.5 miles to Tumalo and turn right on Cook Ave., which soon becomes Cline Falls Hwy. In 4 miles, turn left on Barr Road and follow it 1.5 miles to the trailhead. From Sisters, take Hwy. 20 southeast for 14 miles. Just before the highway heads downhill into Tumalo, turn left on Gerking Market Road. Follow it 4.5 miles to the trailhead.

The Ride: The Cline Buttes themselves rise just northeast of the trailhead, but you can't ride directly to them because the land between is privately owned. The area just east of the trailhead provides hiker-only trails to explore the historic irrigation canals. Horses are permitted in the area to the west and north of the trailhead, where the terrain is juniper-covered and mostly flat, with occasional rock outcroppings and small hills. You'll be able to see the Cascades from several vantage points.

Horse sense is the thing a horse has which keeps it from betting on people.

W. C. Fields

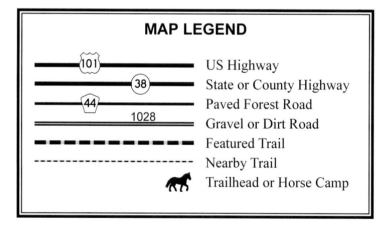

MAP LEGEND

101	US Highway
38	State or County Highway
44	Paved Forest Road
1028	Gravel or Dirt Road
	Featured Trail
	Nearby Trail
	Trailhead or Horse Camp

Cultus Lake
Cultus Corral

Deschutes National Forest

Cultus Lake is located in the heart of the Cascade Lakes District, about an hour southwest of Bend. Horse camping is available at Cultus Corral, a couple of miles from Cultus Lake. The horse camp has 4-horse log corrals, large parking pads at each campsite, and plentiful shade provided by lodgepole pines. To reach additional trailheads you can ride from the horse camp or you can trailer a short distance. Most of the trails in the area are relatively easy and lend themselves to trotting, gaiting, or cantering. The word "cultus" is Chinook jargon that means "worthless." It is believed that the term was used to refer to the lack of adequate forage for horses in the area. It certainly doesn't refer to the nearby trails, which are delightful.

Serviceberry blooms on the shore of Deer Lake.

Getting to Cultus Lake

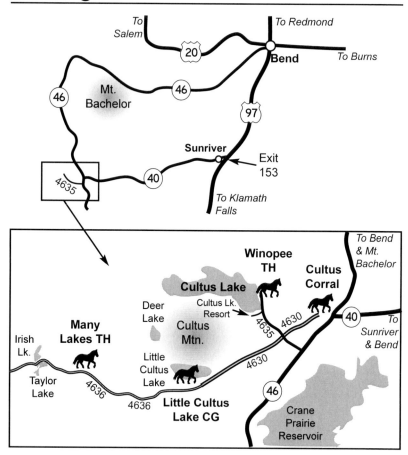

Cultus Lake Trails

Trail	Difficulty	Elevation	Round Trip
Bench Mark Butte	Moderate	4,450-4,800	9 miles
Bench Mark/Cultus Loop	Moderate	4,450-5,100	15 miles
Corral Lakes	Moderate	4,700-5,100	10-16 miles
Irish & Taylor Lakes	Easy	4,750-5,600	12-18 miles
Many Lakes Loop	Moderate	4,750-5,400	11.5-17.5 miles
Teddy Lakes	Moderate	4,450-4,950	13.5 miles
Winopee Lake	Moderate	4,450-5,000	12.5-22.5 miles
Winopee Tie	Easy	4,450-4,800	6-8 miles

Cultus Corral

Directions: From Bend, drive south on Hwy. 97 for 16 miles. Take Exit 153 and head west on Hwy. 40. In 21 miles, turn left on Hwy. 46 and drive 1.2 miles, then turn right on Road 4635 toward Cultus Lake Resort. In 0.7 mile, turn right on Road 4630. The horse camp is on the right in 1.1 miles. The route is well signed. Alternatively, you can take Hwy. 46 (the Cascade Lakes Hwy.) past Mt. Bachelor to Road 4635.

Elevation: 4,450 feet

Campsites: 11 sites with 4-horse corrals. All sites are level and back-in, and most have room for 2 trailers. There is also a day-use area with parking for 8-10 trailers.

Facilities: Vault toilet, manure bin, garbage cans. All sites have fire pits and picnic tables. Stock water from a pump.

Permits: Camping fee, or Northwest Forest Pass for day use

Season: Summer through fall

Contact: Bend/Ft. Rock Ranger District: 541-383-4000, www.fs.usda.gov/centraloregon, then click on "Recreation," "Horse Riding and Camping." Concessionaire: 541-338-7869, www.hoodoo.com, then click on "Campgrounds," "Horse Camping," "Cultus Corral."

Mo and Dixie await dinner at Cultus Corral Horse Camp.

Bench Mark Butte

Trailhead: Start at Cultus Corral

Length: 9 miles round trip from the horse camp to the Corral Swamp trailhead

Elevation: 4,450 to 4,800 feet

Difficulty: Moderate

Footing: Hoof protection recommended

Season: Summer through fall

Permits: Camping fee, or Northwest Forest Pass required for day-use parking at Cultus Corral

Facilities: Toilets, stock water, and parking for 8-10 trailers at Cultus Corral. No stock water on the trail.

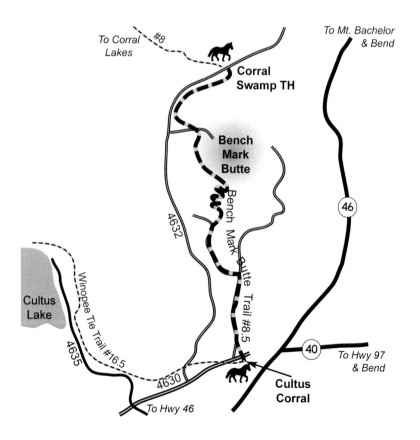

Highlights: This trail departs from Cultus Corral and runs over the flank of Bench Mark Butte to the Corral Swamp trailhead. The trail is fairly rocky in some sections, and has some switchbacks. Otherwise the trail is an easy one.

The Ride: Pick up the Bench Mark Butte Trail #8.5 at Cultus Corral between campsite 11 and the shelter. The trail is marked with gray diamonds and runs on a combination of dirt roads and single-track trails. About 2.5 miles from Cultus Corral there is a sharp right turn (marked with rock cairns) that you could miss if you aren't watching carefully. The trail climbs gradually but steadily over the flank of 5,028-foot Bench Mark Butte, then descends to the Corral Swamp trailhead. About 4 miles into the ride, keep an eye out for some peek-a-boo views of Mt. Bachelor through the trees. Once you reach the Corral Swamp trailhead, you can either continue on toward Corral Lakes on Trail #8 (about 3 miles farther -- see the next several pages for more information) or retrace your steps to Cultus Corral.

Whitney, Diana, Lydia and Connie make a
switchback on the Bench Mark Butte Trail.

Bench Mark Butte/Cultus Lake Loop

Trailhead: Start at Cultus Corral

Length: 15 miles round trip

Elevation: 4,450 to 5,100 feet

Difficulty: Moderate

Footing: Hoof protection recommended

Season: Summer through fall

Permits: Camping fee, or Northwest Forest Pass required for day-use parking at Cultus Corral

Facilities: Toilets, stock water, and parking for 8-10 trailers at Cultus Corral. Stock water is available on the trail.

Connie on Diamond and Whitney on Dixie,
on the Winopee Lake Trail along the shore of Cultus Lake.

Highlights: This is a relatively easy and scenic loop ride. Some of the route is in fir and hemlock forest, and some is in lodgepole forest. The trail passes several pretty lakes and swampy meadows.

The Ride: Pick up the Bench Mark Butte Trail #8.5, which leaves Cultus Corral between campsite 11 and the shelter. The trail follows forest roads and single-track trails for 4.5 miles over the side of Bench Mark Butte to the Corral Swamp trailhead. Then pick up the Corral Swamp Trail #8, which in 2 miles passes the junction with the Met-Win Trail #99 to Lucky Lake. After another mile you'll ride between North and South Corral lakes. Continue 2.3 miles, turn left onto the Winopee Trail #16 and continue 2.4 miles to the Winopee trailhead. From there, take the Winopee Tie Trail #16.5 and follow it 3 miles back to Cultus Corral. For additional information, see the pages in this chapter devoted to the Bench Mark Butte, Corral Lakes, and Winopee Tie Trails.

Corral Lakes

Trailhead: Start at Cultus Corral or at the Winopee trailhead at Cultus Lake

Length: 10 miles round trip from Winopee trailhead, or 16 miles round trip from Cultus Corral

Elevation: 4,700 to 5,100 feet

Difficulty: Moderate

Footing: Hoof protection recommended

Season: Summer through fall

Permits: Camping fee, or Northwest Forest Pass required for day-use parking at either Cultus Corral or Winopee trailhead

Facilities: Toilets, stock water, and parking for 8-10 trailers at Cultus Corral. Parking for 1-2 trailers at Winopee trailhead, with toilets and potable water at nearby Cultus Lake Campground. Stock water is available on the trail.

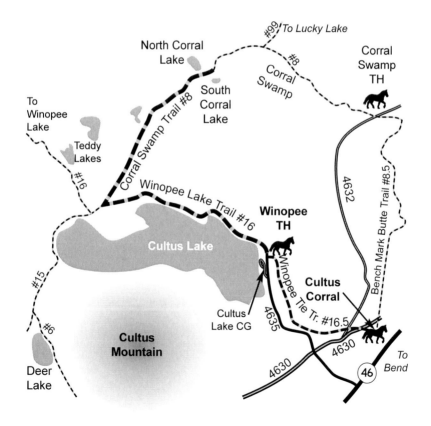

Highlights: This is an enjoyable ride that runs through the forest along the north shore of Cultus Lake, then veers northeast through fir and lodgepole forest to North and South Corral lakes. The views along Cultus Lake are nice, and North Corral Lake makes a good picnic spot.

Finding Winopee Trailhead: Follow the directions to Cultus Corral at the beginning of this chapter, but instead of turning right on Road 4630, go straight and follow the signs toward Cultus Lake Campground and Winopee trailhead. Parking at the trailhead is very limited, so be sure to turn around and park where you can't be blocked by hiker cars.

The Ride: From Cultus Corral, pick up the Winopee Tie Trail #16.5 between campsites 7 and 8 and ride it to the Winopee trailhead on the shore of Cultus Lake. (See the Winopee Tie Trail pages in this chapter for more information.) From Winopee trailhead, take the Winopee Lake Trail #16 west along the shore of Cultus Lake for 2.4 miles. At the first junction, turn right toward Corral Lakes on the Corral Swamp Trail #8. In about 2.3 miles you will reach North Corral Lake.

Whitney and Cody pose near the shore of North Corral Lake.

Irish & Taylor Lakes

Trailhead: Start at Little Cultus Lake Campground or at Cultus Corral

Length: 12 miles round trip from Little Cultus Lake, or 18 miles round trip from Cultus Corral

Elevation: 4,750 to 5,600 feet

Difficulty: Easy

Footing: Hoof protection recommended

Season: Summer through fall

Permits: Camping fee, or Northwest Forest Pass required for day-use parking at Cultus Corral or near Little Cultus Lake Campground

Facilities: Toilet, stock water, and parking for 8-10 trailers at Cultus Corral. Toilet, potable water, and parking for 2-3 trailers near Little Cultus Lake Campground. Stock water is available on the trail.

Highlights: This is a fun road ride that goes past the trailheads for Lemish Lake and Many Lakes and ends at the beautiful Irish and Taylor Lakes near the junction of Road 4636 and the Pacific Crest Trail.

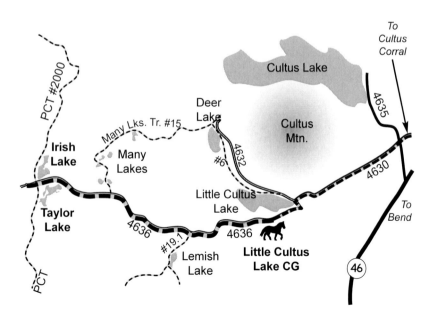

Connie on Diamond and Lydia on Shadow,
relaxing at Irish Lake.

Finding Little Cultus Lake Campground: Follow the directions to
Cultus Corral at the beginning of this chapter, but instead of turning
right on Road 4630, turn left. Continue 2.9 miles to Little Cultus Lake
Campground. You can either park in at the campground (and pay the
camping fee) or drive through the campground to turn around and find
a pull-off on the side of Road 4630 just before the campground.

The Ride: From Cultus Corral, ride Road 4630 west for 2.9 miles to
Little Cultus Lake Campground. From Little Cultus Lake Campground, ride west on Road 4636. The road is too rough for horse trailers, but it makes a great ride on horseback. After about 2.3 miles you
will pass Lemish Lake trailhead, the jumping-off point for the trail to
Lemish Lake (1 mile south) and Charlton Butte. Follow Road 4636
about 2 miles farther and you'll pass the Many Lakes trailhead, the
gateway to dozens of small lakes. Continue on Road 4636 for 1.8
miles to Taylor Lake and Irish Lake. These two scenic lakes are directly across the road from one another, and the Pacific Crest Trail
runs along their western edges.

Many Lakes Loop

Trailhead: Start at Little Cultus Lake Campground or at Cultus Corral

Length: 11.5 miles round trip from Little Cultus Lake Campground, or 17.5 miles round trip from Cultus Corral

Elevation: 4,750 to 5,400 feet

Difficulty: Moderate

Footing: Hoof protection recommended

Season: Summer through fall

Permits: Camping fee, or Northwest Forest Pass required for day-use parking at Cultus Corral or near Little Cultus Lake Campground

Facilities: Toilet, stock water, and parking for 8-10 trailers at Cultus Corral. Toilet, potable water, and parking for 2-3 trailers near Little Cultus Lake Campground. Stock water is available on the trail.

Highlights: The Many Lakes Trail is aptly named, as it weaves among dozens of small lakes that lie scattered through the forest. There is little elevation gain or loss so you can trot or canter if you like, but you won't want to because you'll be savoring the views of the lovely little lakes as you pass them.

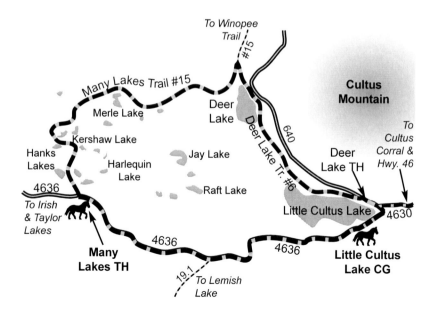

*Lydia on Shadow, Whitney on Cody, and Mona on Eclipse at little
Cultus Lake, at the beginning of the Many Lakes Loop.*

Finding Little Cultus Lake Campground: Follow the directions to
Cultus Corral at the beginning of this chapter, but instead of turning
right on Road 4630, turn left. Continue 2.9 miles to Little Cultus Lake
Campground. You can either park in at the campground (and pay the
camping fee) or drive through the campground to turn around and find
a pull-off on the side of Road 4630 just before the campground. Road
4636 is not suitable for trailers beyond Little Cultus Lake Campground.

The Ride: <u>From Cultus Corral</u>, ride Road 4630 west for 2.9 miles to
Little Cultus Lake Campground. <u>From Little Cultus Lake Camp-
ground</u>, ride west on Road 4636 about 4.3 miles to the Many Lakes
trailhead. Pick up the Many Lakes Trail #15 heading north and follow
it as it winds among dozens of little lakes. After 4 miles it intersects
with the Deer Lake Trail #6. Turn right at this junction and continue
past Deer Lake about 2.3 miles to the Deer Lake trailhead. Go to the
right on Road 640 for 0.4 mile, then turn right on Road 4636 to return
to your trailer at Little Cultus Lake Campground or turn left to ride
Road 4630 back to Cultus Corral.

Teddy Lakes

Trailhead: Start at Cultus Corral
Length: 13.5 miles round trip
Elevation: 4,450 to 4,950 feet
Difficulty: Moderate
Footing: Suitable for barefoot horses
Season: Summer through fall
Permits: Camping fee, or Northwest Forest Pass required for day-use parking at Cultus Corral
Facilities: Parking for 8-10 trailers. Toilet and stock water available at Cultus Corral. Stock water is available on the trail.

Highlights: There are two Teddy Lakes, but only the northern one is visible from the trail. The southern one is hidden back in the forest. The northern lake is a nice destination for a picnic, and along the way you can enjoy the views of Cultus Lake from the trail.

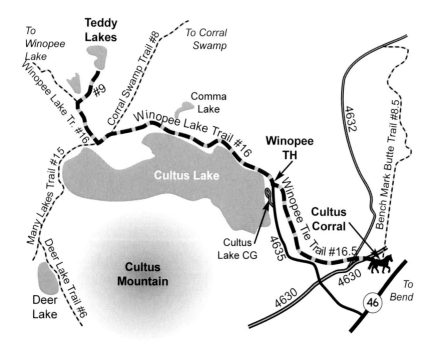

Rhonda on Lizzie and Kenna on Gator, on the trail to Teddy Lakes.

The Ride: Follow the Winopee Tie Trail #16.5 (see the Winopee Tie pages in this chapter) for 3 miles from Cultus Corral to the Winopee trailhead. Pick up the Winopee Lake Trail #16 and ride 2.4 miles. At the junction with the Corral Swamp Trail #8, stay to the left on the Winopee Lake Trail. In 0.3 mile, turn right on the Winopee Lake Trail toward Winopee Lake. In 0.7 mile, turn right on the Teddy Lakes Trail #9. In 0.5 mile you'll arrive at the northern Teddy Lake.

The shore of the north Teddy Lake is a nice lunch spot.

Winopee Lake

Trailhead: Start at Cultus Corral or at the Winopee trailhead at Cultus Lake

Length: From Winopee trailhead it's 12.5 miles to Muskrat Lake or 16.5 miles to Winopee Lake round trip. From Cultus Corral it's 18.5 miles to Muskrat Lake or 22.5 miles to Winopee Lake round trip.

Elevation: 4,450 to 5,000 feet

Difficulty: Moderate

Footing: Hoof protection recommended

Season: Summer through fall

Permits: Camping fee, or Northwest Forest Pass required for day-use parking at Cultus Corral or Winopee trailhead

Facilities: Toilets, stock water, and parking for 8-10 trailers at Cultus Corral. Parking for 1-2 trailers at Winopee trailhead, with toilets and potable water at nearby Cultus Lake Campground. Stock water is available on the trail.

Highlights: This delightful ride has several possible variations. You can start at either Cultus Corral or at the Winopee trailhead, and you can end up at either Muskrat Lake or Winopee Lake, depending on

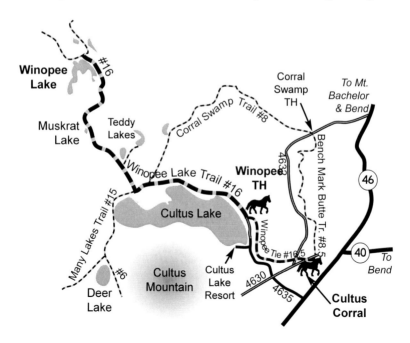

how far you want to ride. Most of the route is forested, and you'll ride along the shore of beautiful Cultus Lake and through several nice meadows along the way.

Finding Winopee Trailhead: Follow the directions to Cultus Corral at the beginning of this chapter, but instead of turning right on Road 4630, go straight and follow the signs toward Cultus Lake Campground and Winopee trailhead. Parking at the trailhead is very limited, so be sure to turn around and park where you can't be blocked by hiker cars.

The Ride: From Cultus Corral, take the Winopee Tie Trail #16.5 to Winopee trailhead. (See the Winopee Tie Trail pages for more information.) From the Winopee trailhead, follow the Winopee Lake Trail #16 along the northern shore of Cultus Lake for 2.4 miles, pass the junction with the Corral Swamp Trail #8, and in another 0.3 mile turn right on the Winopee Lake Trail where it intersects with the Many Lakes Trail #15. After 0.7 mile the trail to Teddy Lakes goes to the right. Stay left and ride 1.2 miles more to reach Muskrat Lake and its derelict shelter. From Muskrat Lake it's 1.4 miles to the south end of Winopee Lake or 2.0 miles to the north end.

In early summer, snow melt swells Muskrat Lake so it covers several acres.

By fall, Muskrat Lake shrinks to a tiny pond just 50 feet across.

Winopee Tie Trail

Trailhead: Start at Cultus Corral

Length: 6 miles round trip to Winopee trailhead, or 8 miles round trip to Cultus Lake Resort

Elevation: 4,450 to 4,800 feet

Difficulty: Easy

Footing: Hoof protection recommended

Season: Summer through fall

Permits: Camping fee, or Northwest Forest Pass required for day-use parking at Cultus Corral

Facilities: Toilets, stock water, and parking for 8-10 trailers at Cultus Corral. Toilets and potable water at Cultus Lake Campground. Stock water is available on the trail.

Highlights: This is an easy, fun ride through the forest from Cultus Horse Camp to the Winopee trailhead on the shore of Cultus Lake. This trail connects with other trails in the area so you can create longer

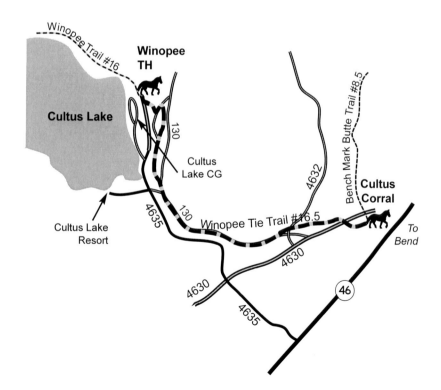

Whitney on Dixie and Diana on Mo, riding the Winopee Tie Trail from Cultus Corral to the Winopee trailhead at Cultus Lake.

rides, or you can ride to Cultus Lake Resort for a good burger, shake, or beer. The route to Winopee trailhead is marked with gray diamonds, and includes both forest roads and single-track trails. The footing is excellent and the terrain slopes gently, creating good opportunities for trotting and cantering.

The Ride: The Winopee Tie Trail #16.5 departs from Cultus Corral between campsites 7 and 8. In the first 0.6 mile it crosses gravel Roads 4630 and 4632 and begins running under the power lines and along gray-cinder Road 130. Ride on Road 130 for 1.1 miles, then veer left on an unnumbered dirt road marked with rock cairns and gray diamonds on the trees. It soon becomes a single-track trail, which you'll continue on for 0.7 mile. Turn left on another unnumbered dirt road marked by rock cairns and gray diamonds. In 0.2 mile the route again veers left on an unnumbered dirt road, and 0.1 mile later it comes out on gravel Road 4635. Turn right and continue 0.1 mile to reach Winopee trailhead. To continue to Cultus Lake Resort, turn left on Road 4635 and ride beside it for 0.8 mile, then veer right at the sign for Cultus Lake Resort and in 0.4 mile you'll arrive at the resort on the lake shore. Tie your horses in the trees and go inside for a good meal or snack.

A horse may be coaxed to drink, but a pencil must be lead.

Stan Laurel

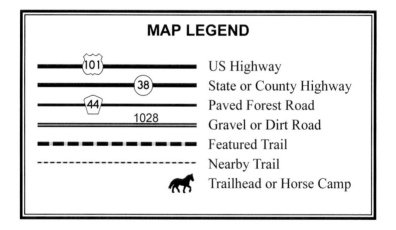

Diamond Peak
Whitefish Horse Camp
Deschutes National Forest

The Diamond Peak Wilderness Area is located near Crescent Lake, at the south end of the Deschutes National Forest. Overnight facilities are available at Whitefish Horse Camp, which provides access to forest and wilderness trails in an area of volcanic peaks dotted with dozens of small lakes. This area is heaven for distance riders because so many longer loop trails are available. Mosquitoes can be fierce here in early summer.

At 8,744 feet, Diamond Peak is the tallest mountain in the area. The peak was named for John Diamond, a member of the party that explored the area in 1852 in search of a wagon route into Central Oregon. The route they selected became the Free Emigrant Road, which crossed Emigrant Pass about 0.5 mile west of Summit Lake. The route was improved in the 1860s and was used until the 1920s when paved roads were opened over other passes in the Cascades.

Crescent Lake, with Odell Butte in the background.

Getting to Diamond Peak

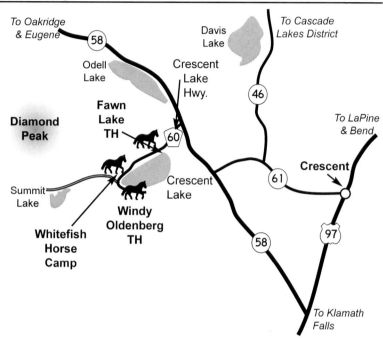

Diamond Peak Trails

Trail	Difficulty	Elevation	Round Trip
Diamond View Lake	Moderate	4,900-5,800	10.5-12.5 miles
Diamond View/Snell Loop	Moderate	4,900-6,250	17.5-19 miles
Fawn Lake	Moderate	4,900-5,600	8-15.5 miles
Fawn Lk./Whitefish Cr. Lp.	Moderate	4,900-6,300	16.5 miles
Meek Lake	Moderate	4,900-5,600	10 miles
Meek/Summit Lakes Loop	Moderate	4,900-5,950	16.5 miles
Oldenberg Lake	Easy	4,900-5,500	10-12.5 miles
Pretty/Fawn Lake Loop	Moderate	4,900-5,900	8-16 miles
Pretty Lake	Moderate	4,900-5,800	5.5-13.5 miles
Snell Lake	Moderate	4,900-5,600	10 miles
Stag Lake	Moderate	4,900-5,800	10-18 miles
Summit Lake	Moderate	4,900-5,550	11.5 miles
Windy Lakes	Moderate	4,900-6,200	9-11.5 miles
Windy/Meek Lakes Loop	Moderate	4,900-6,200	12.5-15 miles
Windy/Oldenberg Lks. Lp.	Moderate	4,900-6,200	14-16.5 miles

Whitefish Horse Camp

Directions: From Bend, drive south on Hwy. 97 for 45 miles to the town of Crescent. Turn right on Hwy. 61 and go west 12 miles to the junction with Hwy. 58, then turn right and go north 3.4 miles. From Eugene, take Hwy. 58 to Oakridge and continue another 35 miles. All, turn southwest on Crescent Lake Hwy. (Road 60). Drive 2 miles, cross the railroad tracks, turn right on Road 60 (the first paved road on the right), and continue 4.3 miles to the horse camp.

Elevation: 4,900 feet

Campsites: 17 sites. Fourteen have 2-horse corrals and 3 have 4-horse corrals. All sites are level and graveled, with room for 2 vehicles.

Facilities: Toilets, potable water spigots, garbage cans, manure pit. Picnic tables and fire pits at each site. No day-use parking at Whitefish, but plenty of parking nearby at the Fawn Lake and Windy Oldenberg trailheads.

Permits: Camping fee. Reservations required. No fee for day-use parking at the Windy Oldenberg or Fawn Lake trailheads.

Season: May to October

Contact: Crescent Ranger District: 541-433-3200, www.fs.usda.gov/centraloregon, then click on "Recreation," "Horse Riding and Camping." Concessionaire: 541-338-7869, www.hoodoo.com, then click on "Campgrounds," "Horse Camping," "Whitefish Horse Camp." Reservations: call 877-444-6777 or go to www.recreation.gov.

Potable water is available from spigots adjacent to each campsite at Whitefish Horse Camp.

Diamond View Lake/Snell Lake Loop

Trailhead: Start at Whitefish Horse Camp or Windy Oldenberg trailhead

Length: From Whitefish Horse Camp, round trip distances are: 17.5 miles for the entire loop, 10.5 miles to Diamond View Lake, or 10 miles to Snell Lake. From Windy Oldenberg trailhead, round trip distances are: 19 miles for the entire loop, 12.5 miles to Diamond View Lake, or 10 miles to Snell Lake round trip.

Elevation: 4,900 to 6,250 feet for the entire loop. Diamond View Lake is at 5,800 feet and Snell Lake is at 5,600 feet.

Difficulty: Moderate

Footing: Hoof protection recommended

Season: Summer through fall

Permits: Camping fee at Whitefish; no fee for day-use parking at Windy Oldenberg trailhead

Facilities: Toilets and potable water at the horse camp. Toilet and plenty of trailer parking at the trailhead. Stock water is available on the trail.

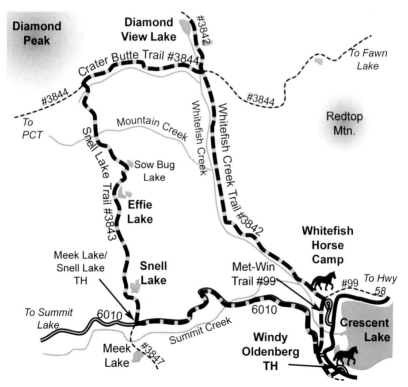

Highlights: As you might expect from the name, Diamond View Lake provides a wonderful view of Diamond Peak. Snell and Effie Lakes are also worthy destinations. The trail travels primarily through lodgepole forest, with stands of hemlock and fir at the higher elevations.

Finding Windy Oldenberg Trailhead: Follow the directions to Whitefish Horse Camp, drive 1 mile past the horse camp and turn left into the trailhead road, which makes a loop back to Road 60.

The Ride: From the Windy Oldenberg trailhead, ride to the Metolius-Windigo Trail #99 and turn right. In 1.5 mile you'll reach the horse camp. From Whitefish Horse Camp, the Whitefish Creek Trail #3842 departs from the north end of the camp. The trail climbs fairly steadily through lodgepole forest along Whitefish Creek for 5.0 miles to Diamond View Lake. The view of Diamond Peak across the lake is impressive. Backtrack 0.7 mile to the junction with the Crater Butte Trail #3844, turn west and travel 2.0 miles to the junction with the Snell Lake Trail #3843. Turn left and continue 2.6 miles to Effie Lake, and then 1.8 miles more to Snell Lake. About 0.6 mile after that you'll reach Road 6010. Turn left and ride 3.8 miles to the junction with the Metolius-Windigo Trail. Turn left and continue 0.7 mile north on the Met-Win to the campground, or turn right and follow the Met-Win south 0.8 mile to the Windy Oldenberg trailhead.

If you want to ride to Snell Lake only, take the Met-Win Trail south (left) out of the horse camp for 0.7 mile. Turn right on Road 6010, go 3.8 miles, turn right on the Snell Lake Trail #3843 and go 0.5 mile north to the lake.

Diamond Peak across Diamond View Lake.

Fawn Lake/Whitefish Creek Loop

Trailhead: Start at Whitefish Horse Camp or Fawn Lake trailhead

Length: From Whitefish Horse Camp, round trip distances are: 16.5 miles for the entire loop, 15.5 miles to Fawn Lake, or 18 miles to Stag Lake. From Fawn Lake trailhead, round trip distances are: 16.5 miles for the entire loop, 8 miles to Fawn Lake, or 10 miles to Stag Lake.

Elevation: 4,900 to 6,300 feet for the entire loop. Fawn Lake is at 5,600 feet, Stag Lake is at 5,800 feet.

Difficulty: Moderate

Footing: Hoof protection recommended

Season: Summer through fall

Permits: Camping fee at Whitefish; no fee for day-use parking at Fawn Lake trailhead

Facilities: Toilets and potable water at the horse camp. Toilet and plenty of trailer parking at the trailhead. Stock water is available on the trail.

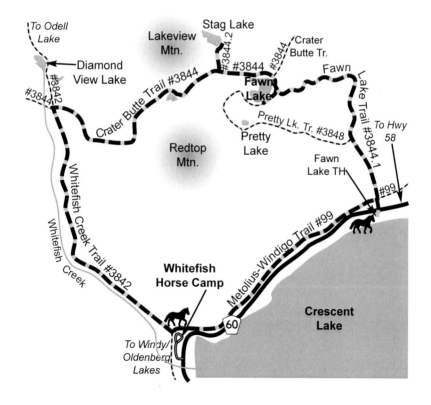

Lakeview Mountain from the south side of Fawn Lake.

Highlights: The Metolius-Windigo Trail runs along the shore of Cultus Lake through stands of enormous old-growth trees. Fawn Lake is very pretty, and the views of Lakeview Mountain and Redtop Mountain are nice. Stag Lake is also a worthy destination.

Finding Fawn Lake Trailhead: Follow the directions toward Whitefish Horse Camp. Before reaching the camp (about 0.9 mile after crossing the railroad tracks), turn left into the trailhead.

The Ride: <u>From Whitefish Horse Camp,</u> the trail begins at the north end of the campground. At the trailhead, turn right on the Metolius-Windigo Trail #99 and follow it 4 miles to the junction with the Fawn Lake Trail. <u>From the Fawn Lake trailhead,</u> pick up the Fawn Lake Trail, and in 0.1 mile you'll reach the junction with the Met-Win. <u>All,</u> head north on the Fawn Lake Trail #3844.1, and in 0.8 mile the Pretty Lake Trail #3848 goes off to the left. Stay right, and in another 2.5 miles you'll arrive at Fawn Lake. The loop trail to Pretty Lake comes in on your left. Stay to the right, and in 0.1 mile the Crater Butte Trail #3844 goes off to the right. Veer left and continue around Fawn Lake, and in about a mile you can take the 0.5-mile detour to the right to Stag Lake. Return to the Crater Butte Trail and continue riding west for 3.3 miles, then turn south on the Whitefish Creek Trail #3842 to return to the horse camp in approximately 4.4 miles. To return to the Fawn Lake trailhead when you reach the horse camp, turn left on the Met-Win Trail and ride 4 miles to the trailhead.

Meek Lake/Summit Lake Loop

Trailhead: Start at Whitefish Horse Camp or Windy Oldenberg trail-head

Length: From either Whitefish Horse Camp or Windy Oldenberg trailhead, round trip distances are: 16.5 miles for the entire loop, 10 miles to Meek Lake, or 11.5 miles to Summit Lake

Elevation: 4,900 to 5,950 feet for the entire loop. Meek Lake is at 5,600 feet, and Summit Lake is at 5,550 feet.

Difficulty: Moderate

Footing: Hoof protection recommended

Season: Summer through fall

Permits: Camping fee at Whitefish; no fee for day-use parking at Windy Oldenberg trailhead

Facilities: Toilets and potable water at the horse camp. Toilet and plenty of trailer parking at the trailhead. Stock water is available on the trail.

Highlights: The portion of the trail that loops from Meek Lake to Summit Lake is shaded by old-growth hemlocks and firs, and is festooned with lakes and lily ponds strung like beads on a necklace. Summit Lake is beautiful and uncrowded compared to the more-accessible

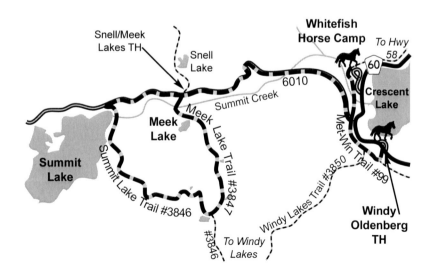

Crescent Lake. Road 6010 is too rutted for horse trailers and there is nowhere to turn around. It has good footing for horses, though, so riding to the Snell/Meek Lakes trailhead is a better choice.

Finding Windy Oldenberg Trailhead: Follow the directions to Whitefish Horse Camp, drive 1 mile past the horse camp and turn left into the trailhead road, which makes a loop back to Road 60.

The Ride: From Whitefish Horse Camp, pick up the Metolius-Windigo Trail #99 along the west side of the campground and turn left. Ride about 1 mile to Road 6010 and turn right. From Windy Oldenberg trailhead, ride to the Met-Win Trail and turn right. Ride 0.7 mile to Road 6010 and turn left. All, ride west on Road 6010 for 3.8 miles to the Meek Lake trailhead. Turn left onto the Meek Lake Trail #3847, which passes its namesake lake after 0.5 mile, winds through stands of old growth mountain hemlock and fir, and provides views of literally dozens of lakes and ponds, including many with lily pads. Two miles after Meek Lake, the trail intersects with the Summit Lake Trail #3846. Turn right, and in 3.5 miles you'll reach Summit Lake. Turn right onto Road 6010 and ride 4.8 miles, then veer left on the Met-Win to return to Whitefish or right to return to the trailhead.

A lily pond on the trail between Meek and Summit Lakes.

Pretty Lake/Fawn Lake Loop

Trailhead: Start at Whitefish Horse Camp or Fawn Lake trailhead

Length: From Whitefish Horse Camp, round trip distances are: 16 miles for the entire ride, or 13.5 miles to Pretty Lake only. From Fawn Lake trailhead, round trip distances are: 8 miles for the entire ride or 4 miles to Fawn Lake only.

Elevation: 4,900 to 5,900 feet

Difficulty: Moderate

Footing: Hoof protection recommended

Season: Summer through fall

Permits: Camping fee at Whitefish; no fee for day-use parking at Fawn Lake trailhead

Facilities: Toilets and potable water at the horse camp. Toilet and plenty of trailer parking at the trailhead. Stock water is available on the trail.

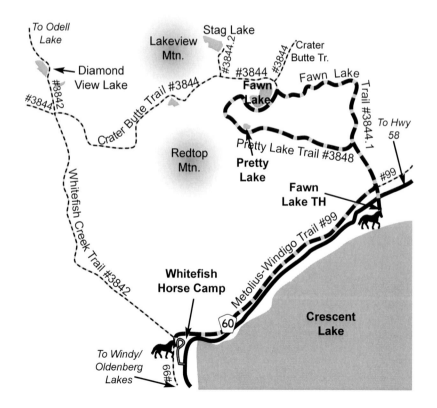

Connie rides Diamond and Lydia rides Shadow past Fawn Lake.

Highlights: This is a fun loop that takes you through varied terrain to two delightful lakes. If you start at Whitefish Horse Camp, you'll also enjoy the pleasant ride among the huge old-growth trees along the shore of Crescent Lake. The trail segment that goes from the Fawn Lake Trail to Pretty Lake is a good climb, gaining 900 feet of elevation in 1.8 miles.

Finding Fawn Lake Trailhead: Follow the directions toward Whitefish Horse Camp. Before reaching the camp (about 0.9 mile after crossing the railroad tracks), turn left into the trailhead.

The Ride: From Whitefish Horse Camp, pick up the trail at the north end of the campground and turn right on the Metolius-Windigo Trail #99. Follow it for 4 miles to the junction with the Fawn Lake Trail. From the Fawn Lake trailhead, pick up the Fawn Lake Trail and in 0.1 mile you'll reach the Met-Win Trail. All, head north on the Fawn Lake Trail #3844.1, and in 0.8 mile turn left on the Pretty Lake Trail #3848. It climbs steadily for 1.8 miles to the shore of Pretty Lake, then continues 1.2 miles to Fawn Lake. Ride along the shore of Fawn Lake for about 0.5 mile, then veer right at the junction and take the Fawn Lake Trail 3.3 miles back to the Met-Win Trail. Go straight ahead to reach the trailhead, or turn right on the Met-Win to return to the horse camp.

Windy Lakes/Meek Lake Loop

Trailhead: Start at Whitefish Horse Camp or Windy Oldenberg trail-head

Length: From Whitefish Horse Camp, round trip distances are: 15 miles for the entire loop, 10 miles to Meek Lake, or 11.5 miles to Windy Lakes. From Windy Oldenberg trailhead, round trip distances are: 12.5 miles for the entire loop, 10 miles to Meek Lake, or 9 miles to the Windy Lakes.

Elevation: 4,900 to 6,200 feet for the entire loop. Meek Lake is at 5,600 feet and the Windy Lakes are at 6,200 feet

Difficulty: Moderate

Footing: Hoof protection recommended

Season: Summer through fall

Permits: Camping fee at Whitefish; no fee for day-use parking at Windy Oldenberg trailhead

Facilities: Toilets and potable water at the horse camp. Toilet and plenty of trailer parking at the trailhead. Stock water is available on the trail.

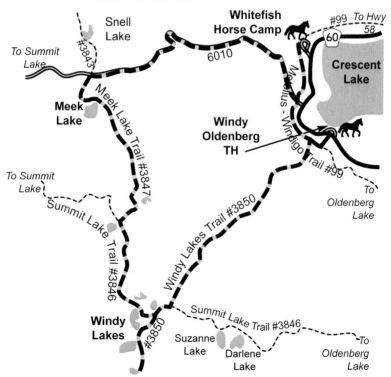

Diamond, Mo, Dixie, and their riders rest awhile at Windy Lakes.

Highlights: The Windy Lakes are beautiful, and the terrain between Meek Lake and the Windy Lakes features large mountain hemlock and fir trees and a smattering of picturesque lakes.

Finding Windy Oldenberg Trailhead: Follow the directions to White-fish Horse Camp, drive 1 mile past the horse camp and turn left into the trailhead road, which makes a loop back to Road 60.

The Ride: From Whitefish Horse Camp, pick up the Metolius-Windigo Trail #99 along the west side of the campground and turn left. Ride about 1.3 miles and turn right on the Windy Lakes Trail. From Windy Oldenberg trailhead, ride to the Met-Win Trail and turn right. In 0.1 mile, turn left on the Windy Lakes Trail. All, follow the Windy Lakes Trail #3850 for 3.3 miles to the junction with the Summit Lake Trail. You can go straight for 1.1 miles to explore all the Windy Lakes. Or you can turn right on the Summit Lake Trail #3846, continue 2 miles, then veer right on the Meek Lake Trail #3847 and ride 2.0 miles to Meek Lake. Continue 0.5 mile farther to reach Road 6010. Turn right and follow Road 6010 for 3.8 miles. Turn left on the Met-Win Trail to return to Whitefish Horse Camp or right to return to the trail-head.

Windy Lakes/Oldenberg Lake Loop

Trailhead: Start at Whitefish Horse Camp or Windy Oldenberg trail-head

Length: From Whitefish Horse Camp, round trips distances are: 16.5 miles for the loop, 11.5 miles to the Windy Lakes, or 12.5 miles to Oldenberg Lake. From the Windy Oldenberg trailhead, round trip distances are: 14 miles for the loop, 9 miles to the Windy Lakes, or 10 miles to Oldenberg Lake

Elevation: 4,900 to 6,200 feet for the entire loop. Windy Lakes are at 6,200 feet and Oldenberg Lake is at 5,500 feet.

Difficulty: Moderate

Footing: Hoof protection recommended

Season: Summer through fall

Permits: Camping fee at Whitefish; no fee for day-use parking at Windy Oldenberg trailhead

Facilities: Toilets and potable water at the horse camp. Toilet and plenty of trailer parking at the trailhead. Stock water is available on the trail.

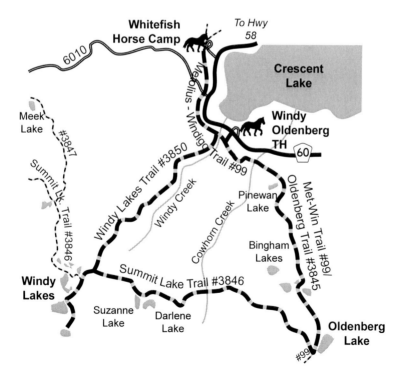

Highlights: The Windy Lakes and Oldenberg Lake are lovely and serene, and the trail between them runs through pretty fir and mountain hemlock forest. If you are doing the entire loop, the trail up to Windy Lakes is best done on the uphill leg of your ride, as it is steeper than the trail to Oldenberg Lake.

Finding Windy Oldenberg Trailhead: Follow the directions to Whitefish Horse Camp, drive 1 mile past the horse camp and turn left into the trailhead road, which makes a loop back to Road 60.

The Ride: From Whitefish Horse Camp, pick up the Metolius-Windigo Trail #99 along the west side of the campground and turn left. Ride about 1.3 miles and turn right on the Windy Lakes Trail. From Windy Oldenberg trailhead, ride to the Met-Win Trail and turn right. In 0.1 mile, turn left on the Windy Lakes Trail. All, follow the Windy Lakes Trail #3850 for 3.3 miles to the junction with the Summit Lake Trail. You can go straight for 1.1 miles to explore all the Windy Lakes, or turn left on the Summit Lake Trail #3846, which takes you past Suzanne and Darlene Lakes to Oldenberg Lake in 4.6 miles. Turn left on the Metolius-Windigo (Oldenberg #3845) Trail and follow it 4.9 miles, then veer right to return to the Windy Oldenberg trailhead. To return to Whitefish, stay on the Met-Win Trail for another 1.4 miles.

Whitney and Dixie, Diana and Mo, and Connie and Diamond
take a break at beautiful Suzanne Lake.

A man on a horse is spiritually, as well as physically, bigger than a man on foot.

John Steinbeck

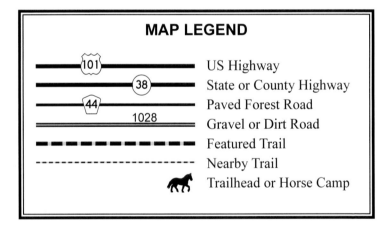

Gray Butte
Cyrus Horse Camp
Crooked River Grasslands

If you're looking for a great place to ride nearly year round, with varied terrain, good footing, nice views, and wonderful spring wildflowers, then Gray Butte is the destination for you. Located about 15 miles north of Redmond, the area offers plenty of good riding, especially during the shoulder seasons when the higher-elevation trails are blanketed with snow. Overnight accommodations are available at Cyrus Horse Camp, which is located along the route of the Ridge Rider Endurance Trail. You can ride the entire endurance trail, or you can do shorter day rides by linking segments of the endurance trail with the dirt roads in the area. And there are additional trails nearby that you can reach from Cyrus Horse Camp or from nearby trailheads.

The trails near Cyrus Horse Camp
offer panoramic views of the surrounding area.

Getting to Gray Butte Trailheads

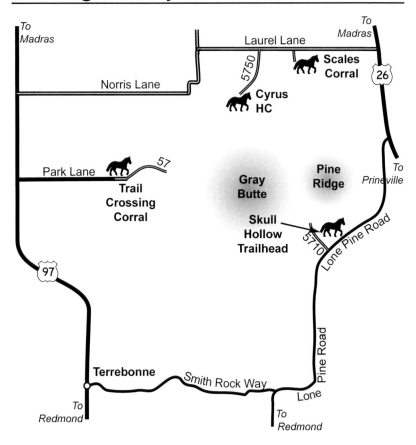

Gray Butte Trails

Trail	Difficulty	Elevation	Round Trip
Cole Loop	Challenging	3,000-4,000	25 miles
Gray Butte	Challenging	2,700-4,250	13-23 miles
Pine Ridge Loop	Moderate	3,000-3,900	8-15 miles
Scales Corral Loop	Moderate	3,200-3,800	11.5 miles
Skull Hollow Loop	Moderate	3,000-4,200	9-13 miles
Tam-a-lau Loop	Moderate	2,500-2,800	12.5 miles
Trail Crossing Corral Lp.	Challenging	2,900-4,250	9-15 miles
Warner Loop	Moderate	2,950-3,400	12.5 miles

Cyrus Horse Camp

Directions: From Redmond, take Hwy. 97 north 5.5 miles to Terre-bonne and turn right on Smith Rock Way. Drive 4.9 miles, turn left on Lone Pine Road, continue 7.4 miles and turn left on Hwy. 26. Go 2 miles and turn left on Laurel Lane. (Note: Norris Lane offers a more direct route, but the road is dusty washboard gravel all the way.) From Madras, drive south on Hwy. 26 for 13 miles and turn right on Laurel Lane. From Prineville, drive north-west on Hwy. 26 for 15 miles and turn left on Laurel Lane. All: Continue 3 miles and turn left on Road 5750, then drive 1.2 miles to the horse camp.

Elevation: 3,350 feet

Campsites: 7 spacious campsites with 4-, 3-, or 1-horse corrals (mostly 4-horse). All sites have room for 2 vehicles. Some sites are more level than others.

Facilities: Vault toilet, manure dump, fire pits, and picnic tables. No potable water, but stock water is available in season. Check with the Crooked River Grasslands office for stock water availability, 541-475-9272.

Permits: None

Season: Spring through early winter. In early spring the trails can be very muddy. To avoid damaging the trails, wait until the terrain has dried out a bit.

Contact: Crooked River Grasslands: 541-475-9272, www.fs.usda.gov/centraloregon, then click on "Recreation," "Horse Riding and Camping"

Directions to Other Area Trailheads

Skull Hollow Trailhead: From Redmond, take Hwy. 97 north 5.5 miles to Terrebonne and turn right on Smith Rock Way. Drive 4.9 miles, turn left on Lone Pine Road, and continue 4.2 miles, then turn left on Road 5710 into the dirt parking area east of the people campground.

Scales Corral: Follow the directions for Cyrus Horse Camp above, but 2 miles after turning onto Laurel Lane you'll come to Scales Corral on your left. There is a parking area next to the corral.

Trail Crossing Corral: From Redmond, drive north on Hwy. 97 for 10 miles, turn right on Park Lane, and continue about 2 miles, past McPheeters Turf, to Road 57. Turn left and drive 0.5 mile to the parking area. Note that an OHV staging area is nearby.

Cole Loop

Trailhead: Start at Cyrus Horse Camp, Scales Corral, Trail Crossing Corral, or Skull Hollow trailhead

Length: 25 miles round trip

Elevation: 3,000 to 4,000 feet

Difficulty: The trails are moderate but the distance is challenging

Footing: Hoof protection recommended

Season: Spring through early winter

Permits: None

Facilities: Toilet, corrals, stock water in season at Cyrus Horse Camp. No facilities at other trailheads. Stock water is available on the trail.

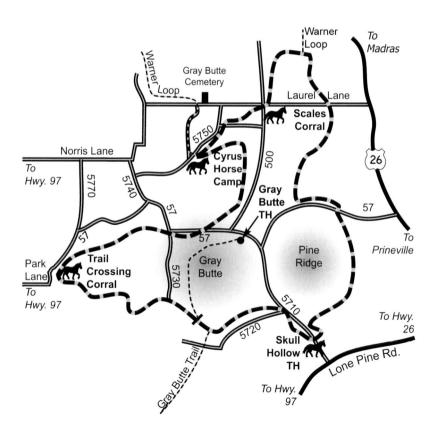

Highlights: Cole Loop is part of the Ridge Rider Endurance Trail system, the site of an annual endurance competition. The trails are also used for day rides. Cole Loop is rideable almost year round, although the segment of the trail on the north side of Gray Butte can be very muddy in winter and early spring.

Finding the Trailheads: See the beginning of this chapter for directions to the various trailheads.

The Ride: The Cole Loop trail travels through the sagebrush flats north of Cyrus Horse Camp, around the eastern flank of Pine Ridge, across the south side of Gray Butte, and through the canyons between Gray Butte and Trail Crossing Corral. The trail is only signed occasionally, but it is well maintained and easy to follow. By connecting segments of Cole Loop with other trails and forest roads, you can break this trail into 4 shorter loop rides: Pine Ridge Loop, Scales Corral Loop, Skull Hollow Loop, and Trail Crossing Corral Loop. See the descriptions of these trails in this chapter for more details.

Lydia on Shadow and Connie on Diamond, enjoying the
Cole Loop Trail near Pine Ridge on a warm December day.

Gray Butte Trail

Trailhead: Start at Cyrus Horse Camp or Skull Hollow trailhead

Length: 13 miles round trip from Skull Hollow trailhead, or 23 miles round trip from Cyrus Horse Camp

Elevation: 2,700 to 3,700 from Skull Hollow or 2,700 to 4,250 feet from Cyrus Horse Camp

Difficulty: Challenging -- very steep side hills, plus frequent mountain bike traffic

Footing: Suitable for barefoot horses

Season: Spring through early winter

Permits: None

Facilities: Toilet, corrals, and seasonal stock water at Cyrus. Plenty of parking at Skull Hollow. Stock water is available on the trail in season.

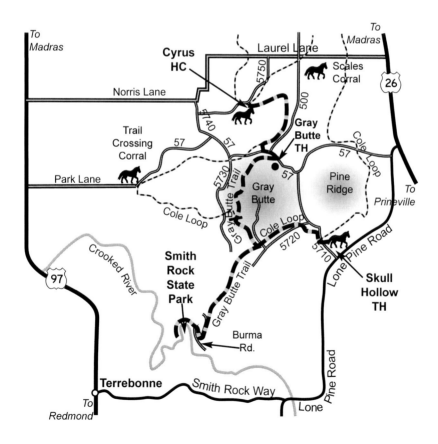

Lydia rides Shadow across a steep ridge toward Smith Rock on the Gray Butte Trail.

Highlights: This trail is popular with mountain bikers, and part of it traverses a very steep ridge where it can be difficult to get off the trail if you meet a bicyclist. However, adventurous equestrians will be rewarded with great views of Smith Rock and the Cascades, and interesting rock outcroppings next to the trail.

The Ride: From Cyrus Horse Camp, pick up the unsigned (no kiosk) Cole Loop Trail on the east side of the campground, next to the camp water supply. After 2 miles the trail drops into a small ravine, crosses a stream bed next to a wooden pole fence, then comes up out of the ravine into an area that has been cleared of juniper. Immediately turn left on an old dirt road and continue 0.1 mile to gravel Road 57. Turn left and ride Road 57 for 0.4 mile to the Gray Butte trailhead at Mc-Coin Orchard. Turn right on the Gray Butte trail. In 2.8 miles the trail forks at a gate, with Cole Loop going off to the right. Go through the gate, and in 1 mile turn right at the junction, toward Smith Rock. From Skull Hollow Trailhead, pick up the trail next to the kiosk on the north end of the parking area. In 0.9 mile it crosses Road 5720 and turns left. Continue 1.6 miles. At the crest of the hill the trail splits. Turn left toward Smith Rock. All: From the trail junction, the trail traverses a steep ridge for about 3 miles. Near the end of the ridge you'll encounter large geologic outcroppings similar to the ones that formed Smith Rock, plus panoramic views to the west. If you continue another 2.5 miles you'll ride down the ridge to Smith Rock State Park and the Crooked River, losing 800 feet of elevation in the process. Retrace your steps to return to your trailer.

Pine Ridge Loop

Trailhead: Start at Cyrus Horse Camp or Skull Hollow trailhead

Length: 8 miles round trip from Skull Hollow, or 15 miles round trip from Cyrus Horse Camp

Elevation: 3,000 to 3,700 feet from Skull Hollow, or 3,000 to 3,900 feet from Cyrus

Difficulty: Moderate -- easy trail, but some trail junctions are not signed

Footing: Suitable for barefoot horses

Season: Spring through early winter

Permits: None

Facilities: Toilet, corrals, and seasonal stock water at Cyrus. Plenty of parking at Skull Hollow. Stock water is available on the trail in season.

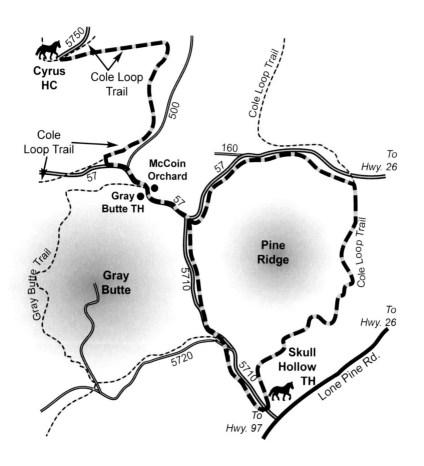

Highlights: This pleasant ride all the way around Pine Ridge is created by linking segments of the Cole Loop Trail and other trails that run along the forest roads between Pine Ridge and Gray Butte.

The Ride: From Cyrus Horse Camp, pick up the unsigned (no kiosk) Cole Loop Trail on the east side of the campground, next to the camp water supply. After 2 miles the trail drops into a small ravine, crosses a streambed next to a wooden pole fence, then comes up out of the ravine into an area that has been cleared of juniper. Immediately turn left on an old dirt road and continue 0.1 mile to gravel Road 57. Turn left and ride Road 57 for 0.4 mile to the Gray Butte trailhead at McCoin Orchard. Stay on Road 57 for another 0.6 mile and turn right on Road 5710. Ride beside it to the Skull Hollow trailhead. From Skull Hollow, pick up the Cole Loop Trail running northeast up onto the flank of Pine Ridge. Follow it counterclockwise around Pine Ridge. In 2.7 miles you'll reach 2 water tanks in a wire enclosure. Ride through the enclosure and continue on the dirt road that runs along the side of the hill. In 0.3 mile, veer left off the dirt road on the single track trail. After another 0.6 mile the trail splits and the Cole Loop Trail continues straight ahead. Veer left and continue around Pine Ridge. In 0.5 mile the trail reaches Road 57 and continues beside it. In 0.4 mile, Road 160 goes off to the right. Stay to the left beside Road 57 and in 0.9 mile, Road 5710 goes to the left. If you parked at Cyrus Horse Camp, turn right on Road 57 and retrace your steps back to the horse camp. If you parked at Skull Hollow, turn left and ride the trail beside Road 5710 back to the parking area.

Debbie, Whitney, and Connie canter their horses along a stretch of the Pine Ridge Loop.

Scales Corral Loop

Trailhead:	Start at Cyrus Horse Camp or at Scales Corral
Length:	11.5 miles round trip
Elevation:	3,200 to 3,800 feet
Difficulty:	Moderate -- some sections of trail are unsigned
Footing:	Hoof protection recommended
Season:	Spring through early winter
Permits:	None
Facilities:	Toilet, corrals, and seasonal stock water at Cyrus. Parking for 4-6 trailers at Scales Corral. Stock water is available on the trail in season.

Highlights: This ride covers the north end of the Cole Loop Trail and completes a loop by using gravel roads and other trails. It offers views of Gray Butte, Pine Ridge, and the open expanses to the north and east. The spring wildflowers are beautiful.

The Ride: From Cyrus Horse Camp, pick up the unsigned (no kiosk) Cole Loop Trail on the east side of the campground, just to the right

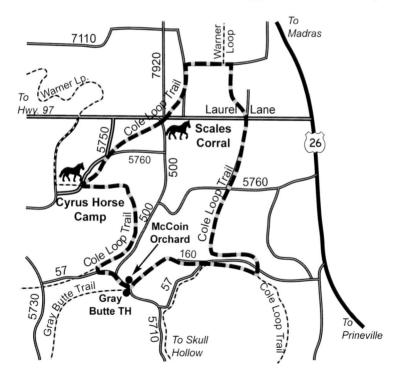

of the camp water supply. After 2 miles the trail drops into a small ravine, crosses a streambed next to a wooden pole fence, then comes up out of the ravine into an area that has been cleared of juniper. Immediately turn left on an old dirt road and continue 0.1 mile to gravel Road 57. Turn left and ride Road 57 for 0.4 mile to the Gray Butte trailhead at McCoin Orchard. Ride past the orchard and turn left along the orchard fence, continuing down the hill to the water trough. To the right of the trough, go through the gate and pick up the trail that at first continues downhill along the orchard fence. It runs for 0.9 mile and at times is indistinct, but you'll be able to see Road 57 ahead of you so aim toward it and the trail will reappear. The trail drops down to a seasonal creek, crosses it, and continues on the right side of Road 160, a well-travelled dirt road that goes slightly to the right. In 0.3 mile Road 160 intersects Road 57. Cross Road 57 and veer left on the trail that runs beside it. In 0.7 mile, turn left on the Cole Loop Trail. Almost immediately the trail crosses Road 57, and 3.0 miles later it crosses Laurel Lane. In 0.8 mile the trail makes a 90-degree turn to the left, and in another 0.1 mile the Warner Loop trail goes off to the right. Continue straight ahead and in 0.6 mile the trail turns sharply left. Follow it 0.9 mile to reach Laurel Lane and Scales Corral. From Scales Corral, the trail runs past the kiosk at Scales Corral, and in 1.6 miles it reaches Cyrus Horse Camp. From there, follow the directions above.

Linda and Beamer on the Scales Corral Loop trail,
with Haystack Butte and Mt. Jefferson in the background.

Skull Hollow Loop

Trailhead: Start at Cyrus Horse Camp or at Skull Hollow trailhead

Length: 9 miles round trip from Skull Hollow, or 13 miles round trip from Cyrus Horse Camp

Elevation: 3,000 to 4,200 feet

Difficulty: Moderate

Footing: Suitable for barefoot horses

Season: Spring through early winter

Permits: None

Facilities: Toilet, corrals, and seasonal stock water at Cyrus. Plenty of parking at Skull Hollow. Stock water is available on the trail in season.

Highlights: This well-maintained trail provides excellent views from the flanks of Gray Butte. It is popular with pleasure and endurance riders, and the Gray Butte Trail segments are also heavily used by

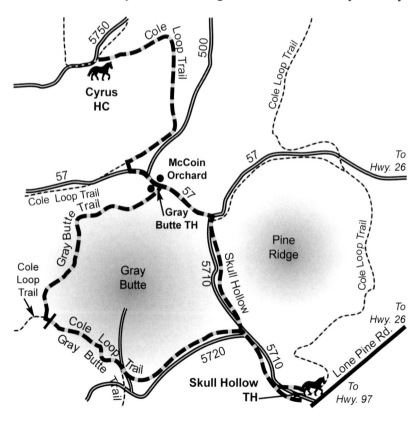

mountain bikers. The trail is accessible about 10 months of the year. Spring wildflowers are plentiful and varied.

The Ride: From Cyrus Horse Camp, pick up the unsigned (no kiosk) Cole Loop Trail on the east side of the campground, next to the camp water supply. After 2 miles the trail drops into a small ravine, crosses a streambed next to a wooden pole fence, then comes up out of the ravine into an area that has been cleared of juniper. Immediately turn left on an old dirt road and continue 0.1 mile to gravel Road 57. Turn left and ride Road 57 for 0.4 mile to the Gray Butte trailhead at Mc-Coin Orchard. Continue on Road 57 for 0.6 mile until it forks, then veer right on Road 5710. Follow the trail beside Road 5710 for 1.9 miles and turn right on the trail next to Road 5720. From Skull Hollow, pick up the trail at the forest service kiosk on the northern end of the parking area. After 1 mile you'll reach Road 5720. All, the trail runs up through a ravine on the north side of Road 5720. After 1.6 miles, at the top of the ravine, the Gray Butte Trail goes off to the left. (There are great views of the Cascades just off the trail to the left here.) Stay right and continue another mile to a gate, where the Cole Loop Trail goes to the left. Stay to the right on the Gray Butte Trail and ride 2.8 miles to the Gray Butte Trailhead at the old McCoin home-stead site. There is a water trough at the bottom of the hill to the right of the orchard. From here, return to Cyrus Horse Camp the way you came. Or loop back to Skull Hollow by following Road 57 southeast for 0.6 mile, then veering right on Road 5710 and following it 2.9 miles back to the trailhead.

Connie rides Diamond on the northern section of the Skull Hollow Loop.

Tam-a-lau Loop

Trailhead: Start at the parking area at the end of Peninsula Road at
Crooked River Ranch

Length: 12.5 miles round trip

Elevation: 2,500 to 2,800 feet

Difficulty: Moderate

Footing: Hoof protection recommended

Season: Early spring through early winter

Permits: None

Facilities: Parking for 3-4 trailers. No water on the trail.

Highlights: Tam-a-lau is a native American word meaning "place of
big rocks on the ground." This certainly describes the peninsula that
lies between the steep gorges of the Deschutes and Crooked rivers. The
terrain is generally flat, with frequent rock outcroppings. The loop portion of the trail at the north end of the peninsula follows the edges of

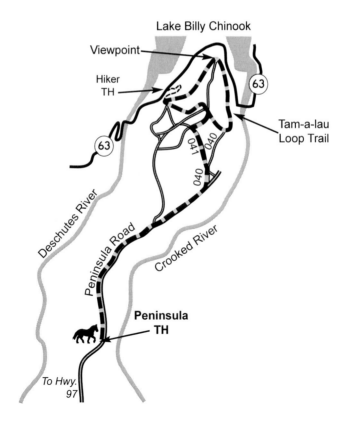

Kim and Jane ride the Tam-a-Lau Loop on a clear winter day.

the canyons, providing spectacular views of the canyon cliffs, and the rivers and Lake Billy Chinook 700 feet below.

Finding the Peninsula Road Trailhead: The official Tam-a-lau trailhead is off Highway 63 (which runs along the south shore of Lake Billy Chinook), but horses are not allowed on the trail that leads from the gorge to the top of the peninsula. Equestrians can access the trail on top of the peninsula by driving through Crooked River Ranch. Take Highway 97 north from Redmond, go 0.5 mile past Terrebonne, and turn left on Lower Bridge Road. Drive 2.2 miles and turn right on NE 43rd. In 1.8 miles go left on Chinook, then in 1.8 miles turn left on Mustang Road. After 1.2 miles, turn left on Shad Road, then in 1.5 miles turn right on SW Peninsula Road. After 3.5 miles the road turns to gravel. Proceed another mile or so, cross the cattle guard, and park.

The Ride: From the parking area, Peninsula Road continues northward, but it is too rough for trailers. Ride along it for 3 miles, then turn left on Road 040. Follow Road 040 for 0.3 mile, then veer left on the unsigned Road 041. Continue 0.7 mile, watching for a gate through the fence on the north side of the road. Turn right, go through the gate, and ride the dirt road for 0.4 mile to where the Tam-a-lau loop trail crosses the road. The trail loops around the northern tip of the peninsula and provides views of Lake Billy Chinook and the Deschutes and Crooked Rivers 700 feet below. After completing the loop, return to the parking area by retracing your steps.

Trail Crossing Corral Loop

Trailhead:	Start at Trail Crossing Corral or Cyrus Horse Camp
Length:	9 miles round trip from Trail Crossing Corral, or 15 miles round trip from Cyrus Horse Camp
Elevation:	2,900-4,250 feet from Trail Crossing Corral
Difficulty:	Challenging -- steep, rocky, some steep side slopes
Footing:	Hoof protection recommended
Season:	Spring through early winter
Permits:	None
Facilities:	Toilet, corrals, and seasonal stock water at Cyrus Horse Camp. Plenty of parking at Skull Hollow and Trail Crossing Corral. Stock water is available on the trail in season.

Highlights: This trail features panoramic views to the west, north, and east, and its significant elevation gains and losses provide good opportunities for conditioning your horse. A partial trail re-route a couple of years ago eliminated the harrowingly steep descent that the trail used to have. The trailhead is adjacent to the Henderson Flat OHV

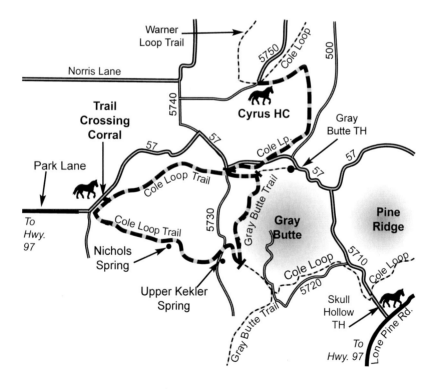

Lydia on Shadow and Connie on Diamond,
on the Gray Butte Trail segment of the loop.

area, but while you are likely to see off-highway vehicles near the trail-head, OHVs are not allowed on this trail. (Note that the OHV area is closed to motor vehicles from December 1 to March 31, so you can ride horses on its 18 miles of trail for 4 months of the year.)

The Ride: From Trail Crossing Corral, begin at the south end of the corrals by the parking area, and at the junction veer left so you are heading eastward. The trail gains elevation steadily for 3.5 miles. About 3 miles from the trailhead it crosses Road 5730 next to its in-tersection with Road 57. The Cole Loop Trail comes in on the left, through a fence. Instead, continue straight ahead on a single-track trail that runs along the right side of the fence, and in 0.5 mile you'll reach a gate and the Gray Butte Trail. From Cyrus Horse Camp, pick up the unsigned (no kiosk) Cole Loop Trail on the east side of camp and ride it 3.0 miles to the junction of Road 57 and Road 5730. Go through the fence and turn left on the single track trail that runs east along the fence. In 0.5 mile you'll reach a gate and the Gray Butte Trail. All, turn right on the Gray Butte Trail (turning left will take you to the Gray Butte trailhead) and follow it about 1.8 miles to a gate at a trail junc-tion. Turn right on the Cole Loop Trail. The trail goes downhill for 0.8 mile to Upper Kekler Spring, then very steeply downhill for 1.6 miles to Nichols Spring. It then descends more gradually, and after 1.7 miles it reaches Road 57 and runs beside it to Trail Crossing Corral. To return to Cyrus Horse Camp, follow the directions above.

Warner Loop

Trailhead: Start at Cyrus Horse Camp or at Scales Corral

Length: 12.5 miles round trip

Elevation: 2,950 to 3,400 feet

Difficulty: Moderate. The trail is easy, but some trail junctions are unsigned

Footing: Suitable for barefoot horses

Season: Early spring through early winter

Permits: None

Facilities: Toilet, corrals, and seasonal stock water at Cyrus Horse Camp. Parking for several trailers at Scales Corral. Stock water is available on the trail in season.

Highlights: The western end of this trail was re-routed a few years ago, creating a more interesting ride. Most of the trail runs across sagebrush flats, with nice views of Gray Butte, Pine Ridge, Haystack Butte, and Grizzly Mountain. The hill segment on the west end provides views of Haystack Reservoir as well. It's easy terrain, and it's accessible most of the winter.

The Ride: <u>From Scales Corral</u>, cross Laurel Lane and pick up the single-track trail that runs northeast. After 0.5 mile it veers north on a dirt

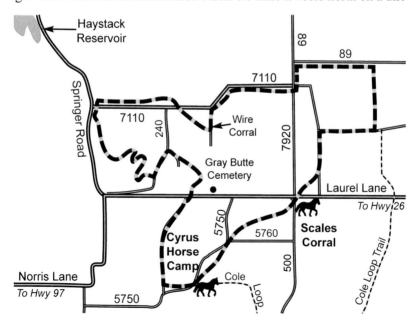

road. For the next 1.1 mile the road runs north, then east. At a fence line the Cole Loop trail goes straight ahead and Warner Loop turns left. Go left, and for the next 2 miles the trail follows the perimeter of a fenced area. Then the trail crosses Road 7920 and continues east for another mile. When you reach a dirt road with a cattle guard, turn left and ride south along the road for 0.2 mile to a barb-wire corral. Turn right and ride through the corral, picking up the trail just north of the corral. Continue westward along Road 7110 for 1.6 miles to Springer Road. The trail veers left when it reaches Springer Road, then travels over a series of small hills that offer several good viewpoints. After 1.8 miles the trail comes out on a dirt road. Turn left and follow it 0.3 mile, then turn right on another dirt road and in 100 yards veer left onto a single-track trail. Follow the trail 0.8 mile, cross Laurel Lane, go through the gate, and pick up the dirt road just inside the gate. Follow it 1.1 mile, then turn left on a single-track trail and continue 0.4 mile to Cyrus Horse Camp. <u>From Cyrus Horse Camp</u>, pick up the trail next to the kiosk on the north side of camp and follow it northeast for 1.6 miles to Scales Corral.

Connie, Diamond, and Joylyn the dog
move out on the Warner Loop Trail.

A horse can lend its rider the speed and strength he or she lacks, but the rider is wise to remember it is no more than a loan.

Pam Brown

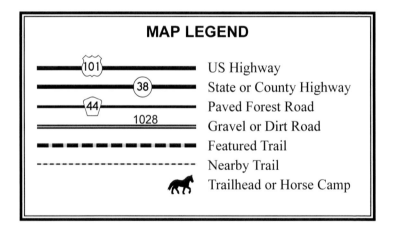

McKenzie Pass

Deschutes & Willamette National Forests

McKenzie Pass is located about 15 miles west of Sisters, on Highway 242. The trails in the area extend into the northern part of the Three Sisters Wilderness and the southern part of the Mt. Washington Wilderness. These trails aren't as heavily used as those along the Cascade Lakes Highway, and they offer more spectacular scenery than many other trails in Central Oregon, with panoramic views, beautiful forests, alpine lakes, lava flows, and mountain vistas. In short, the trails near McKenzie Pass offer the makings of what may be some of the most memorable rides of your life.

If you're inclined to camp nearby, you can stay at either Whispering Pine Horse Camp or Sisters Cow Camp. Both are located off Hwy. 242 not far from McKenzie Pass. See the Sisters Area and Trout Creek Butte chapters for more information.

South Matthieu Lake and North Sister.

165

McKenzie Pass Area

Directions: McKenzie Pass is located about 15 miles west of Sisters, on Hwy. 242. For directions to the nearby trailheads, see "Finding the Trailhead" on the pages for each trail.

Elevation: 5,200 feet

Campsites: Primitive camping is permitted at Lava Camp trailhead. Or you can camp at Whispering Pines Horse Camp or Sisters Cow Camp. See the Trout Creek Butte and Sisters Area chapters for more information.

Facilities: See "Facilities" on the pages for each trail

Permits: See "Permits" on the pages for each trail

Season: Summer through fall

Contact: For information about the Black Crater and Millican Crater/ Matthieu Lakes trails, contact the Sisters Ranger District: 541-549-7700, www.fs.usda.gov/centraloregon, then click on "Recreation," "Horse Riding and Camping."

For information about the Obsidian and Scott Mountain trails, contact the McKenzie Ranger District: 541-822-3381, www.fs.usda.gov/willamette, then click on "Recreation," "Horse Riding and Camping."

Riders head up over Opie Dilldock Pass on the Obsidian Loop.

Getting to McKenzie Pass

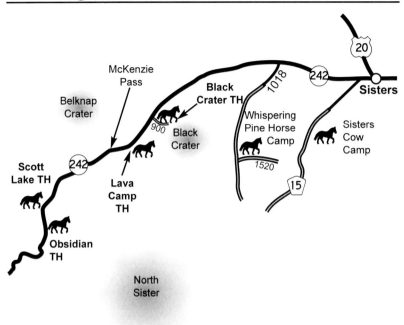

McKenzie Pass Area Trails

Trail	Difficulty	Elevation	Round Trip
Black Crater	Challenging	5,000-7,200	7 miles
Millican Crater/Matthieu Lks.	Moderate	5,200-6,100	10.5 miles
Obsidian Loop	Moderate	4,800-6,900	13-16 miles
Scott Mountain Loop	Moderate	4,800-6,100	8 miles

Black Crater

Trailhead: Start at the Black Crater trailhead
Length: 7 miles round trip
Elevation: 5,000 to 7,200 feet
Difficulty: Challenging -- steep trail
Footing: Hoof protection recommended
Season: Summer through fall
Permits: None
Facilities: Parking for 2-3 trailers (possibly more on a weekday when there are fewer hiker cars). No water on the trail.

Highlights: On a scale of 1 to 10, the views from the summit of Black Crater rate a 15. They are arguably the best views from any horse trail in Central Oregon. On a clear day you can see Mt. Hood, Mt. Jefferson, Three Fingered Jack, and Mt. Washington to the north, and North Sister, South Sister, and Broken Top to the south.

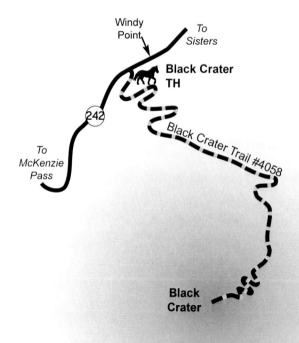

Debbie rides Cowboy near the summit of Black Crater, with North and South Sister and Broken Top in the background.

Finding the Black Crater Trailhead: From Sisters, go west on Hwy. 242 for 11 miles and turn left into the trailhead parking area, located about 0.5 mile past Windy Point.

The Ride: The Black Crater Trail #4058 departs from the south side of the trailhead, next to the kiosk. It climbs steadily (relentlessly) through moss-draped forests of hemlock and fir. For the last 0.6 mile the trail traverses cinder-strewn hillsides punctuated with wind-stunted trees until it arrives at the cinder-covered summit. Be sure to ride this trail on a clear day, as the panoramic views are jaw-dropping.

Whitney and Lydia gaze out at Mt. Jefferson from the cinder summit of Black Crater, while Cody and Shadow wish for some grass to munch.

Millican Crater/Matthieu Lks. Lp.

Trailhead: Start at Lava Camp trailhead
Length: 10.5 miles round trip
Elevation: 5,200 to 6,100 feet
Difficulty: Moderate
Footing: Hoof protection recommended
Season: Summer through fall
Permits: None
Facilities: Toilet and 2 primitive campsites at Lava Camp trailhead. Stock water is available on the trail.

Highlights: This ride goes through dense forest, along a huge lava flow, over Scott Pass, and past the picturesque Matthieu Lakes. Scott Pass offers expansive views of lava flows and cinder cones. Many lodgepoles in the area have been killed by pine beetles, but the forest is regenerating.

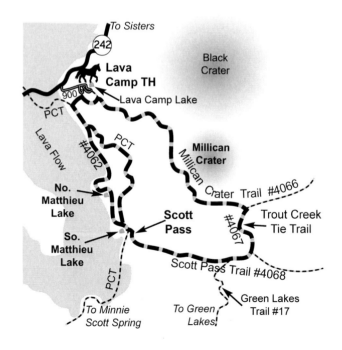

Finding Lava Camp Trailhead: Take Hwy. 242 (McKenzie Hwy.) west from Sisters for 14.5 miles and turn left on Road 900. Continue 0.4 mile to the horse use parking area.

The Ride: On the south side of the parking area, pick up the trail on the left (the Millican Crater Trail #4066). In 0.5 mile, the Lava Camp Lake hiker trail comes in from the left. In 3.5 miles you'll reach the junction with the Trout Creek Tie Trail #4067. Turn right on the Tie Trail toward Scott Pass, and in 1.0 mile you'll reach the Scott Pass Trail #4068. Turn right toward Green Lakes and the PCT. After 0.4 mile, the Green Lakes Trail #17 goes off to the left. Stay right and continue 1.8 mile to Scott Pass, with its impressive views. After a short distance the trail intersects with the PCT. Turn right on the PCT and continue to South Matthieu Lake for a good view of North Sister over the lake. From here you can either stay on the PCT or go left to the very pretty North Matthieu Lake on Trail #4062. Since the detour adds no distance and runs along an interesting lava flow, we recommend taking it. The trail rejoins the PCT in 2 miles. In another 0.7 mile, veer right to return to the Lava Camp trailhead.

Lydia and Shadow relax on the shore of North Matthieu Lake.

Obsidian Loop

Trailhead: Start at the Obsidian trailhead

Length: 13 miles round trip, or 16 miles if you detour to Obsidian Falls

Elevation: 4,800 to 6,900 feet

Difficulty: Moderate

Footing: Hoof protection recommended

Season: Summer through fall

Permits: Advance reservations required to ride this trail (see below). Northwest Forest Pass required.

Facilities: Toilet, parking for many trailers. Stock water is available on the trail.

Highlights: Located in the shadow of North Sister, this scenic ride features soaring obsidian cliffs, lava moonscapes, immense cinder cones, sparkling springs, pretty meadows, and sweeping vistas. To use this trail you must obtain a Limited Entry Permit. This is a fragile environment, so the Forest Service limits the number of riders, hikers, and backpackers in the area at any one time. Call the McKenzie Ranger District at 541-822-3381 to request a permit.

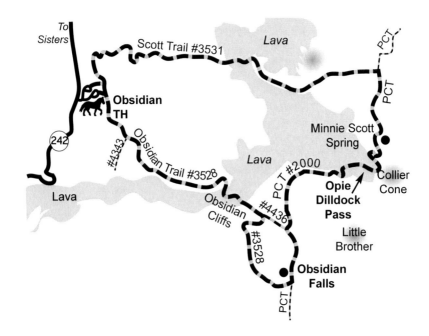

The fabulous Obsidian Loop features lava flows, mountain vistas, beautiful forest, and the amazing Opie Dilldock Pass.

Finding the Obsidian Trailhead: Take Highway 242 west from Sisters for 22 miles and turn left into the Obsidian trailhead. Note that only truck/trailer combinations less than 35 feet are permitted over McKenzie Pass, so you'll need to use a 2-horse trailer or drive the long way around, taking Hwy. 126 toward Eugene and turning left on the McKenzie Hwy.

The Ride: Pick up the trail on the east side of the Obsidian parking lot, and at the first fork go right on the Obsidian Trail #3528. After 3 miles you will see the Obsidian Cliffs, which tower over the forest and lava flows. The trail leads across the lava flow and back into the forest. Shortly afterward, the trail forks. The left fork (Glacier Way Trail #4436) will lead you to the Pacific Crest Trail in 0.6 mile. Or, for a very scenic 3-mile detour, turn right and continue on trail #3528 toward Obsidian Falls. When the trail intersects with the PCT, turn left (north) and soon you will pass Obsidian Falls. Proceed on the PCT for 1 mile to the junction with Trail #4436. Stay to the right and continue on the PCT for 2 miles to Opie Dilldock Pass, where a series of switchbacks will take you over an avalanche of black and red lava that flowed down between two cliffs. Although each switchback is only a couple of horse-lengths long, each is comfortably wide, so while the elevation gain is sizeable there are no steep drop offs. From the pass, continue about a mile past Minnie Scott Spring to the junction with the Scott Trail #3531. Turn left to return to the trailhead.

Scott Mountain Loop

Trailhead: Start at the Hand Lake trailhead in the quarry next to Scott Lake Campground
Length: 8 miles round trip
Elevation: 4,800 to 6,100 feet
Difficulty: Moderate
Footing: Hoof protection recommended
Season: Summer through fall
Permits: Northwest Forest Pass required
Facilities: Toilet and parking for several horse trailers at the trailhead. Stock water is available on the trail.

Highlights: Scott Mountain's open summit offers phenomenal views of the Three Sisters, Mt. Washington, Three Fingered Jack, Mt. Jefferson, and Mt. Hood. The trail is relatively easy except for a couple of steep switchbacks near the top, and it passes several pretty lakes and an interesting lava flow.

Finding the Scott Lake Trailhead: Drive west out of Sisters on Hwy. 242 for 20 miles. Turn right on Road 260 and proceed about a mile to

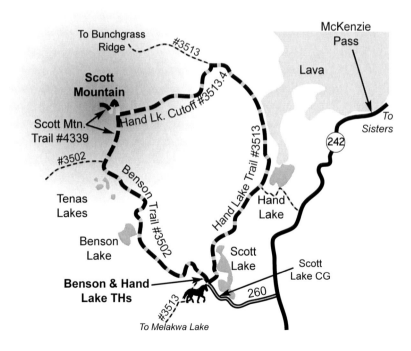

As Whitney and Cody can attest, when you're on top of Scott Mountain, the Three Sisters seem close enough to touch.

the old quarry at the end of the road, near Scott Lake Campground. Note that only truck/trailer combinations less than 35 feet are permitted over McKenzie Pass, so you'll need to use a 2-horse trailer or drive the long way around, taking Hwy. 126 toward Eugene and turning left on the McKenzie Hwy.

The Ride: Take the Hand Lake Trail #3513 from the eastern edge of the parking area. The trail along the shore of Scott Lake may be a bit overgrown with grass, but if you bear left along the lake shore you can't miss the trail as it heads up into the timber. After 1.5 miles you'll reach Hand Lake, and for the next mile or so the trail travels along a lava flow. About 1.5 miles beyond Hand Lake you'll come to a sign indicating that Bunchgrass Ridge is straight ahead. Turn left here on the unsigned Hand Lake Cutoff Trail #3513.4. Continue 1.5 miles and turn right on the Scott Mountain Trail #4339. Ascend another 0.5 mile (including several steep switchbacks) to reach the open, grassy summit with its dazzling views. To complete the loop, follow the Scott Mountain Trail down to the Benson Trail #3502 and turn left.   The Tenas Lakes are 1.5 miles from the summit (2.5 miles from the trailhead), and Benson Lake is 2.5 miles from the summit (1.5 miles from the trailhead).

The daughter who won't lift a finger in the house is the same child who cycles off madly in the pouring rain to spend all morning mucking out a stable.

Sarah Armstrong

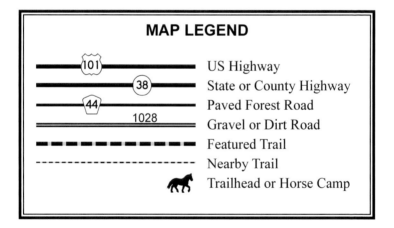

MAP LEGEND

101	US Highway
38	State or County Highway
44	Paved Forest Road
1028	Gravel or Dirt Road
▬ ▬ ▬ ▬ ▬	Featured Trail
- - - - - - -	Nearby Trail
🐎	Trailhead or Horse Camp

Metolius Basin
Sheep Springs Horse Camp
Deschutes National Forest

The Metolius Basin lies about 15 miles northwest of the town of Sisters. This park-like area is flanked by Mt. Jefferson to the north, Black Butte to the south, Green Ridge to the east, and Three Fingered Jack to the west. Sheep Springs Horse Camp provides access to the 150-mile Metolius-Windigo Trail (which originates at the north end of the Basin) as well as other easy low-elevation trails. The basin is also the gateway to several trails that go up into the Mt. Jefferson Wilderness. These higher-elevation trails were affected by the 2003 B&B fire, so you'll see plenty of dead trees, but the fire also opened up some impressive vistas. The forest is regenerating, but the burned trees are beginning to decay and fall so logs blocking the trail can be a problem. Before you ride the wilderness trails, be sure to check with the forest service to make sure the trail you plan to ride has been cleared.

Three Fingered Jack from the Rockpile Lake Trail.

177

Getting to the Metolius Basin

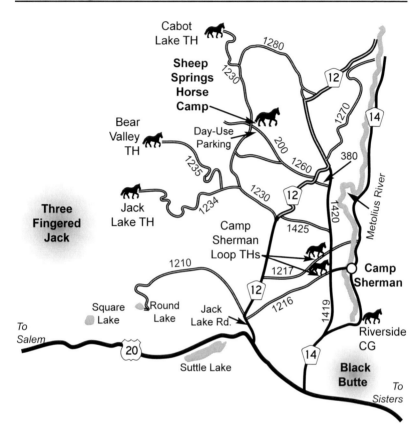

Metolius Basin Trails

Trail	Difficulty	Elevation	Round Trip
Bear Valley	Moderate	3,100-4,200	10 miles
Cabot Lake	Moderate	4,600-4,700+	4-10 miles
Camp Sherman Loop	Moderate	2,950-3,050	7 miles
Camp Sherman/Metolius R.	Moderate	2,950-3,300	17-21 miles
Canyon Creek Meadows Lp.	Moderate	5,150-5,700	5-8 miles
Rockpile Lake	Moderate	4,150-6,300	11.5 miles

Sheep Springs Horse Camp

Directions: From Sisters, drive northwest on Hwy. 20 for 12 miles. Turn right on Jack Lake Road (Road 12) and continue for 6.8 miles, then turn left on Road 1260. Drive about 1.0 mile, veer right on Road 200, and continue another 1.4 miles to the horse camp. The route is well signed. Day riders can park in an unofficial turnout along Road 200, on the left about 0.3 mile before the horse camp.

Elevation: 3,200 feet

Campsites: 11 sites with 4-horse log corrals. A couple are pull-through; the rest are back-in. Most sites have room for 2 vehicles.

Facilities: Vault toilet, manure bins, potable water, garbage cans. All sites have fire pits and picnic tables.

Permits: Camping fee. Reservations required. Day riders can park free at an unofficial turnout on the left 0.3 miles before the horse camp.

Season: May to October

Contact: Sisters Ranger District: 541-549-7700, www.fs.usda.gov/centraloregon, then click on "Recreation," "Horse Riding and Camping." Concessionaire: 541-338-7869, www.hoodoo.com, then click on "Campgrounds," "Horse Camping," "Sheep Springs." Reservations: call 877-444-6777 or go to www.recreation.gov.

Sheep Springs Horse Camp is situated next to a large, sunny meadow, but its campsites are shaded by huge ponderosas.

Bear Valley

Trailhead:	Start at Sheep Springs Horse Camp
Length:	10 miles round trip
Elevation:	3,100 to 4,200 feet
Difficulty:	Moderate
Footing:	Hoof protection recommended
Season:	Summer through fall
Permits:	Camping fee at Sheep Springs. No fee for day parking at turnout to the left of Road 200 about 0.3 mile before Sheep Springs.
Facilities:	Toilets, potable water, and manure bins at the horse camp. Parking for 2-3 trailers at the turnout beside Road 200. No stock water on the trail.

Highlights: This ride follows the Metolius-Windigo Trail from Sheep Springs Horse Camp to the Bear Valley trailhead, the jumping-off point for the Rockpile Lake Trail (which in turn connects with the Pacific Crest Trail). The trail runs in and out of the area burned by the B&B fire, and the contrast between the shade of the unburned forest and the sunny, brushy burned areas is remarkable. You will enjoy filtered views of the mountains along the way.

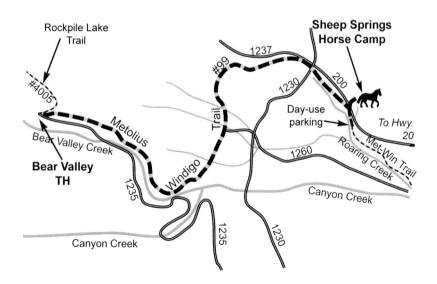

The Ride: <u>From the unofficial day-use parking area</u>, pick up the Metolius-Windigo Trail on the west side of the parking area and head to the right. In 0.3 mile you'll reach Sheep Springs Horse Camp. <u>From Sheep Springs Horse Camp</u>, pick up the Metolius-Windigo Trail #99 directly across Road 200 from the entrance to the camp. Ride about 100 feet and veer right on the Met-Win. The trail is marked with yellow diamonds. The last 2 miles of the trail traverse a ridge above Bear Valley Creek on an old roadbed. Some of the trail goes through forest and grassy meadows, and some goes through burned areas with little shade but nice views of the mountains, the Metolius Basin, and Green Ridge.

Through the burned trees you'll see
Broken Top, Black Butte, and the Three Sisters.

Jane follows the Metolius-Windigo Trail through a forested area unscathed by the fire.

Cabot Lake

Trailhead: Start at the Cabot Lake trailhead

Length: 4 miles round trip to Cabot Lake, 10 miles round trip to Carl Lake

Elevation: 4,600 to 4,700 feet to Cabot Lake, or 4,600 to 5,500 feet to Carl Lake

Difficulty: Moderate to Cabot Lake, but challenging between Cabot and Carl Lakes (very rocky trail)

Footing: Hoof protection strongly recommended

Season: Summer through fall

Permits: None

Facilities: Parking for 2-3 rigs at the trailhead. Stock water is available on the trail.

Highlights: The Cabot Lake trail is one of the few east-side Mt. Jefferson Wilderness Area trails that was not completely burned by the B&B fire in 2003. The terrain is fairly rugged and the trail is rocky, but the scenery is beautiful.

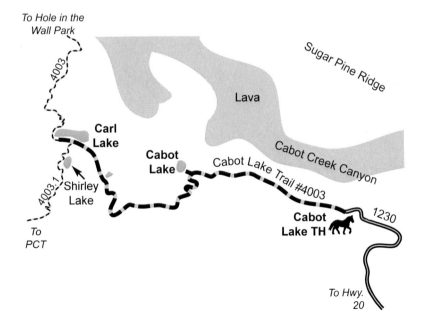

Finding the Cabot Lake Trailhead: Drive northwest from Sisters on Hwy. 20 for 12 miles. Turn right on Jack Lake Road (Road 12) and continue 4.3 miles. Turn left on Road 1230 and drive 8.2 miles to the trailhead.

The Ride: The first mile of the Cabot Lake Trail #4003, which runs along a ridge above Cabot Creek Canyon, was badly burned by the B&B fire. While the fire's devastation is appalling, it opened up views of the lava flows in the canyon below and of Mt. Jefferson looming over Sugar Pine Ridge. Next the trail enters an unburned area, and the contrast between the lovely live forest and the burned area is striking. Two miles from the parking area the trail forks. Take the trail to the right and ride a short distance to Cabot Lake, or take the left fork and go 3 miles farther to Carl Lake. Both lakes are aquamarine gems cradled between rocky ridges, and both make excellent picnic spots. The trail is very rocky between Cabot Lake and Carl Lake. Downed trees in the burned area can be a problem, so before you do this ride check with the forest service to make sure the trail has been logged out.

Riders and horses take a lunch break along the Cabot Lake Trail.

Camp Sherman Loop

Trailhead: Start at the junction of Road 1216 and the Metolius-Windigo Trail

Length: 7 miles round trip

Elevation: 2,950 to 3,050 feet

Difficulty: Moderate -- several creek crossings, and some riding beside actively-used forest roads

Footing: Suitable for barefoot horses

Season: Early spring through late fall

Permits: None

Facilities: No facilities at the parking area. Stock water is available on the trail.

Highlights: It's tough to beat this ride on a hot summer day. It offers plenty of shade, little elevation change, and several refreshing creek

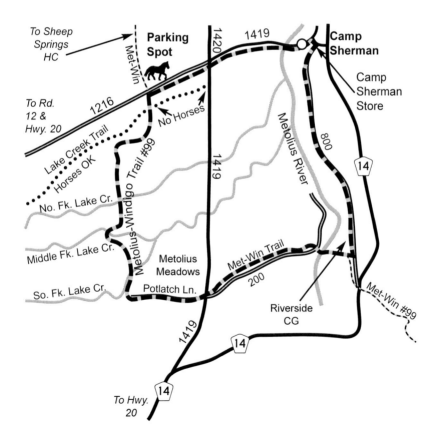

*Debbie, Whitney, and Lee ride Cowboy, Dixie
and Devlin across the Metolius River.*

crossings. Plus, you can get lunch, ice cream, or a cold drink at the
Camp Sherman Store.

Finding the Trailhead: There isn't an official trailhead for this ride,
so just park beside Road 1216. From Sisters, drive 9.5 miles northwest
on Hwy. 20. Turn right on Road 14 (toward Camp Sherman). In 2.7
miles, Road 14 veers to the right. Continue straight ahead on Road
1419 and in another 2.2 miles turn left on Road 1216. Continue 0.5
mile and park on the side of the road where the Met-Win Trail crosses
Road 1216. You can't turn around here, so after your ride just follow
Road 1216 to paved Road 12 and turn left to return to Hwy. 20.

The Ride: From your parking spot beside Road 1216, head south on
the Metolius-Windigo Trail #99, which is marked with yellow diamonds on the trees. In the first 2 miles you'll cross the North, Middle,
and South Forks of Lake Creek. Then the trail will take you around the
perimeter of the Metolius Meadows subdivision and across Road 1419.
A mile after that you'll reach the Metolius River not far from its headwaters. Ford the river (it's easy here) and continue on the Met-Win
Trail, but before you reach paved Road 14 veer left on gravel Road
800 leading past Riverside Campground. Follow it for 1.7 miles to
reach Camp Sherman. After enjoying lunch or a cold drink at the
Camp Sherman Store, cross the bridge over the Metolius River and
ride beside Road 1419 for 0.8 mile to the junction with Road 1216,
then ride along Road 1216 for 0.5 mile to your trailer.

Camp Sherman/Metolius River

Trailhead: Start at Sheep Springs Horse Camp, or at one of the unofficial parking spots where the Metolius-Windigo Trail crosses a forest road

Length: 21 miles round trip from Sheep Springs to the Metolius River, or 17 miles round trip from Sheep Springs to Camp Sherman. Shorter rides are possible.

Elevation: 2,950 to 3,300 feet

Difficulty: Moderate -- several water crossings

Footing: Suitable for barefoot horses

Season: Spring through late fall

Permits: Camping fee at Sheep Springs. No fee at other parking spots.

Facilities: Parking for several trailers near Sheep Springs Horse Camp or at the various roadside locations shown below. The campground has a toilet and potable water. Stock water is available on the trail.

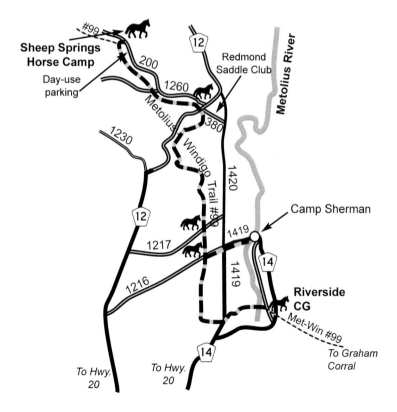

Highlights: This portion of the Metolius-Windigo Trail explores the park-like forest, meadows, and creeks of the beautiful Metolius Basin. It's easy riding, with very little elevation change. Depending on where you park, you can make the ride as long or as short as you like.

Finding the Trailheads: You can park off Road 200 about 0.3 mile before Sheep Springs Horse Camp, or beside the road near Riverside Campground, or beside Roads 1216 or 1217, or at the junction of Roads 12 and 380. If you park beside Roads 1216 or 1217 there is nowhere to turn around, so after your ride just drive straight ahead and you'll soon reach paved Road 12. Turn left to return to Hwy. 20.

The Ride: The Metolius-Windigo Trail #99, which is marked by yellow diamonds, beautifully showcases the huge ponderosas and lush vegetation characteristic of the Metolius Basin. The trail is forested, with frequent crossings of the creeks that are abundant in the basin. You can ride the Met-Win Trail to the Metolius River and beyond, or you can veer left on Road 1216 and follow it and Road 1419 to Camp Sherman instead. If you go to Camp Sherman, be sure to stop at the Camp Sherman Store (located where Road 1419 crosses the Metolius River) for a burger, sandwich, ice cream, or cold drink.

Linda and Beamer gait along the Met-Win Trail.

Canyon Creek Meadows Loop

Trailhead: Start at Jack Lake trailhead

Length: 5 miles round trip for Jack Lake Loop, 6.5 miles round trip for loop plus extension to base of Three Fingered Jack, 8 miles round trip for loop plus extensions to the base of Three Fingered Jack and to Wasco Lake

Elevation: 5,150 to 5,700 feet

Difficulty: Moderate

Footing: Suitable for barefoot horses

Season: Summer through early fall

Permits: Northwest Forest Pass required

Facilities: Toilet, parking for several trailers (depending on the number of hiker cars). Stock water is available on the trail.

Highlights: This is a delightful ride across manzanita-covered hillsides and through dense forest to the flower-filled Canyon Creek Meadows and then along Canyon Creek. Some of the trail was burned in the 2003 B&B fire, but fortunately the lovely meadows were untouched. The western end of the loop offers excellent views of Three Fingered Jack, and a short extension takes you nearly to the base of the

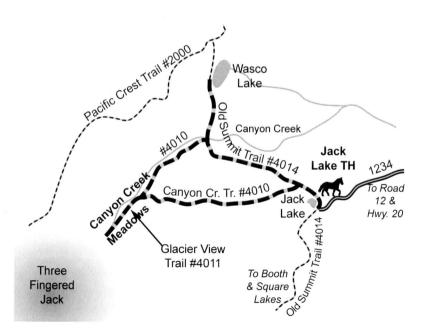

Linda rides Brumby through the wildflowers in Canyon
Creek Meadows, toward cloud-capped Three Fingered Jack.

mountain. If desired, you can also ride a 0.6 mile (one way) extension to Wasco Lake.

Finding the Jack Lake Trailhead: From Sisters, drive northwest for 12 miles on Highway 20. Turn right on Jack Lake Road (Road 12). After 4 miles, turn left on Road 1230 and continue 1.5 miles. Turn left on Road 1234 and go 5 miles to the trailhead. The route is well signed.

The Ride: From the parking lot, pick up the trail going to the right past Jack Lake. After 0.5 mile, the trail forks. Go left on Canyon Creek Trail #4010. In another 1.7 miles you'll reach a junction. Turn left on the Glacier View Trail #4011 to reach Canyon Creek Meadows and good views of nearby Three Fingered Jack. You can ride about 0.7 mile one way, almost to the base of the peak. Then return to the junction and turn left to continue around the loop. The trail follows Canyon Creek for about a mile, after which the 0.6-mile extension to Wasco Lake on the Old Summit Trail turns left, crosses Canyon Creek, and heads north. If you don't want to go to Wasco Lake, don't cross the creek and the trail will return you to the Jack Lake trailhead.

Rockpile Lake

Trailhead: Start at the Bear Valley trailhead
Length: 11.5 miles round trip
Elevation: 4,150 to 6,300 feet
Difficulty: Moderate
Footing: Hoof protection recommended
Season: Summer through fall
Permits: None
Facilities: Parking for 4-6 trailers, but no other facilities. Stock water is available at Rockpile Lake.

Highlights: This trail links the north end of the Metolius-Windigo Trail to the Pacific Crest Trail at Rockpile Lake. It runs alternately through hemlock and fir forest and areas burned by the B&B fire in 2003. The forested areas are beautiful, and the burned areas offer panoramic views of the Metolius Basin, Black Butte, Three-Fingered Jack, Mt. Washington, North and Middle Sister, and Broken Top.

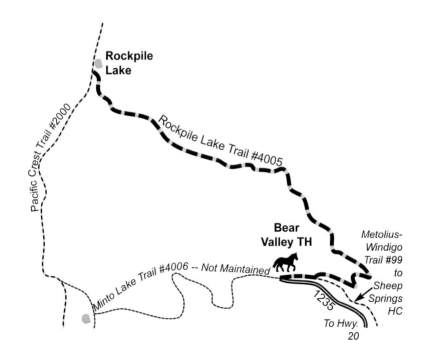

Frank, Doug, Sandy, Dave, Rhonda, Bob, and Kit are the volunteers who used cross-cut saws to clear the Rockpile Lake Trail of downed logs in 2011. They deserve our thanks for keeping this delightful trail accessible to horses.

Finding Bear Valley Trailhead: Drive west from Sisters on Hwy. 20 for 12 miles and turn right on Jack Lake Road (Road 12). In 4 miles veer left on Road 1230. In another 1.5 miles, turn left on Road 1234, and 0.7 mile after that veer right on road 1235. In 4 miles you'll reach the trailhead.

The Ride: Pick up the Metolius-Windigo Trail #99 next to the kiosk on the west end of the parking area. Almost immediately there is a junction, but stay to the right because the trail to Minto Lake is not maintained and is impassible. After 0.3 mile, turn left onto the Rockpile Lake Trail #4005. It makes a couple of switchbacks, then heads up along the nose of a ridge. The trail climbs fairly steadily, but is otherwise not challenging. Rockpile Lake is a delight, and is the only source of stock water along the trail.

I never play horseshoes 'cause Mother taught us not to throw our clothes around.

Mr. Ed (the talking horse
of the 1960's TV series)

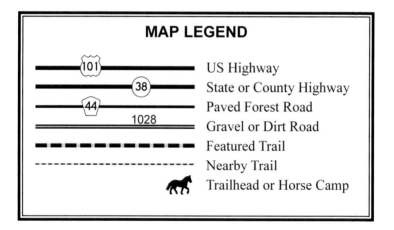

Newberry Crater
Chief Paulina Horse Camp
Deschutes National Forest

Newberry National Volcanic Monument, located about 45 minutes south of Bend, was established in 1990 to preserve the unique geologic features of the Newberry Volcano. The caldera was formed when Newberry Volcano blew its top, and volcanic eruptions occurred there as recently as 1,300 years ago – little more than the blink of an eye in geologic terms. Paulina Lake and East Lake, in the bottom of the caldera, are popular for boating and fishing. At 7,985 feet, Paulina Peak is the tallest of the mountains that ring the crater. From Paulina Peak, North Paulina Peak and various points around the rim you're treated to panoramic views of the Three Sisters, Mt. Bachelor, Mt. Jefferson, and Fort Rock. Many of the features in this area were named for Chief Paulina, a wily Snake Indian chief and skilled horseman who wreaked havoc on the settlers, miners, and trappers in the Oregon Territory. Chief Paulina Horse Camp provides both overnight camping and day-use facilities. La Pine State Park is located nearby, and can be accessed without entering the Monument.

From the Lost Lake Trail you can see Big Obsidian Flow, Paulina Lake, the Three Sisters, and Mt. Bachelor.

Getting to Newberry Crater

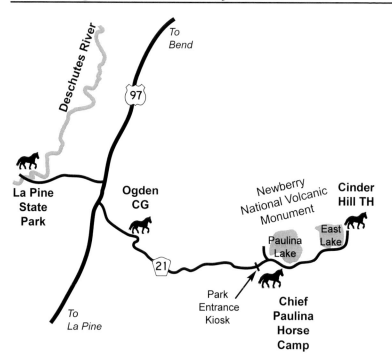

Newberry Crater Area Trails

Trail	Difficulty	Elevation	Round Trip
Crater Rim Loop	Difficult	6,400-7,700	25 miles
East Rim Loop	Moderate	6,400-7,400	11-23 miles
La Pine State Park	Easy	4,100-4,200	3-9 miles
Newberry Crater Trail	Moderate	6,300-6,500	3.5-17 miles
North Paulina Peak	Moderate	6,300-7,600	12.5 miles
North Rim Loop	Challenging	6,300-7,600	17 miles
Paulina Peak	Difficult	6,300-7,600	13 miles
Peter Skene Ogden Trail	Moderate	4,300-6,400	17-20 miles
South Rim Loop	Moderate	6,400-7,300	13.5 miles

Chief Paulina Horse Camp

Directions: From Bend, take Hwy. 97 south for 23 miles and turn left on Paulina Lake Road, Road 21. Continue 11 miles to the park entrance kiosk, then drive 1 mile past it and turn right. The horse camp is ahead on the right in 1.2 miles.

Elevation: 6,400 feet

Campsites: 14 sites. Four sites have 4-horse corrals and the rest are 2-horse. All are back-in, and 6 sites can accommodate 2 vehicles. Some sites cannot accommodate larger trailers.

Facilities: Vault toilet, manure bin, stock water in a large trough. All sites have fire pits and picnic tables. No potable water. Day-use parking area holds 5-6 trailers.

Permits: Campsites may be reserved from July through September. Camping fee, or Northwest Forest Pass required for day use.

Season: May to October

Contact: Bend/Ft. Rock Ranger District: 541-383-4000, www.fs.usda.gov/centraloregon, then click on "Recreation," "Horse Riding and Camping." Concessionaire: 541-338-7869, www.hoodoo.com, then click on "Campgrounds," "Horse Camping," "Chief Paulina." Reservations: call 877-444-6777 or go to www.recreation.gov.

Linda grooms Beamer in the corral at Chief Paulina Horse Camp.

Crater Rim Loop

Trailhead:	Start at Chief Paulina Horse Camp
Length:	25 miles round trip
Elevation:	6,400 to 7,700 feet
Difficulty:	Difficult -- long, with one very steep segment
Footing:	Hoof protection recommended
Season:	Late spring through fall
Permits:	Camping fee, or Northwest Forest Pass for day use
Facilities:	Toilet, stock water, and manure bin at the horse camp. Stock water is available near Paulina Lake Lodge.

Highlights: This ride, which is popular with endurance riders, features expansive views and varied terrain. The trail up Paulina Peak is steep and difficult and the loop is long, so this is a trail for well-conditioned horses and experienced riders.

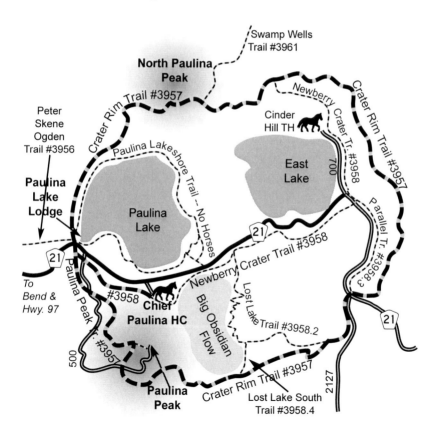

The Ride: From Chief Paulina Horse Camp, pick up the Newberry Crater Trail #3958 between campsites 9 and 10 and ride west for 1.5 miles. Turn left on Crater Rim Trail #3957 toward Paulina Peak. The trail climbs gradually for the next 1.1 mile, then it crosses Road 500 and starts climbing in earnest, gaining 1,300 feet of elevation in the next 1.5 miles. This section of the trail is difficult because in places it is extremely steep. The trail passes near the summit of Paulina Peak, offering breathtaking views. It then levels off for about 3 miles as it runs along the south side of Paulina Peak and past Big Obsidian Flow. The trail then heads gently downhill for about 6.5 miles, passing the junctions with the Lost Lake South #3958.4 and Lost Lake #3958.2 trails. Just after crossing Road 21, veer right to stay on the Crater Rim Trail and continue around the rim. You will reach the junction with the Newberry Crater Trail #3958 about 5.7 miles after crossing Road 21. About 1.6 miles after that you'll pass the junction with the Swamp Wells Trail #3961. In 0.5 mile you'll pass North Paulina Peak, then the trail will head steadily down for 6 miles to near the west shore of Paulina Lake. Return to the horse camp on the Newberry Crater Trail #3958.

The Crater Rim Trail circles
the entire rim of Newberry Caldera.

East Rim Loop

Trailhead: Start at Chief Paulina Horse Camp or Cinder Hill trailhead

Length: 11 miles round trip from Cinder Hill trailhead, or 23 miles round trip from Chief Paulina Horse Camp

Elevation: 6,400 to 7,400 feet

Difficulty: Moderate

Footing: Suitable for barefoot horses

Season: Summer through fall

Permits: Camping fee, or Northwest Forest Pass for day use

Facilities: Toilet, stock water, and manure bins at the horse camp. Toilet at Cinder Hill trailhead. Stock water is available at East Lake.

Highlights: The views from Cinder Hill are a real treat -- you can see East Lake below you, plus Big Obsidian Flow, Paulina Peak, and Paulina Lake in the distance. Once you've made your way up to the

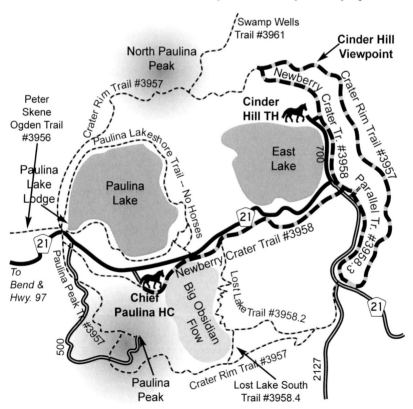

Linda and Beamer take in the huge views from Cinder Hill.
East Lake is below, and Paulina Peak is in the distance.

crater rim, the trail is fairly level until it begins to descend gradually to the lake shore.

Finding the Cinder Hill Trailhead: From Chief Paulina Horse Camp, drive east on Road 21 for 4.5 miles. The road runs into the Cinder Hill campground, and about 0.5 mile after entering the campground you'll see the day-use parking area on the left.

The Ride: <u>From the Cinder Hill trailhead</u>, a short spur trail takes you east to the Newberry Crater Trail #3958. Turn left on it, and in 2.2 miles you'll reach the crater rim, gaining 900 feet of elevation in the process. Turn right on the Crater Rim Trail #3957, and in 0.8 mile you'll arrive at the Cinder Hill viewpoint. After enjoying the views, continue along the rim for about 4.9 miles. When you reach the junction with the Parallel Trail #3958.3, turn right and ride down through the lodgepoles for 1.4 miles to a dirt road where the trail seems to disappear. Turn right on the dirt road, and in 200 feet veer left around a pile of tree stumps to find the trail again. In 0.6 mile you'll reach the Newberry Crater Trail. Turn right on it and in 1.3 miles veer left on the spur trail that will take you back to your trailer. <u>From Chief Paulina Horse Camp</u>, pick up the Newberry Crater Trail #3958 between campsites 2 and 3, and ride 5 miles to the junction with the Parallel Trail #3958.3 just across gravel Road 21. Veer left on the Newberry Crater Trail, and in 1.3 miles you'll reach the Cinder Hill trailhead. Continue by following the directions above.

La Pine State Park

Trailhead: La Pine State Park has two equestrian trailheads, one on each side of the Deschutes River

Length: 3-9 miles, depending on route taken

Elevation: 4,100 to 4,200 feet

Difficulty: Easy

Footing: Suitable for barefoot horses

Season: Late spring through fall

Permits: No fee for day use

Facilities: Plenty of parking for horse trailers. Toilets at several locations around the park. Stock water is available on the trail.

Highlights: The La Pine State Park trails are accessible when the high country is still deep in snow, and they offer nice views of the Deschutes River and Fall River. La Pine State Park also boasts the largest

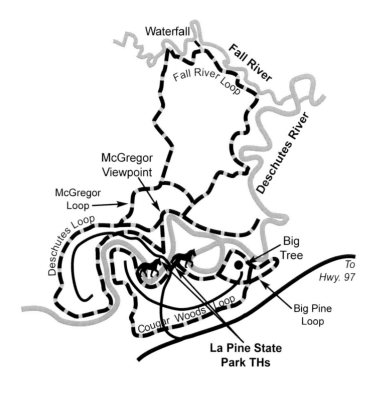

The Deschutes River from McGregor Viewpoint.

ponderosa pine in Oregon. At 191 feet high, 326 inches around, and 500 years old, it's an impressive sight. Several loop rides are possible, so you can tailor your ride to fit your preferences.

Finding the La Pine State Park Trailheads: Take Highway 97 south from Bend for 22 miles (1 mile north of the turnoff to Newberry Crater). Turn right at the sign for La Pine State Park, and drive 4 miles, then veer right into the park and continue straight ahead for 0.5 mile to reach the trailheads on either side of the Deschutes River.

The Ride: There are 5 trails within the park that can be combined to make two loops, or you can link all of the loops to make one longer ride. The Big Pine and Cougar Woods Trails depart from the parking area on the east side of the river and make about a 3.8-mile loop. The Deschutes, McGregor, and Fall River trails are accessible from the west side of the river and make about a 5-mile loop. Trail maps are posted at strategic locations throughout the park.

Newberry Crater Trail

Trailhead: Start at Chief Paulina Horse Camp

Length: 3.5 miles round trip from Chief Paulina to Paulina Lake Lodge, or 12.5 miles round trip from Chief Paulina to Cinder Hill trailhead, or 17 miles round trip from Chief Paulina to the crater rim

Elevation: 6,300 to 6,500 feet for the lake shore portion of the trail, or 6,300 to 7,300 feet to the crater rim

Difficulty: Easy on the crater floor (along Road 21), moderate to the crater rim

Footing: Suitable for barefoot horses

Season: Summer through fall

Permits: Camping fee, or Northwest Forest Pass for day use

Facilities: Toilet, stock water, and manure bins at the horse camp. Stock water is available near Paulina Lake Lodge and at East Lake.

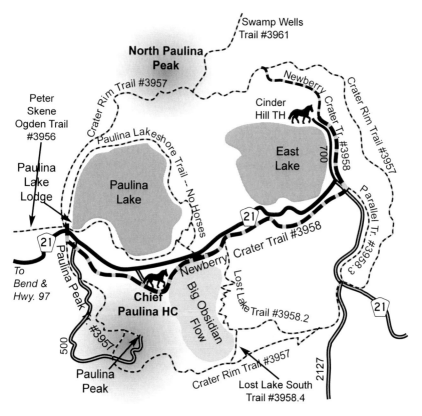

Highlights: The Newberry Crater Trail #3958 runs beside Road 21 at lake level all the way from Paulina Lake Lodge to the Cinder Hill trailhead. From there it climbs to the Crater Rim Trail. This trail provides access to other trails that can take you to the crater rim, or you can ride it to Paulina Lake Lodge for lunch or dinner.

The Ride: From Chief Paulina Horse Camp, you can pick up the westbound Newberry Crater Trail #3958 between campsites 9 and 10 or the eastbound trail between campsites 2 and 3. Heading west, the trail runs mostly under the power lines for 1.5 miles. At the junction with the Crater Rim Trail #3957, you can veer right and cross Road 21 to reach Paulina Lake Lodge, the Peter Skene Ogden Trail #3956, and the Crater Rim Trail toward North Paulina Peak.   Heading east, after 2.3 miles the Lost Lake trail #3958.2 goes off to the right. About 2.7 miles beyond that, the Newberry Crater Trail intersects with the Parallel Trail #3958.3. If you stay to the left you'll reach the Cinder Hill trailhead, where you can detour to East Lake to give your horse a drink. If you continue on the Newberry Crater Trail, you'll climb to the Crater Rim Trail #3957 in another 2.2 miles.

Most of the Newberry Crater Trail has little elevation gain/loss. It has great footing for really moving out -- or for just moseying along.

North Paulina Peak

Trailhead: Start at Chief Paulina Horse Camp
Length: 12.5 miles round trip
Elevation: 6,300 to 7,600 feet
Difficulty: Moderate
Footing: Suitable for barefoot horses
Season: Summer through fall
Permits: Camping fee, or Northwest Forest Pass for day use
Facilities: Toilet, stock water, and manure bins at the horse camp. Stock water is available near Paulina Lake Lodge.

Highlights: The ride is a steady but not very strenuous climb to the crater rim, and the views from the rim near North Paulina Peak are fabulous. As you gaze out at Paulina Lake and Paulina Peak, note that

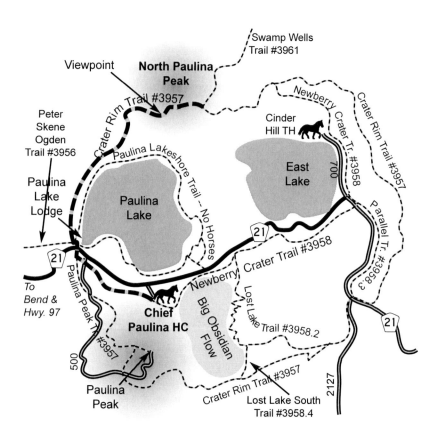

if the west side of the crater hadn't crumbled away and allowed Paulina Creek to flow out, Oregon would have had a second Crater Lake.

The Ride: From Chief Paulina Horse Camp, pick up the Newberry Crater Trail #3958 between campsites 9 and 10 and ride west for 1.5 miles. Turn right on the Crater Rim Trail #3957. Cross Road 21 and the bridge over Paulina Creek, then immediately turn left, skirt the green metal gate, and pick up the Crater Rim Trail #3957. (The Peter Skene Ogden Trail #3956 goes to the left, and the Paulina Lakeshore Trail (no horses allowed) goes to the right.) The trail climbs fairly steadily for 4 miles, following a forest road at first and then becoming a single-track trail. The trail then levels out and runs through a cinder-covered area that provides great views of the lake and the crater rim. If you continue 0.5 mile you'll reach the junction with the Swamp Wells Trail #3961, and 1.6 mile beyond that you'll reach the junction with the Newberry Crater Trail #3958.

Linda and Beamer ride past a viewpoint near North Paulina Peak.
Paulina Lake is below and Paulina Peak is in the background.

North Rim Loop

Trailhead: Start at Chief Paulina Horse Camp
Length: 17 miles round trip
Elevation: 6,300 to 7,600 feet
Difficulty: Challenging -- long
Footing: Hoof protection recommended
Season: Late spring through fall
Permits: Camping fee, or Northwest Forest Pass for day use
Facilities: Toilet, stock water, and manure bins at the horse camp. Toilet at Cinder Hill trailhead. Stock water is available near Paulina Lake Lodge and at East Lake.

Highlights: This is a long ride, though it's much easier than the Paulina Peak and Crater Rim loops. It offers scenic views from the crater rim near North Paulina Peak.

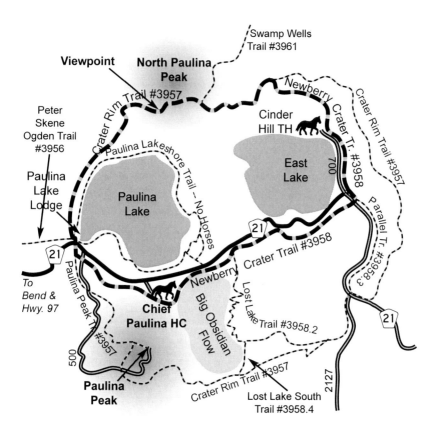

*From the North Rim you have a splendid view
of Paulina Lake and Paulina Peak.*

The Ride: From Chief Paulina Horse Camp, pick up the Newberry Crater Trail #3958 between campsites 9 and 10 and ride west for 1.5 miles to Crater Rim Trail #3957. Turn right on the Crater Rim Trail, then cross Road 21 and the bridge over Paulina Creek. Immediately turn left, skirt the green metal gate, and pick up the Crater Rim Trail #3957 toward North Paulina Peak. The trail climbs fairly steadily for about 4 miles, following a double-track forest road at first and then becoming a single-track trail. Then the trail levels out as it runs along the crater rim.   About 2 miles after passing North Paulina Peak, turn right onto Newberry Crater Trail #3958 and follow it down to the shore of East Lake, about 2.2 miles. Continue another 1.3 miles to where the trail crosses Road 21, then veer right and follow the Newberry Crater Trail #3958 along Road 21 about 5 miles, past Big Obsidian Flow and back to Chief Paulina Horse Camp. Along the way you can water your horses at the boat ramp next to Paulina Lake Lodge and at East Lake near the Cinder Hill trailhead.

Paulina Peak Loop

Trailhead: Start at Chief Paulina Horse Camp

Length: 13 miles round trip for the loop, or 13.6 miles round trip if you detour to the summit of Paulina Peak

Elevation: 6,300 to 7,700 feet for the loop, or 8,000 if you ride to the summit

Difficulty: Difficult -- very steep

Footing: Hoof protection recommended

Season: Late spring through fall

Permits: Camping fee, or Northwest Forest Pass for day use

Facilities: Toilet, stock water, and manure bins at the horse camp. Stock water is available near Paulina Lake Lodge.

Highlights: If your horse is in good condition and you don't want to commit to the 21-mile ride around the entire rim of the crater, this trail is a reasonable alternative. You'll see the spectacular views from the

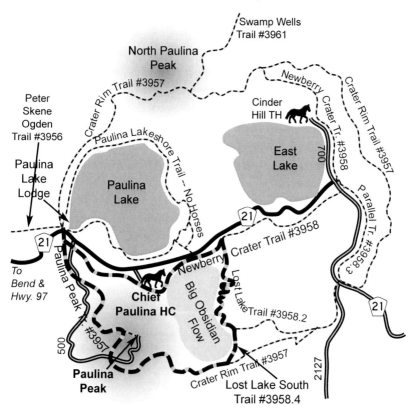

top of Paulina Peak and have an up-close look at Big Obsidian Flow. It's a challenging ride, though, because the first leg of the trail climbs very steeply.

The Ride: From Chief Paulina Horse Camp, pick up the westbound Newberry Crater Trail #3958 between campsites 9 and 10 and ride 1.5 miles. Turn left on the Crater Rim Trail #3957 toward Paulina Peak. The trail runs parallel to Road 500 for a mile or so, crosses it, and then climbs very steeply to near the summit of Paulina Peak, gaining 1,300 feet of elevation in 1.5 miles. The views from the top are amazing, but do not attempt this trail unless your horse is in very good condition. If you want to ride to the summit of Paulina Peak (which can also be accessed by car), veer left on the 0.3-mile spur trail. Continuing on around the loop, the Crater Rim Trail levels out and in 3.4 miles it reaches the junction with the Lost Lake South Trail #3958.4. Turn left, and in 0.7 mile turn left on Lost Lake Trail #3958.2. It will take you down a series of switchbacks along the very impressive eastern edge of Big Obsidian Flow. In 2.7 miles, turn left on the Newberry Crater Trail #3958 to return to the horse camp.

You'll have a panoramic view from the summit of Paulina Peak.

Peter Skene Ogden Trail

Trailhead: Start at Chief Paulina Horse Camp or at Ogden Campground, 25 miles south of Bend on Hwy. 97

Length: 20 miles round trip from Chief Paulina Horse Camp to
Ogden Campground. From Ogden Campground it's
16.5 miles round trip to Paulina Falls or 17.5 miles round
trip to Paulina Lake.

Elevation: 4,300 to 6,400 feet

Difficulty: Moderate

Footing: Suitable for barefoot horses

Season: Summer through fall

Permits: Camping fee, or Northwest Forest Pass for day parking
at Chief Paulina Horse Camp. No fee at Ogden Campground.

Facilities: Toilets, stock water, plenty of parking at both Chief
Paulina and Ogden Campground. Stock water is avail-
able on the trail.

Highlights: The trail winds along beside Paulina Creek, past lovely
pools, waterfalls, and rapids. Wildflowers are abundant along the
creek, which is often just a few feet from the trail. Paulina Falls, located about 0.5 mile from Paulina Lake, spills over a volcanic ledge
into a canyon some 80 feet below. If you want, you can get a burger,
ice cream, or a beer at Paulina Lake Lodge on the shore of the lake.

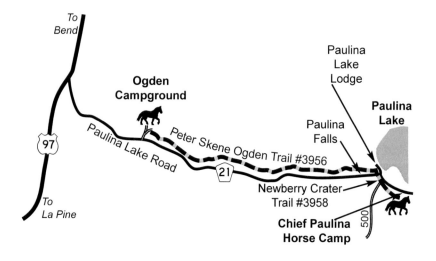

*The double Paulina Falls drops an impressive 80 feet
and is located right beside the trail.*

Finding Ogden Campground: Take Hwy. 97 south of Bend for 23 miles and turn left on Paulina Lake Road toward Newberry National Volcanic Monument. Drive 2 miles and turn left into the campground. Park in the large gravel parking lot to the right of the campground entrance.

The Ride: <u>From Ogden Campground</u>, the trail leaves the gravel parking area, crosses Paulina Creek, and follows the creek steadily uphill to Paulina Lake. <u>From Chief Paulina Horse Camp</u>, pick up the westbound Newberry Crater Trail #3958 between campsites 9 and 10 and ride 1.5 miles. Turn right on the Crater Rim Trail #3957, then cross Road 21 and the bridge over Paulina Creek. Immediately turn left, skirt the green metal gate, and pick up the Peter Skene Ogden Trail #3956 on the left. <u>All</u>, the scenery on this trail is quite varied, as the trail travels past riparian vegetation along the creek, across tree-covered hills, over acres scorched by wildfire several years ago, and through dense stands of lodgepole pine. There are numerous waterfalls of varying sizes all along the creek. Paulina Lake is a nice spot for a picnic, although horses are not allowed in the campground or on the trail that circles the lake. At the lake there are toilets, a cafe, and a small general store at Paulina Lake Lodge. Note that bicyclists are permitted to ride uphill on this trail but are required to ride downhill on a nearby forest road, appropriately dubbed the Paulina Plunge.

South Rim Loop

Trailhead: Start at Chief Paulina Horse Camp
Length: 13.5 miles round trip
Elevation: 6,400 to 7,300 feet
Difficulty: Moderate
Footing: Hoof protection recommended
Season: Summer through fall
Permits: Camping fee, or Northwest Forest Pass for day use
Facilities: Toilet, stock water, and manure bins at the horse camp. No stock water on the trail.

Highlights: This trail runs along the base of Big Obsidian Flow, which towers a hundred feet or more above the trail. It then climbs toward the crater rim on the Lost Lake Trail, offering amazing views of the Big Obsidian Flow, Paulina Lake, Paulina Peak, and the Cascades before descending gently back to lake level.

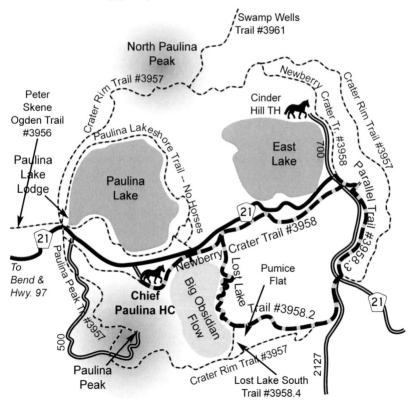

The Ride: Pick up the Newberry Crater Trail #3958 between camp-sites 2 and 3, and in 200 feet veer left at the junction. In 1.5 miles you'll cross the paved road that leads to the Big Obsidian Flow trailhead. About 0.7 mile later, turn right at the junction with the Lost Lake Trail #3958.2. (Lost Lake is located at the base of Big Obsidian Flow, but you can't see it from the trail.) The trail climbs slowly for the next mile, then quickly gains 700 feet of elevation on about 1.4 miles of switchbacks. The huge views in this section are more than adequate compensation for the exertion. Then the trail descends for about 0.2 mile to a junction. Veer left on the Lost Lake Trail toward Pumice Flat, and in 1.5 mile the Lost Lake Trail meets the Crater Rim Trail #3957. Veer left on the Crater Rim Trail, and in 1 mile you'll reach Road 21. Cross it and turn left on the Parallel Trail #3958.3, following it 1.4 miles to a dirt road where the trail seems to disappear. Turn right on the dirt road, and in 200 feet veer left around a pile of tree stumps to find the trail again. In another 0.6 mile turn left on the Newberry Crater Trail #3958 and follow it 4.6 miles back to the horse camp. Where the trail runs through the decommissioned Hot Springs Campground the trail may at times be hard to follow. Just skirt around the base of the lava flow on your left and you'll soon pick up a clearer trail.

*Linda rides Beamer beside the Big Obsidian Flow
on the Lost Lake Trail, part of the South Rim Loop.*

Wherever man has left his footprints in the long as-
cent from barbarism to civilization, we find the
hoofprint of a horse beside it.

John Trotwood Moore

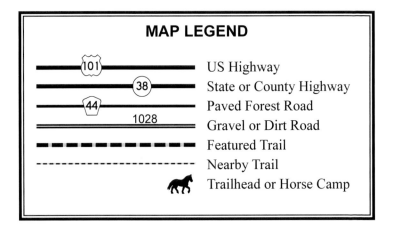

MAP LEGEND

101	US Highway
38	State or County Highway
44	Paved Forest Road
1028	Gravel or Dirt Road
	Featured Trail
	Nearby Trail
	Trailhead or Horse Camp

North Cascade Lakes
Quinn Meadow Horse Camp
Deschutes National Forest

The northern part of the Cascade Lakes district is a rider's paradise. The views in this area can be breathtaking, with mountain peaks soaring above pristine lakes, jagged lava flows next to verdant forests, and sparkling streams flowing through lush meadows. Because of the area's proximity to Bend, the more popular trails may be crowded with hikers, especially on summer weekends. Seek out lesser-known trails during the peak season and you can still have a wonderful wilderness experience without driving for hours to reach the trailhead. Whether you base your riding out of Quinn Meadow Horse Camp (camping only, no day-use parking) or take day rides from the nearby trailheads, there are almost endless opportunities for loop rides on the region's network of intersecting trails. Please keep your horse out of the area lakes, as they are used for drinking water by backpackers. Also note that in this area the Metolius-Windigo Trail is frequently used by mountain bike riders.

Lel and Whitney ride Jane and Dixie across
Wickiup Plain, with South Sister in the background.

Getting to North Cascade Lakes

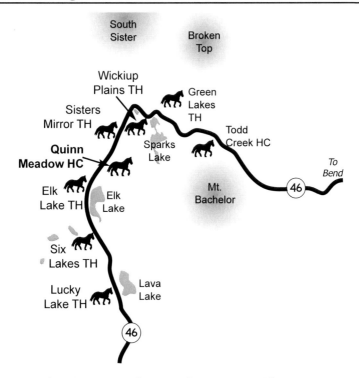

North Cascade Lakes Trails

Trail	Difficulty	Elevation	Round Trip
Appaloosa/Quinn Cr. Lp.	Moderate	5,000-5,450	7 miles
Devils/Quinn Loop	Moderate	5,100-5,700	9.5 miles
Elk Lake	Easy	4,900-5,200	6 miles
Horse Lake Loop	Moderate	4,950-5,300	9-15 miles
Lava Lake	Moderate	4,800-5,100	15-18 miles
Mink Lake Basin	Moderate	4,800-5,700	17 miles
Quinn Springs Loop	Moderate	5,050-5,150	2.2 miles
Senoj Lake	Moderate	4,900-5,600	9 miles
Sink Creek Loop	Moderate	5,050-5,450	5.5 miles
Sisters Mirror/Koosah Lp.	Moderate	5,000-6,500	13-14 miles
Sisters Mirror/Wickiup Lp.	Moderate	5,500-6,300	12-14.5 miles
Sparks Lake/Todd Creek	Moderate	5,000-6,100	6-13 miles
Wickiup Plains Loop	Moderate	5,100-6,300	9-16 miles

Quinn Meadow Horse Camp

Directions: From Hwy. 97 in Bend, take Exit 138 (Colorado Ave.) and head west. Follow the signs toward Mt. Bachelor, which will put you on Hwy. 46 (Century Drive/Cascade Lakes Hwy.) Continue for 30 miles and turn left into the horse camp.

Elevation: 5,100 feet

Campsites: 26 sites with 2- or 4-horse log corrals. 21 sites are back-in, the others are pull-through. All are fairly level and have room for 2 vehicles, and all sites have fire pits and picnic tables.

Facilities: Toilets, manure bins, potable water from a hand pump. Camp host. No day-use parking at Quinn Meadow Horse Camp. Use area trailheads instead.

Permits: User fees for camping. Advance reservations required.

Season: Summer through fall

Contact: Bend/Ft. Rock Ranger District: 541-383-4000, www.fs.usda.gov/ centraloregon, then click on "Recreation," "Horse Riding and Camping." Concessionaire: 541-338-7869, www.hoodoo.com, then click on "Campgrounds," "Horse Camping," "Quinn Meadow." Reservations: call 877-444-6777 or go to www.recreation.gov.

South Sister towers over Quinn Meadow Horse Camp.

Appaloosa/Quinn Creek Loop

Trailhead: Start at Quinn Meadow Horse Camp

Length: 7 miles round trip

Elevation: 5,000 to 5,450 feet

Difficulty: Moderate -- water crossing, bridge, and challenging switchbacks on the Quinn Creek Trail

Footing: Hoof protection recommended

Season: Summer through fall

Permits: Camping fee. No day-use parking at Quinn Meadow.

Facilities: Toilets, potable water, and manure bins at the horse camp. Stock water is available on the trail.

Highlights: This is a delightful ride that offers tree-filtered views of South Sister, Mt. Bachelor, and Hosmer Lake. It runs along Quinn Creek at the beginning and end of the ride, and goes through several different types of forest along the way. The switchbacks on the Quinn

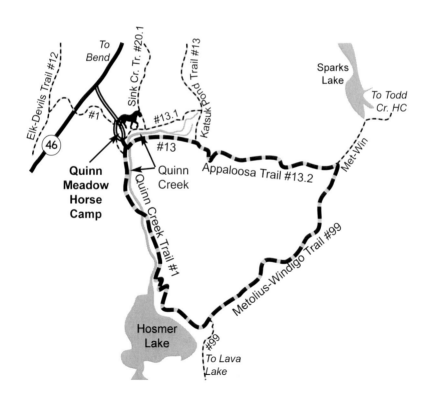

Part of the trail runs beside Quinn Creek.

Creek Trail coming down toward Hosmer Lake are a bit challenging, but are manageable.

The Ride: Pick up the Katsuk Pond Trail #13 next to campsite 15. In 300 feet, veer left on the Katsuk Pond Trail and cross the creek. The trail runs beside Quinn Creek for 0.8 mile, and in this stretch you'll get some filtered views of South Sister. At the trail junction, veer right on the Appaloosa Trail #13.2, and follow it up some gentle switchbacks and over a low ridge. You'll have some views of Mt. Bachelor in this section. After 1.6 miles you'll come to the Metolius-Windigo Trail #99. Turn right toward Lava Lake. The trail runs gently downhill for 2.3 miles. At the next junction the Met-Win jogs to the left and the Quinn Creek Trail #1 goes straight ahead. Go straight, and as the trail runs along the ridge above Hosmer Lake you'll get filtered views of the lake below you. Then the trail makes a series of steep switchbacks that will bring you to the bank of Quinn Creek near where it flows into Hosmer Lake. About 1.2 miles after turning onto the Quinn Creek Trail, you'll come to a small waterfall and a bridge over the creek. Continue along the trail for 1 mile to return to the horse camp.

Devils/Quinn Loop

Trailhead: Start at either the Wickiup Plains trailhead or at Quinn Meadow Horse Camp

Length: 9.5 miles round trip

Elevation: 5,100 to 5,700 feet

Difficulty: Moderate

Footing: Hoof protection recommended

Season: Summer through fall

Permits: Northwest Forest Pass required at Wickiup Plains trailhead. Camping fee at Quinn Meadow.

Facilities: Toilet and plenty of trailer parking at Wickiup Plains trailhead. Camping facilities at Quinn Meadow. Stock water is available on the trail.

Highlights: The trail runs primarily through lodgepole pine and mountain hemlock forest. On the east side of Hwy. 46, the Katsuk Pond Trail passes fascinating lava outcroppings and the delightful

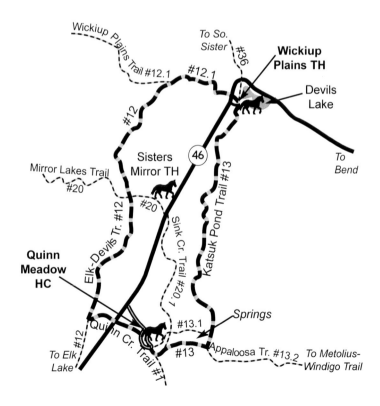

springs that create Quinn Creek. On the west side of the highway the Elk-Devils Trail follows the track of an old wagon road.

Finding the Wickiup Plains Trailhead: From Bend, drive west on Hwy. 46 (the Cascade Lakes Hwy.) for 28 miles, then just past Devils Lake turn left into the trailhead.

The Ride: From Wickiup Plains trailhead, take the Katsuk Pond Trail #13 south toward Quinn Meadow Horse Camp. There are amazing lava outcroppings all along this portion of the trail. After 3.2 miles the Quinn Springs Trail #13.1 goes off to the right. It will take you to Quinn Meadow in 1.2 miles. Or, for an easier route you can stay to the left and continue 0.2 mile to the next junction, then veer right on the Katsuk Pond Trail and continue 0.8 mile to Quinn Meadow. Either way, just before the horse camp you'll ford Quinn Creek and veer right to get to Quinn Meadow Horse Camp. From Quinn Meadow, pick up the Quinn Creek Trail #1 next to campsite #1. Follow it 0.5 mile to the underpass under Hwy. 46, then another 0.4 mile to the Elk-Devils Trail #12. Turn right on the Elk-Devils Trail toward Devils Lake. You'll cross the Sisters Mirror Trail in 1.6 miles. Continue another 1.7 miles, and at the junction with the Wickiup Plains Trail #12.1 (which also goes to Sisters Mirror Lake), stay to the right. Continue another 0.9 mile to the Wickiup Plains trailhead. Follow the directions above to return to Quinn Meadow.

Lydia rides Shadow through a lava outcropping on the Katsuk Pond Trail.

Elk Lake

Trailhead: Start at Quinn Meadow Horse Camp
Length: 6 miles round trip
Elevation: 4,900 to 5,200 feet
Difficulty: Easy
Footing: Hoof protection recommended
Season: Summer through fall
Permits: Camping fee. No day-use parking at Quinn Meadow.
Facilities: Toilets, potable water, and manure bins at the horse camp. Stock water is available on the trail.

Highlights: While you're camping at Quinn Meadow, it's a short jaunt down the Elk-Devils trail to get lunch, dinner, or an ice cream at Elk Lake Lodge on the shore of beautiful Elk Lake.

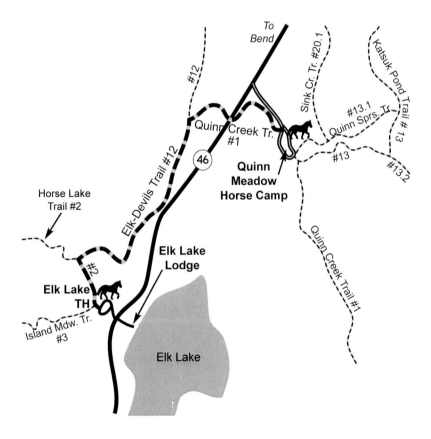

Diana and Mo lead the group down the Elk-Devils Trail.

The Ride: From Quinn Meadow, pick up the Quinn Creek Trail #1 next to campsite #1. In 0.5 mile it will take you to the underpass under Hwy. 46, and in another 0.4 mile you'll reach the Elk-Devils Trail #12. Turn left on it toward Elk Lake, and in 1.5 mile you'll reach the junction with the Horse Lake Trail #2. Turn left, and in 0.3 mile you'll reach the trailhead. Ride down the trailhead entrance road, cross Hwy. 46, and continue about 0.1 mile to Elk Lake Lodge. Tie your horses in the trees behind the Lodge, take in the view, and enjoy a relaxing meal. Life is good!

Elk Lake Lodge has a pretty view of Mt. Bachelor and the lake, and the burgers are good, too.

Horse Lake Loop

Trailhead: Start at the Elk Lake trailhead or at Quinn Meadow Horse Camp

Length: 9 miles round trip from Elk Lake trailhead, or 15 miles round trip from Quinn Meadow

Elevation: 4,950 to 5,300 feet

Difficulty: Moderate

Footing: Hoof protection recommended

Season: Summer through fall

Permits: Northwest Forest Pass required at Elk Lake trailhead. Camping fee at Quinn Meadow.

Facilities: Toilet and parking for several trailers at Elk Lake trailhead. Camping facilities at Quinn Meadow. Stock water is available on the trail.

Highlights: This is a very nice ride over forested terrain, and Horse Lake is a pretty destination. The large meadow just east of Horse Lake makes a good picnic spot. The lakes in this area are heavily used by backpackers for drinking water, so please keep your horse out of the lakes.

Finding the Elk Lake Trailhead: From Bend, drive west on Hwy. 46 (the Cascade Lakes Hwy.) for 32.5 miles and turn right into the trailhead, which is directly across from the entrance to Elk Lake Lodge.

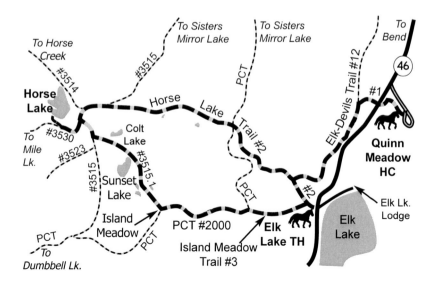

The Ride: <u>From Elk Lake trailhead</u>, pick up the trail on the west side of the parking area. Almost immediately Trail #3 goes off to the left toward the Pacific Crest Trail (PCT) and Island Meadow. This is your return route, so for now continue straight. In 0.3 mile, the Elk-Devils Trail #12 to Quinn Meadow goes off to the right. Stay left, and in another 1.2 miles the trail crosses the PCT. Continue straight for 2.0 miles more, at which point Trail #3515 to Sisters Mirror Lake goes off to the right. In another 0.2 mile you'll reach a junction where Trail #3514 goes to the right to Horse Creek. Turn left on Trail #3515 toward Dumbbell Lake, and in another 0.2 mile veer to the right on Trail #3530 toward Mile Lake. Shortly after this junction the trail passes a large meadow (a good lunch spot). Just beyond the meadow, look for an unmarked spur trail to your right. This unmaintained user trail will take you to the south shore of Horse Lake. After that, retrace your steps to the junction of Trails #3530 and #3515. Turn right on Trail #3515 toward Dumbbell Lake and continue about 0.2 mile, then turn left on Trail #3515.1 toward Sunset Lake. After 1.4 miles you'll reach Island Meadow. Turn left at the junction with the Pacific Crest Trail #2000 and follow it 1.4 miles, then veer right on the Island Meadow Trail #3 to return to the Elk Lake trailhead. <u>From Quinn Meadow Horse Camp</u>, pick up the Quinn Creek Trail #1 near campsite 1, ride 0.9 mile (crossing under the highway) and turn left on the Elk-Devils Trail #12. Continue 1.5 miles to reach the junction with the Horse Lake Trail #2. Turn right and follow the directions above.

Eli and Dottie and ride Dakota and Hope on the Horse Lake Loop.

Lava Lake

Trailhead: Start at the Lucky Lake trailhead or at Quinn Meadow Horse Camp

Length: 15 miles round trip from Quinn Meadow to Lava Lake, or 18 miles round trip from Lucky Lake trailhead to Quinn

Elevation: 4,800 to 5,100 feet

Difficulty: Moderate

Footing: Hoof protection recommended

Season: Summer through fall

Permits: Northwest Forest Pass required at Lucky Lake trailhead. Camping fee at Quinn Meadow.

Facilities: Toilet and parking for 4-5 trailers at Lucky Lake trailhead. Camping facilities at Quinn Meadow. Stock water is available on the trail.

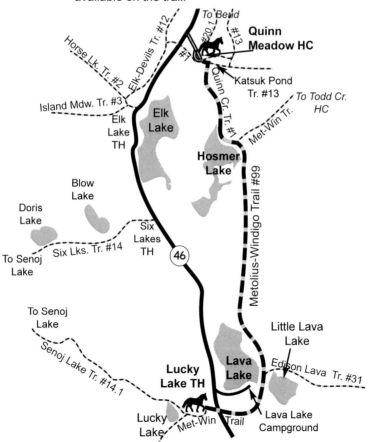

Suzanne rides Mick along the shore of Lava Lake.

Highlights: The trail runs though lodgepole pine forest and past both Lava Lake and Hosmer Lake along the Metolius-Windigo Trail. You'll encounter interesting lava outcroppings near the south end of Hosmer Lake. Watch for mountain bike riders on this stretch of the Met-Win.

Finding the Lucky Lake Trailhead: From Bend, take Hwy. 46 (the Cascade Lakes Hwy.) west for 38.5 miles and turn right into the trailhead.

The Ride: <u>From the Lucky Lake trailhead</u>, cross Highway 46 and pick up the clearly-marked Metolius-Windigo Trail #99 to Lava Lake. The trail travels 1.5 miles through mixed conifer forest, past Lava Lake Campground and between Lava Lake and Little Lava Lake. Then it runs along the shore of lovely Lava Lake for 1.5 miles. Once the trail leaves Lava Lake, it travels through mostly-lodgepole forest for 3.5 miles. For the last mile or so it parallels the shore of Hosmer Lake some distance away, with filtered views of the lake through the trees. Turn left at the junction with the Quinn Creek Trail #1 and continue about 2.2 miles to Quinn Meadow. <u>From Quinn Meadow Horse Camp</u>, pick up the Katsuk Pond Trail #13 next to campsite 15, and in 300 feet veer right on the Quinn Creek Trail #1. Ride along the creek and up some steep switchbacks, and in 2.2 miles turn right on the Metolius-Windigo Trail. Ride it for 5 miles to Lucky Lake.

Mink Lake Basin

Trailhead: Start at the Six Lakes trailhead

Length: 17 miles round trip to Mink Lake, or 19.5 miles if you circle Mink Lake

Elevation: 4,800 to 5,700 feet

Difficulty: Moderate

Footing: Hoof protection recommended

Season: Summer through fall

Permits: None

Facilities: Toilet and parking for many trailers at Six Lakes trailhead. Stock water is available on the trail.

Highlights: The Mink Lake Basin is on the west side of the Cascades, so the forest there is quite different than it is near Doris and Blow Lakes. In the basin, the undergrowth beneath the old-growth trees is lush and green, and if you throw a rock in any direction it will probably land in a lake. Please keep your horse out of the lakes, as they are used for drinking water by backpackers. Mosquitoes can be fierce early in the season.

Finding the Six Lakes Trailhead: From Bend, take Hwy. 46 (the Cascade Lakes Hwy.) west for 34 miles. Just past the south end of Elk Lake, turn right into the trailhead parking area.

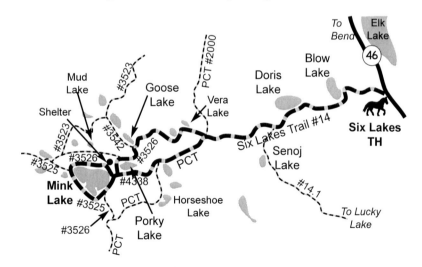

The Ride: Several lollipop-style loop rides are possible in the Mink Lake Basin. To begin any of the loops, go west 3.4 miles on the Six Lakes Trail #14, passing Blow Lake and Doris Lake along the way. At the junction with the Senoj Lake Trail #14.1, go right toward the PCT. Continue 2 miles, then turn left on the Pacific Crest Trail #2000 toward Horseshoe Lake. To make the loop to Mink Lake, follow the PCT southwest for 1.4 miles. At this point an unmarked spur trail goes off to the left. Stay to the right and in 100 feet turn right on Trail #4338 toward Porky Lake. In 1.1 miles you'll reach a junction where Mink Lake is straight ahead and Trail #3526 to Goose Lake is to the right. Go straight, and in 0.2 mile you'll reach Mink Lake. At the lake shore, take the trail to the right a short distance to find a dilapidated forest shelter and a good spot to water your horses. To return to the trailhead, go back to the last junction and turn left on Trail #3526 toward Goose Lake. In 0.3 mile turn right toward Goose Lake. In another mile you'll reach Goose Lake and the junction with Trail #3542. Veer right on Trail #3526 toward Vera Lake. In 2.2 miles you'll be back at the PCT. Cross it and continue straight ahead on the Six Lakes Trail to return to the trailhead. Other loops in the basin are possible, so go exploring!

Mona on Eclipse and Linda on Brumby,
relaxing on the shore of Mink Lake.

Quinn Springs Loop

Trailhead: Start at Quinn Meadow Horse Camp
Length: 2.2 miles round trip
Elevation: 5,050 to 5,150 feet
Difficulty: Moderate
Footing: Hoof protection recommended
Season: Summer through fall
Permits: Camping fee. No day-use parking at Quinn Meadow.
Facilities: Toilet, potable water, and manure bins at the horse camp. Stock water is available on the trail.

Highlights: This is an amazing little loop. It's very short, but it's unique and so scenic you must make the time to ride it. From Quinn Meadow Horse Camp the trail runs along one side of the lovely Quinn Creek, past all of the springs that feed this crystal-clear waterway. (This area is known as Quinn Meadow, the source of the horse camp's name. Please stay on the trail in this fragile environment.) After a mile the trail loops around and returns along the other side, giving you

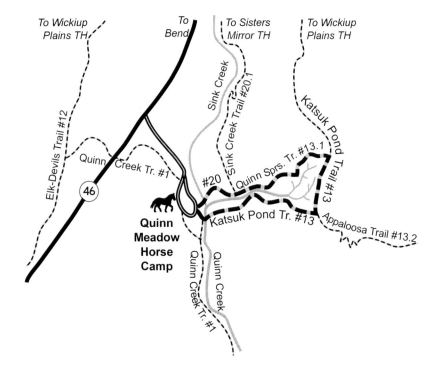

a different view of the springs and the creek. Along the way you'll ride through lush forest and stark lava outcroppings. The contrasts are striking.

The Ride: Pick up the Sink Creek Trail #20, which departs next to campsite #15. Cross the creek and follow the trail for 0.3 mile, and at the trail junction veer to the right on the Quinn Springs Trail #13.1. In 0.8 mile, turn right again on the Katsuk Pond Trail #13, and 0.2 mile later turn right again on the Katsuk Pond Trail. After 0.8 mile you'll ford Quinn Creek and reach the junction with the Quinn Creek Trail #1 in a meadow. Veer right to return to Quinn Meadow in 0.1 mile.

Mt. Bachelor is visible above sparkling Quinn Creek.

Cowboy, Moose, Diamond, and Mo carry their riders through the lava outcroppings along the Quinn Springs Trail.

Senoj Lake

Trailhead: Start at the Six Lakes trailhead

Length: 9 miles round trip to Senoj Lake, or 5.5 miles round trip to Doris Lake, or 2.6 miles round trip to Blow Lake

Elevation: 4,900 to 5,600 feet to Senoj Lake, or 4,900 to 5,300 feet to Doris Lake, or 4,900 to 5,100 feet to Blow Lake

Difficulty: Moderate -- may encounter downed logs on the Senoj Lake Trail

Footing: Hoof protection recommended

Season: Summer through fall

Permits: None

Facilities: Toilet, hitching post, and parking for many trailers at the trailhead. Stock water is available on the trail.

Highlights: Senoj Lake was named in honor of someone named Jones -- spelled backward. This is a nice ride on a forested trail that runs

past Blow Lake and Doris Lake and ends on the grassy shore of Senoj Lake.

Finding the Six Lakes Trailhead: From Bend, take Hwy. 46 (the Cascade Lakes Hwy.) west for 34 miles. Just past the south end of Elk Lake, turn right into the parking area.

The Ride: Pick up the Six Lakes Trail #14 on the west side of the trailhead. It winds through the forest and reaches Blow Lake in 1.3 miles. After another 1.4 miles, Doris Lake appears. Both lakes are worth a detour, and both are good destinations for short, easy rides. About 0.6 mile beyond Doris Lake, turn left on the Senoj Lake Trail #14.1. In another mile you'll reach Senoj Lake. Its grassy banks are an inviting spot for a picnic, for both you and your horse. Retrace your steps to return to the trailhead.

Debbie and Mel relax at Senoj Lake.

Sink Creek Loop

Trailhead: Start at Quinn Meadow Horse Camp or Sisters Mirror trailhead

Length: 5.5 miles round trip

Elevation: 5,050 to 5,450 feet

Difficulty: Moderate

Footing: Hoof protection recommended

Permits: No fee at Sisters Mirror trailhead. Camping fee at Quinn Meadow.

Facilities: Toilet and parking for 2-3 trailers (depending on the number of hiker cars) at Sisters Mirror trailhead. Camping facilities at Quinn Meadow. Stock water is available on the trail.

Highlights: The Elk-Devils Trail runs along an old wagon road through mixed conifer forest, including some old-growth areas. The

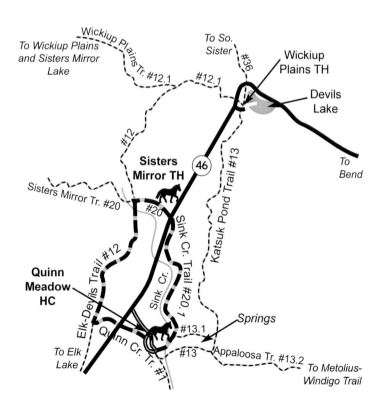

Ray rides Moose and Connie rides Diamond
past a 30-foot high lava flow.

Sink Creek Trail runs beside Sink Creek and through some impressive lava flows.

Finding the Sisters Mirror Trailhead: From Bend, take Hwy. 46 (the Cascade Lakes Hwy.) west from Bend for 29 miles and turn right into the trailhead.

The Ride: From Quinn Meadow, pick up the Quinn Creek Trail #1 near campsite 1. In 0.5 mile you'll reach the underpass under Hwy. 46, and 0.4 mile later you'll reach the Elk-Devils Trail #12. Turn right toward Devils Lake. In 1.5 miles the trail crosses Sink Creek, and 0.1 mile later you'll come to the junction with the Sisters Mirror Trail #20. Turn right toward the Sisters Mirror trailhead, and in 0.5 mile you'll arrive at the trailhead. From Sisters Mirror trailhead, pick up the Sink Creek Trail #20.1 directly across Hwy. 46 from the parking area. Ride it for 1.7 miles, and at the junction turn right toward Quinn Meadow. In 0.4 mile you'll reach Quinn Meadow Horse Camp. Follow the directions above to return to your trailer if you parked at Sisters Mirror trailhead.

Sisters Mirror/Koosah Mtn. Loop

Trailhead: Start at Quinn Meadow Horse Camp, Sisters Mirror Trailhead, or Elk Lake Trailhead

Length: 13 miles round trip from Sisters Mirror or Elk Lake trailheads, or 14 miles round trip from Quinn Meadow

Elevation: 5,000 to 6,500 feet

Difficulty: Moderate -- creek crossings and a couple of short but steep side hills to traverse

Footing: Hoof protection recommended

Season: Summer through fall

Permits: Northwest Forest Pass required at Elk Lake. No fee at Sisters Mirror. Camping fee at Quinn Meadow.

Facilities: Toilets at the trailheads. Limited trailer parking at Sisters Mirror, but plenty at Elk Lake. Camping facilities at Quinn Meadow. Stock water is available on the trail.

Highlights: Sisters Mirror Lake is a pretty spot for a leisurely picnic, and the summit of Koosah Mountain offers excellent views of South

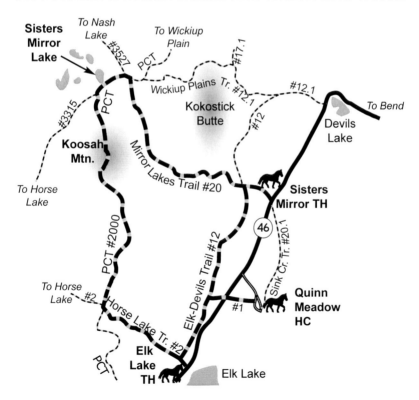

Debbie on Cowboy and Lydia on Shadow, riding through a blowdown on Koosah Mountain that opened up an amazing view of South Sister.

Sister, Broken Top, and Mt. Bachelor. Dogs must be on leash on this trail.

Finding the Sisters Mirror and Elk Lake Trailheads: From Bend, drive west on Hwy. 46 (the Cascade Lakes Hwy.) for 29 miles to reach the Sisters Mirror trailhead or 32.5 miles to reach the Elk Lake trailhead.

The Ride: From Quinn Meadow Horse Camp, pick up the Quinn Creek Trail #1 near campsite 1 and ride it 0.9 mile, through the tunnel under Hwy. 46, to the Elk-Devils Trail #12. Turn right, and in 1.5 miles turn left on the Mirror Lakes Trail #20. From Sisters Mirror trailhead, pick up the Mirror Lakes Trail and ride 0.5 mile to the junction with the Elk-Devils Trail #12. From Elk Lake trailhead, pick up the Elk-Devils Trail #12 and in 0.3 mile veer right on it. Ride 3.1 miles and turn left on the Mirror Lakes Trail #20. All, ride west on the Mirror Lakes Trail #20. In 3.2 miles you'll reach the Pacific Crest Trail #2000. Turn left and ride 0.3 mile to Sisters Mirror Lake or one of the other nearby lakes for a good lunch stop. Continue south on the PCT for 1.5 miles to the top of Koosah Mountain, which offers nice views of nearby peaks and the surrounding forest. Ride the PCT another 3 miles to the Horse Lake Trail #2, then turn left and ride 1.5 miles to the Elk-Devils Trail #12. Go straight ahead to reach the Elk Lake trailhead, or turn left, ride about 1.6 miles, and turn right to go back to Quinn Meadow. To reach the Sisters Mirror Trail, stay on the Elk-Devils Trail and ride 1.5 miles farther to the junction with the Mirror Lakes Trail, then turn right.

Sisters Mirror/Wickiup Plain Loop

Trailhead: Start at Quinn Meadow Horse Camp, Wickiup Plains trailhead, or Sisters Mirror trailhead

Length: 12 miles round trip from Sisters Mirror trailhead, 13 miles round trip from Wickiup Plains trailhead, or 14.5 miles round trip from Quinn Meadow

Elevation: 5,500 to 6,300 feet

Difficulty: Moderate

Footing: Hoof protection recommended

Season: Summer through fall

Permits: Northwest Forest Pass required at Wickiup Plains. No fee at Sisters Mirror. Camping fee at Quinn Meadow.

Facilities: Toilets at the trailheads. Limited trailer parking at Sisters Mirror, but Wickiup Plains has plenty. Camping facilities at Quinn Meadow. Stock water is available on the trail.

Highlights: This loop near the base of South Sister is a great way to take in both Sisters Mirror Lake and Wickiup Plain. On a clear, calm

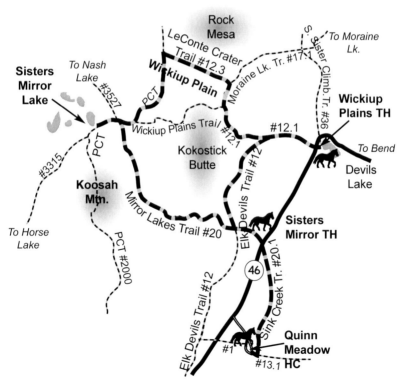

Linda and Beamer on the LeConte Crater Trail, with South Sister in the background.

day, South Sister is beautifully re-flected in the lake. The open expanse of Wickiup Plain is a stark contrast to the forest that flanks it. Please ride horses single file on the plain to avoid damaging this fragile area. Dogs must be on leash on this trail.

Finding the Wickiup Plains and Sisters Mirror Trailheads: From Bend, drive west on Hwy. 46 (the Cascade Lakes Hwy.) for 28 miles to reach Wickiup Plains trailhead or 29 miles to Sisters Mirror Lake trailhead.

The Ride: From Wickiup Plains trailhead, pick up the Wickiup Plains Trail #12 and ride it 0.9 mile. Turn left on the Elk-Devils Trail #12, and continue 1.7 miles, then turn right on the Mirror Lakes Trail #20. From Quinn Meadow Horse Camp, pick up the Sink Creek Trail #20.1 next to campsite 15 and ride it 2.1 miles to the Sisters Mirror trailhead. From Sisters Mirror trailhead, ride the Mirror Lakes Trail #20 for 0.5 mile. All, head west on the Mirror Lakes Trail #20 for 3.2 miles. Turn left on the PCT and make a 0.3 mile detour to Sisters Mirror Lake. Return to the junction with the Mirror Lakes Trail and follow the PCT 0.3 mile. At the junction with the Wickiup Plains Trail #12.1, stay to the left on the PCT and continue 1.7 more miles, crossing Wickiup Plain. At the next junction, turn right on the LeConte Crater Trail #12.3. In 1.4 mile, turn right at the junction with the Moraine Lake Trail #17.1. After 0.5 mile, veer right on the Wickiup Plains Trail #12.1 and follow it for a mile. To return to Wickiup Plains trailhead, continue straight ahead on the Wickiup Plains Trail. To return to Sisters Mirror trailhead or Quinn Meadow, turn right on the Elk-Devils Trail. In 1.7 miles turn left on the Mirror Lakes Trail to return to Sisters Mirror trailhead. To continue to Quinn Meadow, cross Hwy. 46 and return on the Sink Creek Trail #20.1.

Sparks Lake/Todd Creek

Trailhead: Start at Quinn Meadow Horse Camp
Length: 6 miles round trip from to Sparks Lake or 13 miles round trip to Todd Creek Horse Camp
Elevation: 5,000 to 6,100 feet
Difficulty: Moderate
Footing: Hoof protection recommended
Season: Summer through fall
Permits: Camping fee. No day-use parking at Quinn Meadow.
Facilities: Horse camping facilities at Quinn Meadow. Toilet and stock water at Todd Creek. Stock water is available on the trail.

Highlights: This is a mostly-forested ride that connects the two horse camps in the area with Sparks Lake. Along the way you'll enjoy views of South Sister, Mt. Bachelor, and Sparks Lake. The shore of Sparks Lake is a beautiful place for a picnic. You may encounter mountain bikes on this stretch of the Met-Win Trail.

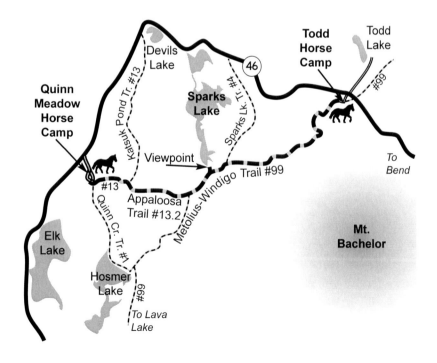

The Ride: Pick up the Katsuk Pond Trail #13 next to campsite 15. In 300 feet, veer left on the Katsuk Pond Trail and cross the creek. The trail runs beside Quinn Creek for 0.8 mile and offers glimpses of South Sister. At the junction, veer right on the Appaloosa Trail #13.2 and follow it up some gentle switchbacks and over a low ridge. Watch for filtered views of Mt. Bachelor. After 1.6 miles you'll come to the Metolius-Windigo Trail #99. Turn left, and in 0.5 mile you'll reach a short spur trail that will take you to the shore of Sparks Lake. To continue to Todd Creek, stay on the Metolius-Windigo Trail. About 0.5 mile past Sparks Lake the Soda Creek Trail #4 goes off to the left. Stay right on the Met-Win, and in 3.5 miles you'll reach Todd Creek Horse Camp. In this last section you'll have more views of Mt. Bachelor. It's pretty much uphill all the way from Quinn to Todd Creek, and interestingly enough, it's downhill all the way back.

Walk along the eastern shore of Sparks Lake
to get this fabulous view of South Sister.

Wickiup Plain Loop

Trailhead: Start at the Wickiup Plains trailhead or Quinn Meadow Horse Camp

Length: 9 miles round trip from Wickiup Plains trailhead, or 16 miles round trip from Quinn Meadow

Elevation: 5,500 to 6,300 feet from Wickiup Plains trailhead, or 5,100 to 6,300 from Quinn Meadow

Difficulty: Moderate

Footing: Hoof protection recommended

Season: Summer through fall

Permits: Northwest Forest Pass required at Wickiup Plains trailhead. Camping fee at Quinn Meadow.

Facilities: Toilet and plenty of trailer parking at Wickiup Plains trailhead. Horse camping facilities at Quinn Meadow. Stock water is available on the trail.

Highlights: Wickiup Plain, a huge pumice plain at the base of South Sister, offers expansive views of the surrounding peaks and contrasts

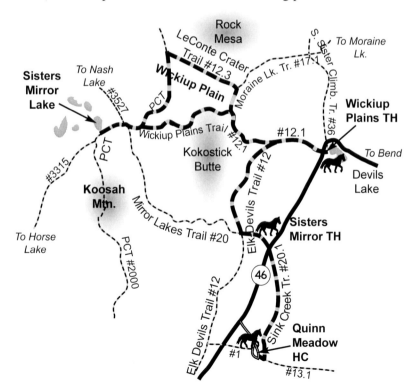

Lel and Whitney ride Jane and Dixie across Wickiup Plain in front of Rock Mesa and South Sister.

sharply with the dense forest you ride through to reach it. Please ride horses single file on the plain to avoid damaging this fragile area. If desired, you can detour 1.2 miles round trip to reach Sisters Mirror Lake. Dogs must be on leash on this trail.

Finding the Wickiup Plains Trailhead: From Bend, take Hwy. 46 (the Cascade Lakes Hwy.) west for 28 miles. Just past Devils Lake, turn left into the trailhead.

The Ride: <u>From Wickiup Plains trailhead</u>, pick up the Wickiup Plains Trail #12 and ride west for 0.9 mile. At the first junction, stay to the right on the Wickiup Plains Trail and continue another mile. At the second junction, stay to the left on the Wickiup Plains Trail and follow it 1.7 miles to the Pacific Crest Trail. Turn right on the PCT. (If desired you can turn left and detour 0.6 mile each way to Sisters Mirror Lake, then return to this junction.) Ride north on the PCT and in 1.7 miles it will take you to Wickiup Plain and the LeConte Crater Trail #12.3. Turn right here and ride past the Rock Mesa lava flow at the base of South Sister. In 1.4 miles turn right on the Moraine Lake Trail #17.1. In 0.5 mile, turn left on the Wickiup Plains Trail and follow it 1.0 mile. Continue straight on the Wickiup Plains Trail to return to the Wickiup Plains trailhead, or turn left on the Elk-Devils Trail to return to Quinn Meadow or the Sisters Mirror trailhead. <u>From Quinn Meadow Horse Camp</u>, pick up the Sink Creek Trail #20.1 next to campsite 15 and follow it 2.1 miles to the Sisters Mirror trailhead. Take the Mirror Lakes Trail #20, and in 0.5 mile turn right on the Elk-Devils Trail #12. Follow it 1.7 miles, veer left on the Wickiup Plains Trail #12.1, then follow the directions above.

Feeling down? Saddle up.

Anonymous

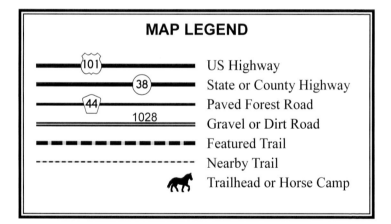

MAP LEGEND

═══(101)═══	US Highway
═══(38)═══	State or County Highway
═══(44)═══	Paved Forest Road
═══1028═══	Gravel or Dirt Road
▬ ▬ ▬ ▬ ▬	Featured Trail
- - - - - - -	Nearby Trail
🐎	Trailhead or Horse Camp

Oregon Badlands Wilderness

Bureau of Land Management

Oregon's newest wilderness area is located in the high desert just 12 miles east of Bend. There are no camping facilities in the Badlands--the closest camping spots are at Sisters Cow Camp or Cyrus Horse Camp--but excellent day rides showcase the unique geological features of this area. In the Badlands you'll find ancient junipers (some over 1,000 years old), sagebrush and bunchgrass, dry creek beds, and interesting rock outcroppings. The footing is sandy volcanic ash and pumice, so the riding is excellent in the winter and spring, but can be dusty in summer. Please stay on the trails to avoid damaging this fragile ecosystem.

The Badlands were formed by an ancient volcanic vent that slowly oozed lava in the Badlands area. The outer layers of lava cooled as they flowed, and were pushed up by the hotter lava below to form pressure ridges like Badlands Rock and Flatiron Rock.

A gnarled old juniper along the trail in the Badlands.

Oregon Badlands Wilderness

Directions: The Oregon Badlands Wilderness Area is located about 15 miles east of Bend, off Hwy. 20. It has 4 trailheads that can accommodate horse trailers. For directions, see "Finding the Trailhead" on the pages for each trail.

Elevation: 3,600 feet

Campsites: No camping facilities, but primitive camping is permitted anywhere other than at trailheads. Only certified weed-free hay may be used in the Oregon Badlands.

Facilities: Toilet at Reynolds Pond trailhead on a seasonal basis. Parking varies at each trailhead -- see "Facilities" on the pages for each trail

Permits: None

Season: Year-round

Contact: BLM Prineville District: 541-416-6700, www.blm.gov/or/resources/recreation/badlands

Along every trail you'll find fascinating lava outcroppings, complete with rifts, fissures, and small caves.

Getting to the Oregon Badlands

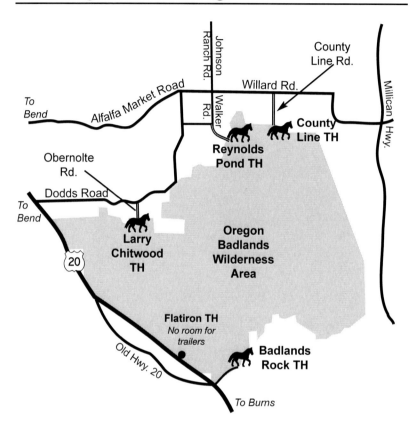

Oregon Badlands Wilderness Trails*

Trail	Difficulty	Elevation	Round Trip
Badlands Rock/Dry River Lp.	Easy	3,450-3,600	13 miles
Badlands/Flatiron Rocks Lp.	Easy	3,550-3,775	8-11 miles
Black Lava Trail	Easy	3,375-3,500	9.5 miles
Dry River/Sand Trail Loop	Easy	3,350-3,500	10 miles
Larry Chitwood Loops	Easy	3,450-3,600	6-11 miles
Tumulus Trail	Easy	3,375-3,550	13.5-20 miles

* Trails are subject to change upon completion of BLM's Wilderness Management Plan.

Badlands Rock/Dry River Loop

Trailhead: Start at the Badlands Rock trailhead
Length: 13 miles round trip
Elevation: 3,450 to 3,600 feet
Difficulty: Easy
Footing: Suitable for barefoot horses
Season: Year-round
Permits: None
Facilities: Parking for 6-8 trailers at the trailhead. No stock water on the trail.

Highlights: The focal point of the Badlands Rock Trail is Badlands Rock itself, a large volcanic pressure ridge covered with fissures and

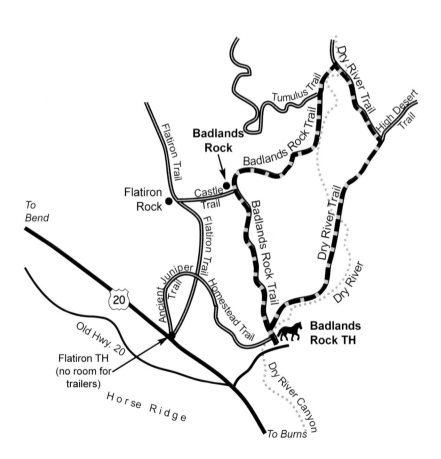

rifts. Along the Badlands Rock Trail you'll also see small and medium-sized rock outcroppings. The Dry River Trail follows a dry river bed through terrain that is fairly open, with lots of sagebrush and old junipers. Combining the two trails makes a good loop.

Finding the Badlands Rock Trailhead: From Bend, drive east on Hwy. 20. Just before the 18-mile marker, turn left on a paved road marked by an Oregon Badlands sign. Follow it 1 mile and turn left into the Badlands Rock trailhead parking area.

Ride: Pick up the trail heading north from the Badlands Rock trailhead. After 3 miles the trail passes Badlands Rock. Veer right here and continue on the Badlands Rock Trail. There are some interesting lava outcroppings in the area beyond Badlands Rock, including rocks with fissures large enough to ride through. About 3.2 miles past Badlands Rock, the trail intersects with the Tumulus Trail. Turn right and follow the Tumulus Trail 0.4 mile to the Dry River Trail. Turn right again and follow the Dry River Trail about 5.7 miles back to the Badlands Rock Trail. Turn left and ride 0.3 mile to return to the trailhead.

Debbie on Cowboy, Whitney on Dixie, and Diana on Mel,
ambling down the Dry River Trail.

Badlands Rock/Flatiron Rock Loop

Trailhead: Start at Badlands Rock trailhead

Length: 8 miles round trip to Badlands Rock and Flatiron Rock, or 11 miles if you include the Ancient Juniper Trail loop

Elevation: 3,550 to 3,650 feet for the shorter loop; 3,550 to 3,775 feet for the longer loop

Difficulty: Easy

Footing: Suitable for barefoot horses

Season: Year-round

Permits: None

Facilities: Parking for 6-8 rigs at the trailhead. No stock water on the trail.

Highlights: This nice, easy loop trail goes past three of the most prominent rock formations in the Badlands: Badlands Rock, Castle Rock, and Flatiron Rock. Both Castle Rock and Flatiron Rock have

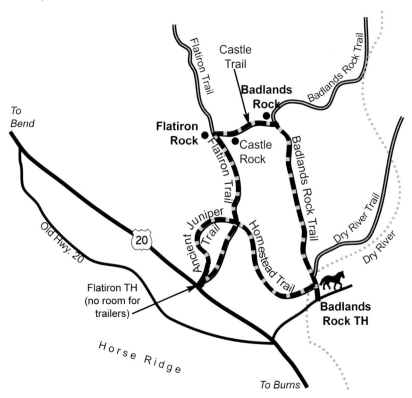

*Debbie, Whitney, and Suzi ride through a fissure in
a rock formation near the Badlands Rock Trail.*

deep fissures at the top that you can walk through on foot, so tie your
horses at the base and climb up to have a look--it's worth it. If you
want to extend your ride you can add a detour along the Ancient Juniper Trail, which offers slightly elevated views of the Badlands.

Finding the Badlands Rock Trailhead: From Bend, drive east on
Hwy. 20. Just before the 18-mile marker, turn left on a paved road
marked by an Oregon Badlands sign. Follow it 1 mile and turn left
into the Badlands Rock trailhead parking area.

The Ride: The Badlands Rock Trail goes north from the trailhead, following an old dirt road. In 0.3 mile the Homestead Trail comes in from
the left. Continue on the Badlands Rock Trail for another 2.7 miles to
Badlands Rock, a large mound of fractured basalt. Turn left on the
Castle Trail and ride 0.7 mile to Castle Rock, then 0.4 mile farther to
Flatiron Rock. Turn left on the Flatiron Trail and follow it 1.5 miles
to the junction with the Homestead Trail. Here you can do a loop detour on the Ancient Juniper Trail to add 3.3 miles to your journey, or
you can head back to the trailhead by veering left and riding 2.1 miles
on the Homestead Trail. When the Homestead Trail intersects with the
Badlands Rock Trail, turn right to return to the trailhead.

Black Lava Trail

Trailhead: Start at the Reynolds Pond trailhead
Length: 9.5 miles round trip
Elevation: 3,375 to 3,500 feet
Difficulty: Easy
Footing: Hoof protection recommended
Season: Year-round
Permits: None
Facilities: Parking for many rigs at Reynolds Pond trailhead. Portable toilet on seasonal basis. Stock water on the trail during irrigation season.

Highlights: The Black Lava trail goes through an area with many small to mid-sized lava outcroppings. Many are deeply fissured and fractured, with hardy juniper trees growing out of the rocks. The trail ends at an old corral that is cleverly built into a basalt outcropping.

Finding the Reynolds Pond Trailhead: From Bend, drive east on Hwy. 20 for 4.7 miles. Turn left on Powell Butte Highway, and in 0.9

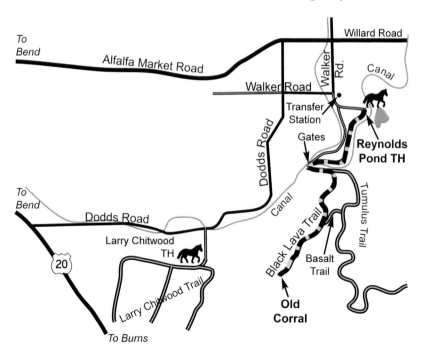

You'll marvel at the fascinating lava outcroppings along the Black Lava Trail.

Debbie and Cowboy check out a historic corral built into the rocks.

mile turn right on Alfalfa Market Road. Follow it 9.4 miles to Walker Road and turn right. In 1 mile Walker Road makes a 90-degree turn to the right. Go straight instead and drive 0.2 mile, past the entrance to the transfer station. About 200 feet later, turn left and drive over the cattle guard. Continue on this pot-holed dirt road for 0.6 mile to the trailhead.

The Ride: From the Reynolds Pond trailhead, pick up the dirt road that runs south along the west side of the irrigation canal. Ride the canal road for 1.9 miles, go through the horse step-over next to a gate, and continue 0.3 mile to a second gate and horse step-over. Cross the bridge over the canal, turn left and ride back along the canal for 0.5 mile to the signed junction of the Black Lava and Tumulus Trails. Turn right on the Black Lava Trail. In 2 miles you'll reach an interesting old corral that was used for rounding up stock many years ago. To return to Reynolds Pond, retrace your steps.

Dry River/Sand Trail Loop

Trailhead: Start at the County Line trailhead
Length: 10 miles round trip
Elevation: 3,350 to 3,500 feet
Difficulty: Easy
Footing: Suitable for barefoot horses
Season: Year-round
Permits: None
Facilities: Parking for up to 3 trailers. No stock water on the trail.

Highlights: The Dry River Trail roughly follows the dry bed of the Dry River. Both this trail and the Sand Trail (the return leg of the ride) travel through old-growth junipers and open sagebrush steppe areas. You'll find many small lava outcroppings, but nothing like the dra-

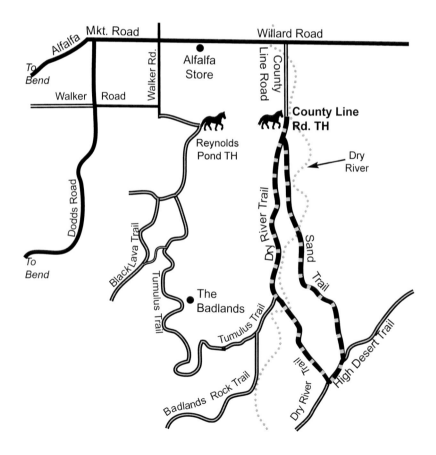

matic formations in other parts of the Badlands. Out here you can spot plenty of wildlife, though, including deer, rabbits, hawks, and coyotes. You may even see Rachael Scdoris training her sled dogs using a wheeled sled, a permitted use that was specifically grandfathered for her by the legislation that created the wilderness area. A Bend resident, Rachael was the first legally-blind person to enter and finish the Iditarod dog sled race.

Finding the County Line Trailhead: From Bend, drive east on Hwy. 20 for 4.7 miles. Turn left on Powell Butte Highway, then in 0.9 mile turn right on Alfalfa Market Road. After about 10 miles it becomes Willard Road. Two miles past the Alfalfa Store, turn right on County Line Road and drive 1 mile, then turn right into the trailhead parking area.

The Ride: Ride out on the gravel road that runs south from the trailhead. In 0.3 mile, veer right onto the Dry River Trail. It runs through sagebrush and juniper with little elevation change. About 3 miles from the trailhead you'll reach the junction with the Tumulus Trail. Stay to the left, and in 1.8 miles you'll come to the junction with the High Desert Trail. Turn left and ride 0.5 mile, then veer left onto the Sand Trail. The High Desert Trail becomes rather indistinct beyond this point. The Sand Trail runs northward, rejoining the Dry River Trail about 0.3 mile from the trailhead.

Debbie and Cowboy admire a juniper growing out of the rocks on the Dry River Trail.

Larry Chitwood Loops

Trailhead:	Start at the Larry Chitwood trailhead
Length:	6 miles around the East Loop, 7 miles around the West Loop, 7.5 miles around the perimeter, or 11 miles around both loops in a figure eight
Elevation:	3,450 to 3,600 feet
Difficulty:	Easy
Footing:	Suitable for barefoot horses
Season:	Year-round
Permits:	None
Facilities:	The parking area is too small for trailers, but you can turn around at the trailhead and park 3-4 trailers on the side of Obernolte Road. No stock water on the trail.

Highlights: This is an easy, relaxing ride that lacks the impressive lava outcroppings of some of the other Badlands trails, but it runs past many gnarled, ancient junipers that are quite interesting. You can tell

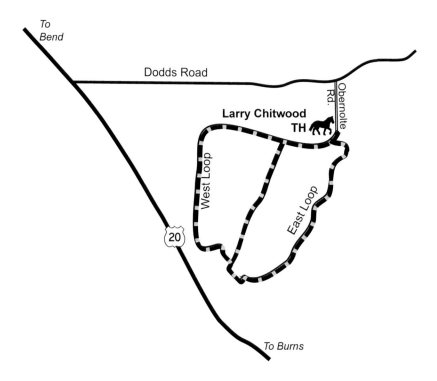

*Debbie and Cowboy enjoy a leisurely amble
past an ancient juniper on the Larry Chitwood Loops.*

which junipers are old by looking at their tops: younger junipers have
pointed tops, and the older ones are rounded. Like all the other Badlands trails, the Obernolte Loops are suitable for green horses and inexperienced riders.

Finding the Larry Chitwood Trailhead: From Bend, drive east on
Hwy. 20 for 8.6 miles. Turn left on Dodds Road and continue 3.3
miles. Turn right on Obernolte Road and drive 0.5 mile to the trailhead. The parking area is too small for horse trailers, so turn around
and park on the side of Obernolte Rd.

The Ride: Go through the trailhead gate and ride about 0.3 mile to the
junction with the loop trails. You can ride these loops in a variety of
ways, doing the east loop, the west loop, the perimeter, or both loops
in a sort of sideways figure eight (riding the center leg twice). The far
eastern leg is a bit rocky, but the rest of the trails are not.

Tumulus Trail

Trailhead: Start at Reynolds Pond trailhead

Length: 13.5 miles round trip to interesting rock outcroppings, or 20 miles round trip to the Dry River Trail

Elevation: 3,375 to 3,550 feet

Difficulty: Easy

Footing: Hoof protection recommended

Season: Year-round

Permits: None

Facilities: Parking for many trailers at Reynolds Pond trailhead. Portable toilet on seasonal basis. Stock water on the trail during irrigation season.

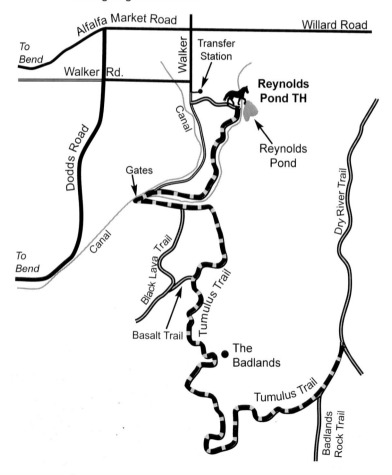

*Debbie rides Cowboy through a fracture in a
rock outcropping along the Tumulus Trail.*

Highlights: The amazing rock outcroppings you'll see along this trail
qualify it as the most scenic ride in the Badlands.

Finding the Reynolds Pond Trailhead: From Bend, drive east on
Hwy. 20 for 4.7 miles. Turn left on Powell Butte Highway, and in 0.9
mile turn right on Alfalfa Market Road. Follow it 9.4 miles to Walker
Road and turn right. In 1 mile, Walker Road makes a 90-degree turn
to the right. Go straight instead and drive 0.2 mile, past the entrance
to the transfer station. About 200 feet later, turn left and drive over the
cattle guard. Continue on this pot-holed dirt road for 0.6 mile to the
trailhead.

The Ride: From Reynolds Pond trailhead, pick up the dirt road that
runs south along the west side of the irrigation canal. Ride the canal
road for 1.9 miles, go through the horse step-over next to a gate, and
continue 0.3 mile to a second gate and horse step-over. Cross the
bridge over the canal, turn left and ride back along the canal for 0.5
mile to the signed junction of the Black Lava and Tumulus trails.
Continue straight for another 0.2 mile and veer right on the Tumulus
Trail. After about 4 more miles you'll reach an area of huge rock outcroppings known as The Badlands. Some of the outcroppings are split
by deep rifts, and some feature small caves. You'll also find many ancient junipers along the trail. About 9.3 miles from the trailhead the
Badlands Rock Trail comes in on the right, and 0.6 mile later the trail
intersects with the Dry River Trail.

A woman needs two animals -- the horse of her dreams, and a jackass to pay for it.

Robert Louis Stevenson

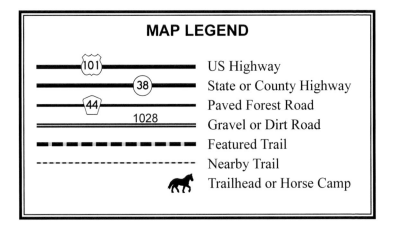

MAP LEGEND

US Highway
State or County Highway
Paved Forest Road
Gravel or Dirt Road
Featured Trail
Nearby Trail
Trailhead or Horse Camp

Peterson Ridge

Deschutes National Forest

Located just southeast of the town of Sisters, Peterson Ridge offers over 20 miles of easy horse trails that feature spectacular views of the Cascades. While there are no horse camps within riding distance, you can easily trailer to Peterson Ridge from Sisters Cow Camp or Graham Corral. Or you can stay at a local hotel while boarding your horse at the full-care Eagle Bear Ranch. Peterson Ridge is very popular with mountain bikers, but the mountain bike trails are completely separate from the horse trails. Please don't ride on the bike trails, as horse hooves tear up the trail tread and ruin the riding experience for the bicyclists. Members of the mountain bike community helped build the horse trail system, so please be neighborly and respect the integrity of their trails. Also, note that this trail system utilizes many forest roads. The road number signs aren't always present, but you can easily find your way by following the Sisters Trails Alliance signs.

Whitney and Dixie, at the Lazy Z viewpoint.

Getting to Peterson Ridge

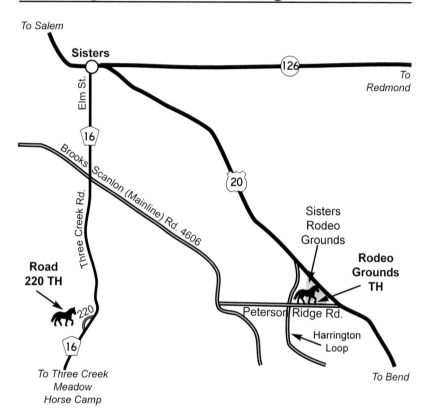

Finding the Rodeo Grounds Trailhead: On Hwy. 20, drive 4.5 miles southeast from Sisters or 16.5 miles northwest from Bend and turn west on Peterson Ridge Road. Continue 0.5 mile to the parking area, just outside the southwest corner of the Sisters Rodeo grounds.

Peterson Ridge Area Trails

Trail	Difficulty	Elevation	Round Trip
Lazy Z Loop	Easy	3,200-3,500	7.5 miles
Peterson Ridge	Easy	3,300-3,800	7-12 miles
Road 16 to Whychus Creek	Moderate	3,400-3,900	10 miles
Rodeo Short Loop	Easy	3,200-3,300	4.5 miles
Whychus Creek Trail	Easy	3,200-3,400	8.5 miles

Eagle Bear Ranch

Address: 69437 Crooked Horseshoe Road, Sisters, OR 97759

Directions: On the east end of Sisters, turn north on Locust St. and drive 1.3 miles. Turn left on Crooked Horseshoe Road. Eagle Bear Ranch is 0.8 mile ahead on the left.

Facilities: Full-care boarding in stalls with outside runs or in large outdoor paddocks. Automatic waterers, secure tack room, outdoor riding arena and round pen, hot-water wash rack, choice quality hay fed per your specifications, full-care managers on site, trailer parking, picnic area and lunchroom, miles of trails on adjacent forest service land.

Fees: Boarding fee

Season: Year-round

Contact: TK NoBear, 541-504-1234, www.eaglebearranch.com

While you are staying in the Sisters area at one of the local hotels, you can board your horses in style at Eagle Bear Ranch, a full-care boarding facility with access to trails right outside the back gate. Peterson Ridge is a short trailer drive away.

Guests head out the back gate for a carriage ride on the forest roads and trails behind Eagle Bear Ranch.

Two boarders hang out in the large outdoor paddocks. The barn with stalls and outdoor runs is in the background.

Lazy Z Loop

Trailhead: Start at the Rodeo Grounds trailhead

Length: 7.5 miles round trip

Elevation: 3,200 to 3,500 feet

Difficulty: Easy -- two water crossings during irrigation season

Footing: Suitable for barefoot horses

Season: Early spring through late fall

Permits: None

Facilities: Parking for 6-8 trailers at the rodeo grounds.   Stock water is available on the trail only in summer.

Highlights: This is an easy trail that runs on a combination of forest roads and single-track trails. The route is clearly marked with Sisters

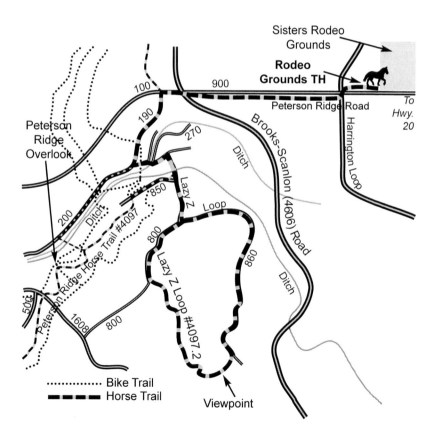

Trails Alliance signs on the trees. When you reach the south end of the loop you'll have a splendid view of the Three Sisters and Broken Top.

The Ride: From the parking lot, ride west beside Peterson Ridge Road. In 0.2 mile, cross Harrington Loop and pick up the trail on the left side of Peterson Ridge Road (Road 900). After another mile you'll cross the red cinder Brooks-Scanlon Road (Road 4606). Continue straight, and in 0.1 mile turn left on Road 190. Follow the Sisters Trails signs on the trees, and in 0.5 mile make a sharp left turn and ride up onto Peterson Ridge. Near the top of the hill, veer right and cross an irrigation ditch, then almost immediately veer right again at another road junction. In 0.2 mile you'll reach another irrigation ditch. Cross it and continue straight ahead for 0.5 mile to reach the loop. Turn right onto the loop (you are now on Road 800), ride 0.5 mile, and then veer left onto a single-track trail. Follow it 0.7 mile to the edge of the ridge, near a rock outcropping where you'll have a great view of the Three Sisters and Broken Top. Continue 0.2 mile to Road 860 and veer left, then ride 1.4 miles to where you entered the loop. Turn right and retrace your steps to the trailhead.

Margie and Spook explore the Lazy Z Loop.

Peterson Ridge

Trailhead: Start at the Rodeo Grounds trailhead

Length: 7 miles round trip to the Peterson Ridge Overlook, 10.5 miles round trip to the Eagle Rock 2 viewpoint, or 12 miles round trip to the Peak View viewpoint

Elevation: 3,300 to 3,800 feet

Difficulty: Easy -- two water crossings during irrigation season

Footing: Suitable for barefoot horses

Season: Early spring through late fall

Permits: None

Facilities: Parking for 6-8 trailers. Stock water is available on the trail only during the summer irrigation season.

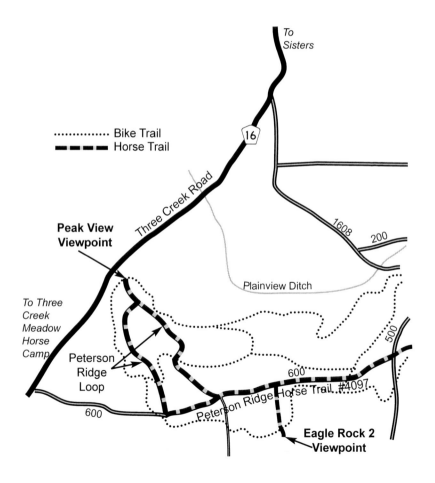

Highlights: This easy trail follows the Peterson Ridge Horse Trail #4097 through beautiful Ponderosa forest, offering several viewpoints along the way that provide splendid views of the Cascades. The directions below are fairly detailed to help you stay on the trail you want to be on, but the entire route is marked with Sisters Trails signs so it's easier than it looks.

The Ride: From the parking lot, ride west beside Peterson Ridge Road. In 0.2 mile, cross Harrington Loop and pick up the trail on the left side of Peterson Ridge Road. After another mile you'll cross the red cinder Brooks-Scanlon Road. Continue straight, and in 0.1 mile turn left on Road 190. Follow the Sisters Trails signs on the trees, and in 0.5 mile make a sharp left turn and ride up onto Peterson Ridge. Near the top of the hill, veer right, cross an irrigation (continued on next page)

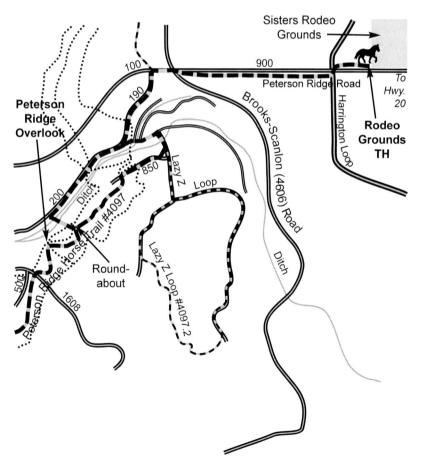

Peterson Ridge (continued)

(continued from previous page) ditch, then almost immediately veer right again at another road junction. In 0.2 mile you'll reach another irrigation ditch. Just past the second ditch, turn right on a single-track trail that will take you to Road 850 in 200 yards. Turn right on Road 850 and follow it 0.3 mile, then make a sharp left onto a single track trail. Continue on the trail 0.4 mile to the Roundabout, an intersection where 2 bike trails meet in a jumble of logs and stumps right next to the horse trail. The signs indicate that the horse trail goes to the left, and to the right across the bike trails. Stay to the left and don't cross the bike trails. In 0.3 mile you'll reach a hitching rail and picnic table at the Peterson Ridge Overlook, your first viewpoint.

Continue another 0.3 mile and cross red cinder Road 1608 near its junction with Road 500, a wide red cinder road. In another 0.5 mile the trail crosses Road 500 and continues along Road 600 for about 0.7 mile. In this stretch you'll start to see Ponderosas growing in rows (planted by machine after the Peterson Burn). Turn left and ride down any row of

The Peak View Viewpoint, one of several viewpoints on Peterson Ridge, provides sweeping views to the north.

*Dottie on Hope and Ann on Spook, riding along
the Peterson Ridge Trail with North Sister behind them.*

trees for 0.3 mile to Eagle Rock 2 at the edge of the ridge. There are great views of the Three Sisters from near this interesting rock pinnacle.

Return to Road 600 and continue west another 0.4 mile to reach the Peterson Ridge Loop. The east leg of the loop goes to the right immediately after a forest road veers off Road 600 to the left. Continue straight ahead on Road 600 for 0.3 mile to reach the west leg of the loop, and turn right at the sign that points to Peterson Ridge Loop. In 0.8 mile the west leg joins the east leg of the loop. Turn left and continue 0.2 mile to the viewpoint, then follow the east leg of the loop back to Road 600.

To return to the trailhead, retrace your steps back to the Roundabout. Here you can vary your return route by turning left and crossing the bike trails, riding down the hill, across two irrigation ditches, and along a single-track trail for 0.1 mile, then turning right on Road 200. Follow Road 200 for 0.6 mile to the spot where you rode up onto the ridge on the first leg of the ride. Stay to the left and return to Peterson Ridge Road for the final leg back to the trailhead.

Road 16 to Whychus Creek

Trailhead: Start at the Road 220 trailhead. You can also reach this trail from the Rodeo Grounds trailhead or from Sisters Cow Camp.

Length: 10 miles round trip from Road 220, or 19.5 miles round trip from the Rodeo Grounds trailhead

Elevation: 3,400 to 3,900 feet from the Road 220 trailhead

Difficulty: Moderate -- crossing Whychus Creek may be challenging during spring runoff

Footing: Suitable for barefoot horses

Season: Late spring through late fall

Permits: None

Facilities: Parking for 2-3 trailers on Road 220, or 6-8 trailers at the rodeo grounds. Stock water is available on the trail.

Highlights: This is a terrific out-and-back ride that roughly parallels Whychus Creek. It showcases the canyon carved by the creek, some interesting rock formations, and even the Three Sisters.

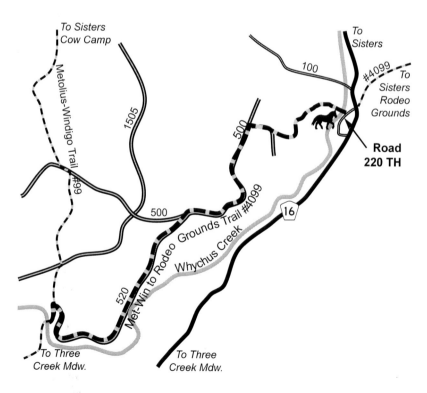

Linda and Beamer enjoy the view of North and Middle Sister while riding the Road 16 to Whychus Creek trail.

Finding the Road 220 Trailhead: You can ride this trail from the Sisters Rodeo grounds but it's a long ride. Instead, we prefer to park at a primitive campground on Road 220, just off Road 16. From Sisters, go south on Elm St., which becomes Road 16/Three Creeks Road. Just past the 3-mile marker, pass the first Road 220 and turn right at the second Road 220, then park in the campground along Whychus Creek. If you choose to start at the Sisters Rodeo Grounds instead, follow the directions for the Whychus Creek Trail later in this chapter.

The Ride: Near the east end of the primitive campground, look for the Sisters Trails Alliance signs that will lead you to the Whychus Creek ford and the Met-Win to Rodeo Grounds Trail #4099. The entire trail is well marked with Sisters Trails signs. Cross the creek and follow the trail up the hill. After about 1.5 miles the trail veers left onto Road 500, then it veers left again on Road 520. In this section the trail runs along the canyon rim above Whychus Creek. After 3.1 miles of riding the roads, you'll reach the Metolius-Windigo Trail. Turn left on the Met-Win and in 0.2 mile it will take you to Whychus Creek, where you can water your horses. If you go north on the Met-Win from here, you'll reach Sisters Cow Camp in 5 miles.

Rodeo Short Loop

Trailhead: Start at the Rodeo Grounds trailhead
Length: 4.5 miles round trip
Elevation: 3,200 to 3,300 feet
Difficulty: Easy
Footing: Suitable for barefoot horses
Season: Early spring through late fall
Permits: None
Facilities: Parking for many trailers. No stock water on the trail.

Highlights: This is a nice, easy loop for riding a green horse, or for those times when you can only do a short ride but still want a pleasant forest experience.

The Ride: From the Rodeo Grounds trailhead, ride north toward the far end of the parking area. Sisters Trails Alliance signs, which mark the entire route, will direct you to veer left onto a dirt road. You are now on the Met-Win to Rodeo Grounds Trail #4099. In 0.3 mile you'll

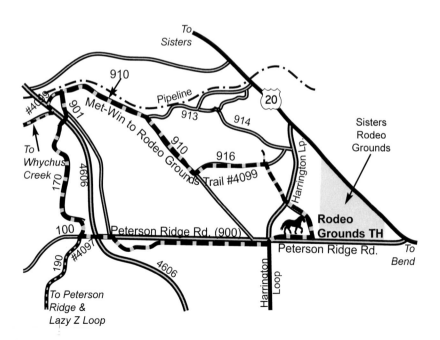

Tex moves out along the Rodeo Short Loop.

cross Harrington Loop, a well-traveled gravel road. The trail becomes a single track and continues 0.3 mile to dirt Road 916. A user trail continues straight ahead, but you'll turn left on Road 916, continue 0.4 mile and turn right on Road 910. Follow Road 910 for 0.4 mile and you'll reach a covered irrigation pipeline. Veer left and ride along the pipeline for 0.5 mile. Turn left on Road 901, and in 0.1 mile veer right on a single track trail that will take you across Road 4606 (the red cinder Brooks-Scanlon Road) and up a small hill. At the crest of the hill, the trail veers to the left and follows Road 170 for 0.6 mile. Then the trail goes up another small hill and in 0.1 mile it reaches Road 100. If you go straight, you'll be on Road 190 and on your way to Peterson Ridge. Instead, turn left on Road 100 and follow it 0.1 mile. Cross Road 4606 and continue straight on Peterson Ridge Road. In less than 0.1 mile you'll pass an irrigation ditch. Just beyond the ditch, pick up the single track trail on the right side of the road and follow it 1 mile to Harrington Loop. Cross Harrington Loop and ride along Peterson Ridge Road for 0.2 mile to return to the parking area.

Whychus Creek Trail

Trailhead: Start at the Rodeo Grounds trailhead
Length: 8.5 miles round trip
Elevation: 3,200 to 3,400 feet
Difficulty: Easy
Footing: Suitable for barefoot horses
Season: Early spring through late fall
Permits: None
Facilities: Parking for 6-8 trailers. Stock water is available on the trail.

Highlights: This ride is a fun, relaxing trail that takes you through beautiful Ponderosa forest to the bank of Whychus Creek, at the spot where the Met-Win to Rodeo Grounds Trail fords the creek.

The Ride: From the Rodeo Grounds trailhead, ride north toward the far end of the parking area. Sisters Trails Alliance signs, which mark the entire route, will direct you to veer left onto the dirt road that marks the east end of the Met-Win to Rodeo Grounds Trail #4099. In 0.3 mile you'll cross Harrington Loop, a well-traveled gravel road. The trail becomes a single track and continues 0.3 mile to dirt Road 916.

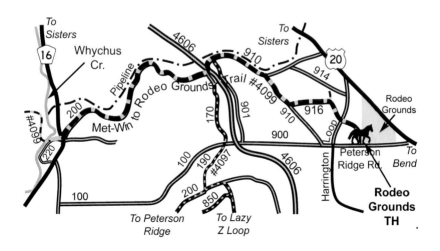

(Watch for the Sisters Trails sign; an unmarked user trail continues straight ahead.) Turn left on Road 916 and continue 0.4 mile, then turn right on Road 910. In 0.9 mile you'll see a sign on the left indicating the route to the Lazy Z Loop and Peterson Ridge. Continue straight, toward the Whychus Creek ford. About 0.1 mile beyond the sign you'll reach the red cinder Road 4606 (Brooks Scanlon Mainline Road). Veer left on it for 200 feet, then turn right and follow the Sisters Trails sign up a small hill. The trail veers right, then left onto an unmarked dirt road. Follow it for 2 miles. For part of this distance you'll be traveling next to a covered irrigation pipeline. The trail stays to the left of the pipeline and joins Road 200. When you reach paved Road 16 (Three Creek Road), cross it and continue 0.1 mile on Road 220, which will take you to a primitive campground on the bank of Whychus Creek. This campground is the parking area for the Road 16 to Whychus Creek ride earlier in this chapter. (The Met-Win to Rodeo Grounds Trail continues across Whychus Creek and on to the Metolius-Windigo Trail.) After watering your horse at the creek, return to the Rodeo Grounds trailhead.

Whychus Creek offers a nice mid-ride watering spot for the horses.

If your horse says no, either you asked the wrong question, or asked the question wrong.

Pat Parelli

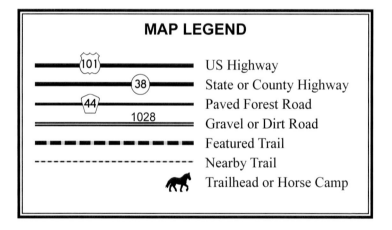

Santiam Pass

Deschutes National Forest

The trails near Santiam Pass provide access to the southern Mt. Jefferson and northern Mt. Washington Wildernesses. Most of these trails, which are easily accessed from Hwy. 20, go through the area burned in the 90,000-acre B&B fire in 2003. You'll see thousands of burned trees as you ride, but the fire also opened up tremendous mountain views that you wouldn't otherwise have. And it's interesting to watch the forest grow back year by year: dense undergrowth, wildflowers, and young trees now cover the area that in 2004 was nothing but gray ash and blackened tree trunks.

If you want to camp nearby, Sheep Springs Horse Camp is not far away. See the Metolius Basin chapter for more information.

The trails near Santiam Pass
provide amazing mountain views.

Santiam Pass Area

Directions:	Santiam Pass is located about 20 miles northwest of Sisters, on Hwy. 20. For directions to the nearby trailheads, see "Finding the Trailhead" on the pages for each trail.
Elevation:	4,800 feet
Campsites:	The nearest horse camping facilities are at Sheep Springs Horse Camp. See the Metolius Basin chapter for more information.
Facilities:	See "Facilities" on the pages for each trail
Permits:	See "Permits" on the pages for each trail
Season:	Summer through fall
Contact:	For information about the Old Summit and Square/Round Lake Trails, contact the Sisters Ranger District: 541-549-7700, www.fs.usda.gov/centraloregon, then click on "Recreation," "Horse Riding and Camping." For information about the Patjens Lake Trail, contact the McKenzie Ranger District: 541-822-3381, www.fs.usda.gov/willamette, then click on "Recreation," "Horse Riding and Camping." For information about the Santiam Lake Trail contact the Detroit Ranger District: 503-854-3366, www.fs.usda.gov/willamette, then click on "Recreation," "Horse Riding and Camping."

Santiam Pass Trails

Trail	Difficulty	Elevation	Round Trip
Old Summit Trail	Moderate	4,750-5,400	15 miles
Patjens Lakes	Moderate	4,400-4,800	6 miles
Santiam Lake	Moderate	4,850-5,450	12 miles
Square & Round Lakes	Moderate	4,300-5,000	9.5 miles

Getting to Santiam Pass Trailheads

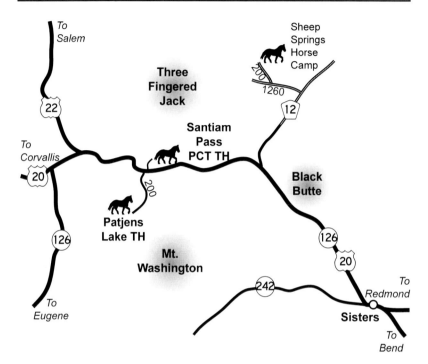

*Debbie rides Cowboy beneath Three Fingered Jack
on the Santiam Lake Trail.*

Old Summit Trail

Trailhead: Start at the Pacific Crest Trail trailhead at Santiam Pass
Length: 15 miles round trip
Elevation: 4,750 to 5,400 feet
Difficulty: Moderate
Footing: Hoof protection recommended
Season: Summer through fall
Permits: Northwest Forest Pass required
Facilities: Toilet, hitching posts, parking for several trailers. Stock water is available on the trail.

Highlights: The Old Summit Trail used to be a beautifully forested ride over the shoulder of Three Fingered Jack, but the 2003 B&B fire changed all that. On the entire 7.5-mile trail, you won't see more than a couple hundred full-size living trees. The underbrush is recovering, though, and silvery tree trunks now frame good views of Mt. Wash-

ington, the North and Middle Sisters, Broken Top, Black Crater, Black Butte, and Three Fingered Jack.

Finding the Santiam Pass PCT Trailhead: From Sisters, drive northwest on Hwy. 20 for 19 miles. Turn right at the Santiam Pass trailhead for the Pacific Coast Trail (PCT), and drive 0.4 mile to the parking area.

The Ride: Pick up the trail next to the kiosk on the east side of the parking loop and turn left on the PCT. After 0.2 mile, turn right on the Old Summit Trail #4014 (aka the Summit Lakes Trail) toward Square Lake and Jack Lake. In 2 miles you'll come to Square Lake. Ride along the lake for 0.2 mile and turn left at the trail junction on its shore. About 1.5 miles later you'll pass Booth Lake. Continue another 3.8 miles to reach Jack Lake. Retrace your steps to return to the trailhead.

Three Fingered Jack is reflected in a tiny unnamed lake along the trail.

Through the trees burned in the B&B fire, you'll get great views of North & Middle Sister and Mt. Washington.

Patjens Lakes

Trailhead: Start at Patjens Lake trailhead

Length: 6 miles round trip

Elevation: 4,400 to 4,800 feet

Difficulty: Moderate

Footing: Hoof protection recommended

Season: Summer through fall

Permits: None

Facilities: Toilet and potable water at nearby Big Lake campground. Parking for 2-3 trailers at the trailhead. Stock water is available on the trail.

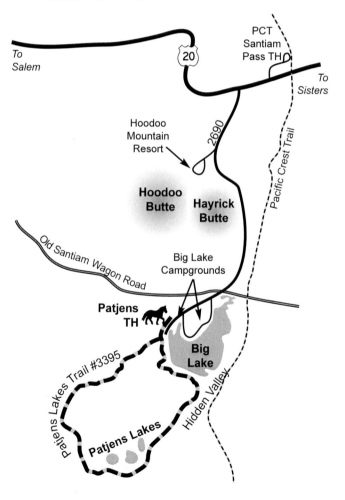

Teresa on Radar and Lydia on Shadow at the Patjens Lakes.

Highlights: This is a fun forested loop ride that provides good views of Big Lake and the tiny Patjens Lakes. In late June and early July it features more blooming bear grass than any other trail in Central Oregon.

Finding the Patjens Lake Trailhead: From Sisters, drive northwest on Highway 20 to Santiam Pass, about 19 miles. Turn left on Road 2690 toward Hoodoo Ski Area and Big Lake. Continue toward Big Lake for 3.7 miles. Drive past the first Big Lake campground and park in the trailhead parking area on the right, just outside the second campground.

The Ride: Head south from the trailhead. The trail forks after about 0.3 mile. Take the left fork, which follows the shore of Big Lake and goes through Hidden Valley, turns west and passes the Patjens Lakes, then loops north over a ridge and back to the trailhead. The bear grass is at its most beautiful in late June and early July. Unfortunately, that's when the mosquitoes are hungriest, and both Bug Lake -- oops, I mean Big Lake -- and the Patjens Lakes produce a bumper crop of them. Be sure to slather yourself and your horse with mosquito repellent if riding early in the season.

Santiam Lake

Trailhead: Start at the Pacific Crest Trail trailhead at Santiam Pass
Length: 12 miles round trip
Elevation: 4,850 to 5,450 feet
Difficulty: Moderate
Footing: Hoof protection recommended
Season: Summer through fall
Permits: Northwest Forest Pass required
Facilities: Toilet, hitching rails, and parking for several trailers. Stock water is available on the trail.

Highlights: This absolute gem of a ride is mostly on the west side of the Cascades, so technically speaking it may not be in Central Oregon. But it starts in Central Oregon, so that counts, right? The trail takes you through the area burned by the B&B fire, with impressive

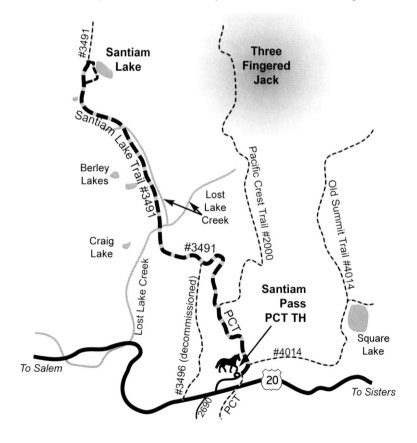

views of the Cascade peaks to the south. Next it goes through dense fir and hemlock forest to the shore of beautiful Santiam Lake. Be sure to do this ride on a clear day, because the reflection of Three Fingered Jack in the lake is stunning.

Finding the Santiam Pass PCT Trailhead: From Sisters, drive northwest on Hwy. 20 for 19 miles. Turn right at the Santiam Pass trailhead for the Pacific Crest Trail (PCT), and drive 0.4 mile to the parking area.

The Ride: Pick up the trail next to the kiosk on the east end of the parking loop, and turn left on the PCT. In 0.2 mile, the Old Summit Trail #4014 goes off to the right. Stay to the left on the PCT, and in 1 mile turn left on Trail #3491 toward Santiam Lake. In another mile you'll reach the unsigned junction with the decommissioned Trail #3496. Veer right to stay on Trail #3491. In about 0.5 mile an unsigned user trail goes off to the left. Stay to the right, and for the next 2 miles you'll ride beside Lost Lake Creek (dry in late summer). Shortly after leaving the creek you'll pass a pretty little unnamed lake on the left. Ride 0.3 mile farther and watch for an unsigned trail on the right that will take you downhill to Santiam Lake. (The lake is not visible from the main trail.) Walk along the lake shore and on the northern end you'll find another spur trail that will return you to the main trail.

Three Fingered Jack reflected in Santiam Lake.

Square and Round Lakes

Trailhead: Start at the Pacific Crest Trail trailhead at Santiam Pass

Length: 9.5 miles round trip

Elevation: 4,300 to 5,000 feet

Difficulty: Moderate

Footing: Suitable for barefoot horses

Season: Summer through fall

Permits: Northwest Forest Pass required

Facilities: Toilet, hitching rails, and parking for several trailers. Stock water is available on the trail.

Highlights: The Round Lake Trail follows the Old Summit Trail to Square Lake, then branches off to Round Lake. The entire ride is within the area burned by the B&B fire in 2003. While the black and silver skeletons of the burned trees remain, the forest is regenerating. Undergrowth is plentiful, and the juvenile lodgepoles are growing. Plus, the trail now offers mountain views that were formerly obscured by the forest.

Finding the Santiam Pass PCT Trailhead: From Sisters, drive northwest about 19 miles on Highway 20. Turn right at the Santiam Pass trailhead for the Pacific Crest Trail (PCT), and drive 0.4 mile to the parking area.

The Ride: Pick up the trail next to the kiosk on the east end of the parking loop and turn left on the PCT. About 0.2 mile later turn right

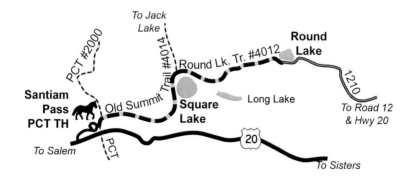

Suzanne and Skipper ride past Square Lake.

on the Old Summit Trail #4014 (aka the Summit Lakes Trail). In another 2 miles you'll reach Square Lake. After following the lake shore for 0.2 mile, the Old Summit Trail turns left and heads toward Jack Lake, while Round Lake Trail #4012 goes straight ahead. Stay straight, and in 0.1 mile you'll reach a good place to take your horse down to Square Lake for a drink. Continue on the trail for 2 miles farther to reach Round Lake. The trail ends at the hiker trailhead at Round Lake, at the end of Road 1210. Unfortunately, there isn't a trail to the shore of Round Lake.

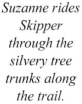

Suzanne rides Skipper through the silvery tree trunks along the trail.

Somewhere in time's own space
There must be some sweet pastured place
Where creeks sing on and tall trees grow
Some paradise where horses go,
For by the love that guides my pen
I know great horses live again.

Stanley Harrison

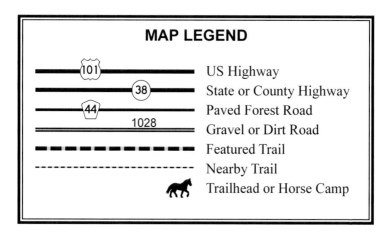

MAP LEGEND

US Highway
State or County Highway
Paved Forest Road
Gravel or Dirt Road
Featured Trail
Nearby Trail
Trailhead or Horse Camp

Sisters Area
Sisters Cow Camp
Deschutes National Forest

The area near the town of Sisters offers wonderful low- to mid-elevation riding. Some trails offer excellent mountain views, while others are primarily in beautiful ponderosa pine forest. The low-elevation trails originate at Sisters Cow Camp, which at one time was used by ranchers to gather cows to take them off their summer range. The camp has a historic storage shed, large corrals, and a loading chute to remind us of its original purpose. Nowadays, though, Sisters Cow Camp is a popular camping area and trailhead for horseback riders. You can also ride from the Sisters Tie trailhead, or you can go to the Pole Creek trailhead, which provides access to several very nice higher-elevation trails on the flank of North Sister.

Katherine, Debbie, and Suzi ride the Cow Camp Loop,
with Mt. Jefferson in the background.

Getting to Sisters Area

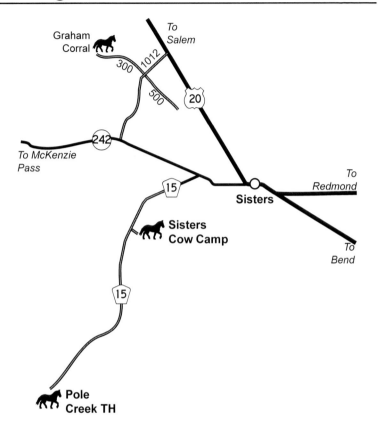

Sisters Area Trails

Trail	Difficulty	Elevation	Round Trip
Camp Lake	Challenging	5,300-7,000	13 miles
Cow Camp Loop	Moderate	3,400-4,100	9 miles
Demaris Lake	Challenging	5,300-6,400	11 miles
Graham Corral	Easy	3,250-3,550	13.5 miles
Marquis Loop	Moderate	3,400-4,300	13 miles
Park Meadow	Moderate	5,300-6,200	12 miles
Short Loop	Easy	3,300-3,400	3 miles
Sisters	Moderate	3,200-3,400	8.5 miles
Sisters Tie	Easy	3,200-3,250	13 miles
Whychus Creek	Moderate	3,400-3,900	7-10 miles

Sisters Cow Camp

Directions: From Sisters, drive west 1.5 miles on Hwy. 242 and turn left on Road 15. Continue 2.5 miles and turn left toward Sisters Cow Camp at the sign (which is on the right side of the road). Drive 0.4 mile to reach the camp.

Elevation: 3,300 feet

Campsites: 5 campsites with fire pits and picnic tables. Level parking areas. Two 2 large corrals in center of camp.

Facilities: Toilet, stock water in season, central corrals. Plenty of parking for day-riders. Please haul your manure home with you.

Permits: None

Season: Spring through late fall

Contact: Sisters Ranger District: 541-549-7700, www.fs.usda.gov/centraloregon, then click on "Recreation," "Horse Riding and Camping"

*The two large corrals at Sisters Cow Camp
can hold plenty of horses.*

Camp Lake

Trailhead: Start at Pole Creek trailhead

Length: 13 miles round trip

Elevation: 5,300 to 7,000 feet

Difficulty: Challenging -- trail is steep, rocky, and narrow near the end; potentially hazardous crossing of glacier-fed stream

Footing: Hoof protection recommended

Season: Late summer through early fall

Permits: Northwest Forest Pass required

Facilities: Toilet and parking for 2-3 trailers (depending on the number of parked hiker cars) at Pole Creek Trailhead. Stock water is available on the trail.

Highlights: This fabulous ride gives you a chance to see all Three Sisters up close. Much of the distance is a moderate climb through

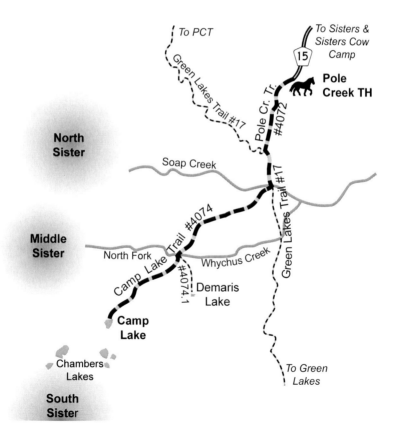

the forest.   Midway through the ride you'll go through old growth forest punctuated by interesting rock outcroppings.   As you near Camp Lake, the forest thins out and the trail gets steep, narrow, and rocky. You'll come out above timberline, where the Three Sisters seem close enough to touch, and the views of Middle Sister's glaciers are impressive.   Some years you may not be able to reach Camp Lake because of lingering snowfields.

Finding Pole Creek Trailhead: Take Hwy. 242 west from Sisters for 1.5 miles, turn left on Road 15, and follow it for 10.5 miles. Pole Creek trailhead is very popular with hikers doing multi-day hiking trips around the Sisters, so be sure to turn your trailer around when you arrive so you cannot be blocked in by hiker cars.

The Ride: Ride south from the trailhead on the Pole Creek Trail #4072 for 1.5 miles. At the first junction veer left on the Green Lakes Trail #17. Continue 0.7 mile, and after crossing Soap Creek turn right toward the Chambers Lakes on the Camp Lake Trail #4074. After 2.5 miles you'll cross the fast-flowing, glacier-fed North Fork of Whychus Creek (you can't see the bottom because of the glacial silt in the water) and come to the junction with the Demaris Lake Trail #4074.1. Keep right and continue 2 miles to Camp Lake.

*Lydia and Shadow check out the view of North Sister
on the trail to Camp Lake.*

Cow Camp Loop

Trailhead: Start at Sisters Cow Camp

Length: 9 miles round trip

Elevation: 3,400 to 4,100 feet

Difficulty: Moderate -- some of this ride is on unsigned forest roads, so the Sisters Ranger District map and a GPS will be useful

Footing: Hoof protection recommended

Season: Early spring through late fall

Permits: None

Facilities: Toilet, stock water in season, corrals, and plenty of trailer parking at Sisters Cow Camp.

Highlights: To do a nice loop ride from Sisters Cow Camp, take the Metolius-Windigo Trail to Pole Creek, then follow forest roads to complete the loop.

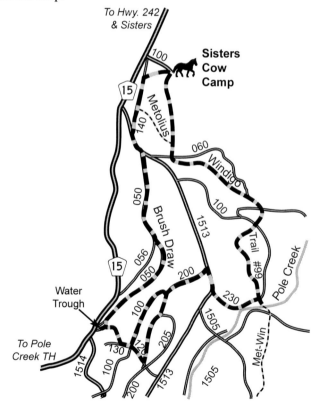

The Ride: Pick up the unsigned trail on the south side of Sisters Cow Camp (between the toilet and the fence). On your way up the hill, look behind you at the expansive mountain views. In 0.8 mile this trail merges with the Metolius-Windigo Trail #99. About 3.3 miles from camp you'll reach Pole Creek. After watering your horses, backtrack to Road 230 (the road you crossed just before reaching the creek), turn left, and follow it 0.7 mile. Turn right on gray-gravel Road 1513 and continue 0.2 mile, then turn left on red-cinder Road 200, the first road on the left. Follow it 0.5 mile and turn right on Road 100, a very overgrown dirt road marked by a rock cairn. The sign for the road is 100 feet in and not visible from Road 200. Follow Road 100 for 0.8 mile to the junction with Roads 120 and 130. (Or, continue straight on Road 200 for another 0.8 mile (this is a great road for cantering), turn right on Road 120 and follow it 0.2 mile.) At the junction of the 100, 120, and 130 Roads, pick up Road 130. In 0.2 mile, an indistinct single-track trail marked by a rock cairn goes off to the right. Follow this trail 0.3 mile through the forest and down a steep hill. At the bottom of the hill you can turn left and ride 200 yards to a stock water trough. Then turn around and follow the dirt road downhill 0.1 mile until it ends, pick up the single-track trail to the left, and follow it to Road 050. Ride Road 050 down through Brush Draw for 2.2 miles to gray-gravel Road 1513 and turn left. Ride 0.1 mile, then veer right on Road 140 and in 0.3 mile the Metolius-Windigo Trail comes in from the right and you'll begin seeing yellow diamonds on the trees. Follow the Met-Win about 0.3 mile back to Sisters Cow Camp.

Donita and Toby travel through Brush Draw on the Cow Camp Loop.

Demaris Lake

Trailhead: Start at the Pole Creek Trailhead

Length: 11 miles round trip

Elevation: 5,300 to 6,400 feet

Difficulty: Challenging -- glacier-fed stream crossing can be hazardous early in the season

Footing: Hoof protection recommended

Season: Summer through early fall

Permits: Northwest Forest Pass required

Facilities: Toilet and parking for 2-3 trailers (depending on the number of parked hiker cars) at Pole Creek Trailhead. Stock water is available on the trail.

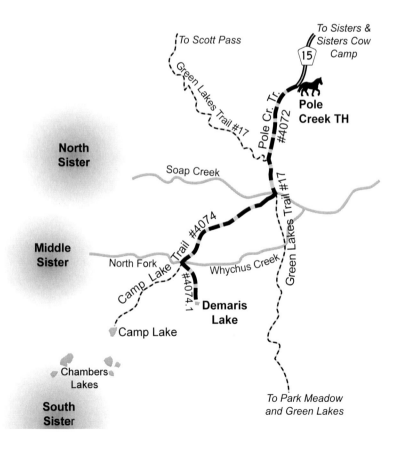

North Sister is reflected in the calm surface of Demaris Lake.

Highlights: At several points this forested trail offers filtered views of the Three Sisters and Broken Top. As you approach the North Fork of Whychus Creek you'll ride through stands of old-growth trees and past interesting rock outcroppings. When you reach the lake, tie your horse in the trees and hike to the left along the east side of the lake (the trail is not suitable for horses) to see the Three Sisters.

Finding Pole Creek Trailhead: Take Hwy. 242 west from Sisters for 1.5 miles, turn left on Road 15, and follow it for 10.5 miles. Pole Creek trailhead is very popular with hikers doing multi-day hiking trips around the Sisters, so be sure to turn your trailer around when you arrive so you cannot be blocked in by hiker cars.

The Ride: Ride south from the trailhead on the Pole Creek Trail #4072 for 1.5 miles. At the first junction veer left on the Green Lakes Trail #17. Continue 0.7 mile, and after crossing Soap Creek turn right toward the Chambers Lakes on the Camp Lake Trail #4074. After 2.5 miles you'll cross the fast-flowing, glacier-fed North Fork of Whychus Creek (you can't see the bottom because of the glacial silt in the water) and come to the junction with the Demaris Lake Trail #4074.1. Turn left and continue 0.7 mile to Demaris Lake.

Graham Corral

Trailhead: Start at Sisters Cow Camp

Length: 13.5 miles round trip

Elevation: 3,250 to 3,550 feet

Difficulty: Easy

Footing: Suitable for barefoot horses

Season: Early spring through late fall

Permits: None

Facilities: Toilet, stock water in season, corrals, and plenty of trailer parking at Sisters Cow Camp. Toilet, potable water and corrals at Graham Corral.

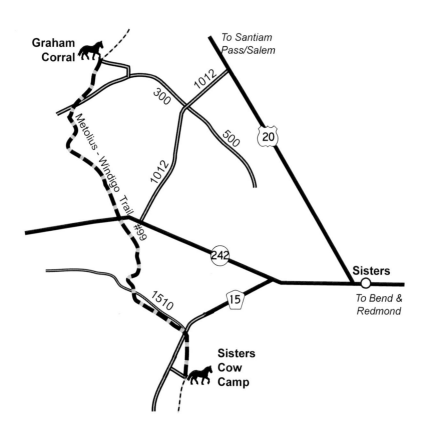

Highlights: This is a nice forested ride on the segment of the Metolius-Windigo Trail that runs between Sisters Cow Camp and Graham Corral.   The trail goes over a small ridge that offers nice mountain views through the trees.   With its low elevation and easy terrain, this is a good springtime ride for getting your horse in shape for the summer riding season.

The Ride: Pick up the Metolius-Windigo Trail #99 on the north edge of Sisters Cow Camp and head north.   Part of the route is on single-track trail and part is on old forest roads.   The way is clearly marked with yellow diamonds.   In 0.6 mile you'll cross the gravel Road 15 and the trail will run beside Road 1510 for 1.1 miles.   Then it crosses Road 1510, goes 1.8 miles, and crosses Hwy. 242.   A short distance beyond the highway, the trail drops into a small grotto with interesting rock outcroppings, lots of grass, and old growth ponderosas.   About 1.9 miles beyond the grotto, the trail goes over a low ridge that offers nice mountain views to the west.   About 1.5 miles after the ridge top, the trail crosses Road 300 and continues 0.7 mile to Graham Corral.

Connie on Diamond, Lydia on Shadow, and Debbie on Mel,
on the way to Graham Corral.

Marquis Loop

Trailhead: Start at Sisters Cow Camp

Length: 13 miles round trip

Elevation: 3,400 to 4,300 feet

Difficulty: Moderate -- most of this ride is on unsigned forest roads, so a Sisters Ranger District map and a GPS are helpful

Footing: Hoof protection recommended

Season: Early spring through late fall

Permits: None

Facilities: Toilet, stock water in season, corrals, and plenty of trailer parking at Sisters Cow Camp

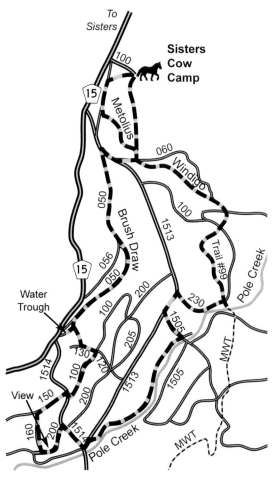

Highlights: Oregon Equestrian Trails sponsors an annual fundraising ride for St. Jude's Hospital, and each year Pat and Rhonda Marquis lay out a loop trail for the riders. The route varies from year to year, and this particular loop is their best ever: it features a beautiful stretch along the bank of Pole Creek and nice views of the Three Sisters at the midpoint of the ride.

The Ride: Pick up the unsigned trail on the south side of Sisters Cow Camp (between the toilet and the fence). As you ride up the hill, be sure to look over your shoulder at the fabulous mountain views. In 0.8 mile this trail merges with the Metolius-Windigo Trail #99. About 3.3 miles from camp you'll reach Pole Creek. After watering your horse, backtrack about 100 yards and turn left on Road 230. Follow it 0.7 mile, turn left on gravel Road 1513, and in 0.2 mile turn left again on Road 1505. In 0.3 mile you'll reach Pole Creek. Don't cross the creek. Instead, turn right on the dirt road that runs beside the creek. Follow it 1.6 miles, then turn left on Road 1513 and in a few hundred yards turn right on red cinder Road 1514. Ride 0.3 mile and turn left on Road 200. In about 0.2 mile you'll get a nice view of The Sisters. Continue another 0.2 mile and turn right on Road 160. Ride 0.5 mile and turn right on Road 150. In 0.4 mile you'll reach the red cinder Road 1514. Turn right, and in about 100 feet turn left on Road 100. About 0.6 mile farther, turn left on Road 130. In 0.2 mile, a single-track trail marked by a rock cairn goes off to the right. Follow it 0.3 mile through the forest and down a steep hill. At the bottom of the hill you can turn left and ride 200 yards to a stock water trough. Then turn around and follow the dirt road downhill 0.1 mile until it ends, pick up the single-track trail to the left, and follow it to Road 050. Ride Road 050 down through Brush Draw for 2.2 miles to Road 1513, turn right on it and ride 0.2 mile, then turn left on Road 060. In 0.1 mile, just before the gate, turn left on the Metolius-Windigo Trail and follow it back to Cow Camp.

North Sister towers above as Debbie and Lydia ride Cowboy and Shadow on the Marquis Loop trail.

Park Meadow

Trailhead:	Start at Pole Creek trailhead
Length:	12 miles round trip
Elevation:	5,300 to 6,200 feet
Difficulty:	Moderate -- crossing Whychus Creek in early summer may be hazardous if the water level is high
Footing:	Hoof protection recommended
Season:	Summer through fall
Permits:	Northwest Forest Pass required
Facilities:	Toilet and parking for 2-3 trailers (depending on the number of parked hiker cars) at Pole Creek trailhead. Stock water is available on the trail.

Highlights: Most people ride to the beautiful Park Meadow using the trail that originates near Three Creek Meadow Horse Camp. The route described here is more difficult, with more elevation change and a potentially challenging crossing of Whychus Creek early in the season.

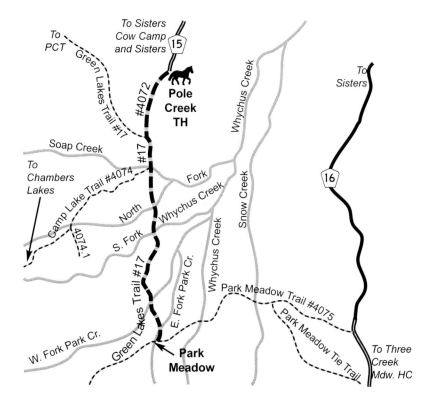

But the views and solitude on this trail-less-travelled are ample rewards for the extra exertion.

Finding Pole Creek Trailhead: Take Hwy. 242 west from Sisters for 1.5 miles, turn left on Road 15, and follow it for 10.5 miles. Pole Creek Trailhead is very popular with hikers doing multi-day hiking trips around The Sisters, so be sure to turn your trailer around when you arrive so you cannot be blocked in by hiker cars.

The Ride: From the trailhead, ride south on the Pole Creek Trail #4072 for 1.5 mile. At the first junction veer left on the Green Lakes Trail #17 and continue 0.7 mile. Just across Soap Creek, the Camp Lake Trail #4074 goes off to the right. Stay to the left, and in 0.8 mile you'll cross the North Fork of Whychus Creek. About 0.6 mile after that you'll cross the South Fork of Whychus Creek. The trail then climbs a steep ridge and enters an area burned several years ago by a forest fire. Be sure to look behind you and take in the views. About 0.8 mile after crossing the South Fork of Whychus Creek you'll pass a tiny unnamed lake, and 1.5 miles after that the trail reaches Park Meadow.

Riders cross Park Meadow, in the shadow of South Sister.

Short Loop

Trailhead: Start at Sisters Cow Camp
Length: 3 miles round trip
Elevation: 3,300 to 3,400 feet
Difficulty: Easy, but a Sisters Ranger District map and a GPS will come in handy
Footing: Suitable for barefoot horses
Season: Early spring through late fall
Permits: None
Facilities: Toilet, stock water in season, and plenty of trailer parking at the horse camp. No stock water on the trail.

Highlights: This ride uses the Metolius-Windigo Trail, a neighborhood trail, and double-track forest roads to create a loop that is good for training a green horse, or for those occasions when you want to ride but don't have a lot of time. Most of the forest roads are unsigned so this route will test your navigation skills.

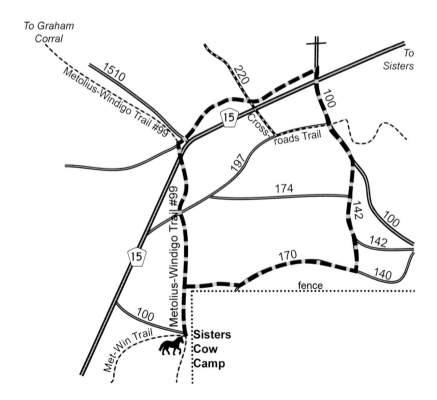

This short, pleasant ride uses forest roads to make a loop southeast of Sisters Cow Camp.

The Ride: From Sisters Cow Camp, pick up the Metolius-Windigo Trail #99 on the north side of camp and follow it 0.8 mile. The trail crosses gravel Road 15 and almost immediately crosses a small dirt road. Instead of continuing on the Met-Win, turn right on the dirt road. In about 100 feet you'll reach Road 1510. Cross it and pick up the trail directly in front of you, next to a small rock cairn. The trail roughly parallels Road 15 for 0.6 mile, then intersects with the wide gravel Road 100. (If you look left down Road 100 you'll see a green gate across it that marks the boundary of the Crossroads subdivision.) Turn right, cross Road 15, and follow Road 100 for 0.4 mile. (The Crossroads Trail crosses Road 100 in 0.2 mile.) Veer right on Road 142, an unmarked dirt road that heads south. Ride it for 0.5 mile, ignoring the smaller dirt roads that branch off it and staying on the most well-traveled road. After 0.5 mile, in an area of young trees, the road makes a T-intersection with the well-traveled dirt Road 170. Turn right and follow Road 170 for 0.5 mile to where it dead-ends at a fence. Veer right and ride cross-country beside the fence for 0.2 mile, then turn left on the Metolius-Windigo trail to return to Sisters Cow Camp.

Sisters

Trailhead: Start at Sisters Cow Camp
Length: 8.5 miles round trip
Elevation: 3,200 to 3,400 feet
Difficulty: Moderate - some riding in traffic
Footing: Suitable for barefoot horses
Season: Early spring through late fall
Permits: None
Facilities: Toilet, stock water in season, and plenty of trailer parking at the horse camp. No stock water on the trail.

Highlights: This route links single-track trails and forest roads to go from Sisters Cow Camp to the town of Sisters. You'll have some nice mountain views along the way. The Sisters Trails Alliance has proposed creating a route that will be almost all single-track trail, but as of this writing the trail is still in the proposal stage. When/if it is completed, it will be marked with Sisters Trails signs. The last mile of this route runs along the side of Hwy. 242. The road shoulder is very wide so unless your horse is afraid of traffic this should not be a problem. Once you arrive in town, you can get a burger or ice cream at the Sno-

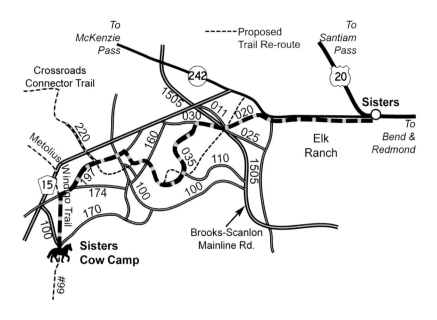

Lydia and Shadow saunter along the trail to Sisters.
That's Black Crater in the background.

Cap Drive-in, pick up groceries at Ray's Food Place, or get some good barbecue at Slick's Que Co. There are no hitching rails in town, though, so someone in your group will need to hold the horses.

The Ride: From Sisters Cow Camp, pick up the Metolius-Windigo Trail #99 on the north side of camp. Follow it for 0.5 mile and turn right on well-worn dirt Road 197. (If you come to Road 15, a wide gray gravel road, you've gone too far.) Follow Road 197 for 0.8 mile. The Crossroads Connector trail comes in on Road 220, and after that you will see Sisters Trails Alliance trail signs marking the way. Follow the Sisters Trails signs for 4 miles to Hwy. 242. When you reach Hwy. 242, turn right and ride along the very wide shoulder of the road, past the elk ranch, for about a mile to reach the town of Sisters. On the return journey, note that at the junction of Roads 197 and 220, the Crossroads Connector trail goes straight ahead but you should veer left on Road 197. Follow Road 197 back to the Metolius-Windigo Trail (marked with yellow diamonds) and turn left on the Met-Win to return to the horse camp.

Sisters Tie

Trailhead: Start at the Sisters Tie trailhead
Length: 13 miles round trip
Elevation: 3,200 to 3,250 feet
Difficulty: Easy
Footing: Suitable for barefoot horses
Season: Early spring through late fall
Permits: None
Facilities: Parking for 2-3 trailers at the trailhead. Stock water is available on the trail.

Highlights: The Sisters Tie Trail is an easy ride that runs through open Ponderosa forest, connecting the town of Sisters with the Metolius-Windigo trail. Watch for evidence of beaver activity along the stretch next to Indian Ford Creek.

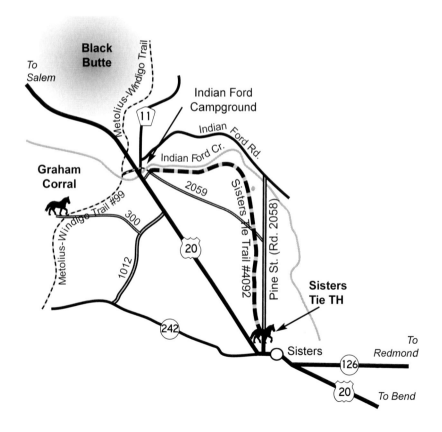

Beavers are hard at work along Indian Ford Creek.

Finding the Sisters Tie Trailhead: In downtown Sisters, turn north on Pine Street and drive 0.5 mile to where the road turns to gravel. Turn around and park beside the road and ride north 100 yards to the trailhead kiosk.

The Ride: At the kiosk, pick up the Sisters Tie Trail #4092, which is marked with Sisters Trails Alliance signs to distinguish it from the user trails that lace the area. In 2.0 miles the trail goes under some power lines. In another 0.4 mile it reaches dirt Road 2059. A mile after that you'll pass a small pond (may be dry in summer) in an excavated area. In another 1.9 miles the trail begins running beside Indian Ford Creek, and 1.5 miles later you'll arrive at Indian Ford Campground. Skirt around the west perimeter of the campground to reach a good place to water your horse at Indian Ford Creek.

If you want to continue on to the Metolius-Windigo Trail #99, cross Indian Ford Creek using the campground bridge, then continue skirting the campground (horses are not permitted in the campground), cross Road 11 and Hwy. 20, and follow the Sisters Trails Alliance signs to the Met-Win Trail.

Whychus Creek

Trailhead: Start at Sisters Cow Camp
Length: 10 miles round trip to Whychus Creek, or 7 miles round trip to Pole Creek
Elevation: 3,400 to 3,900 feet
Difficulty: Moderate
Footing: Hoof protection recommended
Season: Late spring through fall
Permits: None
Facilities: Toilet, stock water in season, and plenty of trailer parking at the horse camp. No stock water on the trail.

Highlights: This trail travels mostly through ponderosa forest, and has little elevation change after climbing the hillside immediately south of Cow Camp. The treeless hillside above the camp has wonderful views of Mt. Jefferson, Mt. Washington, and the Three Sisters.

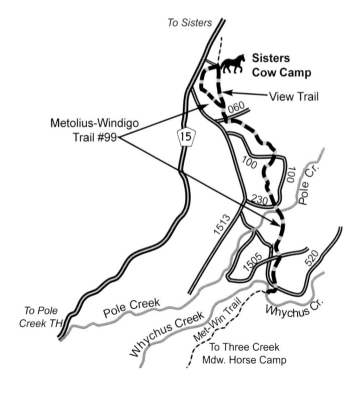

Suzi on Frosti, Debbie on Cowboy, and Katherine on Mel, enjoying the mountain views on the Met-Win Trail not far from Cow Camp.

The Ride: You can pick up the southbound Metolius-Windigo Trail #99 on the west side of Cow Camp. Instead, we suggest departing on the unsigned trail that begins on the south side of camp between the toilet and the fence. After climbing the treeless ridge, be sure to look behind you because on a clear day you'll have memorable views of the mountains. The trail then enters the forest and continues with little elevation gain. About 0.8 mile from camp, the trail you're on joins the Met-Win Trail. After another 0.4 mile the Met-Win (marked with yellow diamonds) crosses gravel Road 060, and 2.4 miles farther it reaches Pole Creek. Cross the bridge, and in a mile the trail crosses gravel Road 1505. About 0.5 mile after that you'll cross Road 520, and 0.2 mile later you'll descend to Whychus Creek. The entire route is clearly marked with yellow diamonds. On your return trip, you can make a bit of a loop back to camp by veering left on the Met-Win Trail about 0.1 mile after crossing Road 060 and following the Met-Win back to Cow Camp.

All horses deserve, at least once in their lives, to be loved by a little girl.

Anonymous

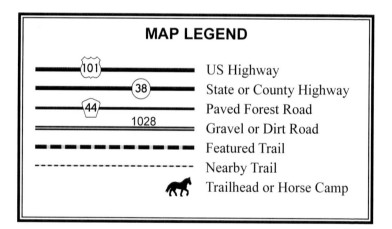

Skyline Forest

Bend, Oregon

If you're one of the many equestrians who enjoy riding the forest trails near Tumalo Reservoir, you may be surprised to know that these trails are not on public land. In fact, generations of Central Oregonians have benefitted from the open-access policies of the timber companies that historically owned Skyline Forest, though most never realized they were on private land. This 33,000 acre private forest spans from Bend to Sisters. Now owned by a Fortune 500 corporation, the forest is today at risk of development and loss of public access. Fortunately, the Deschutes Land Trust is leading a community effort to purchase the land, turn it into a Community Forest, and preserve it forever for wildlife, public recreation, and scenic views. Special legislation passed in 2009 to facilitate the transaction provides for continued public access while the landowner and Deschutes Land Trust work on a permanent deal. Since, it can take years to accomplish a purchase like this, the Land Trust needs the support of equestrians in order to make it happen. So if you'd like to continue to enjoy the beautiful trails of Skyline Forest, please consider becoming a member of the Deschutes Land Trust (www.deschuteslandtrust.org) and do your part to help preserve this wonderful place.

Debbie and Whitney ride Mel and Dixie beside Tumalo Reservoir, near the equestrian parking area for Skyline Forest.

Skyline Forest

Directions: Most of the trails in this chapter depart from the end of Tumalo Reservoir Road. To reach the trailhead, drive northwest from Bend on Hwy. 20 to Tumalo and turn left on Bailey Rd. Drive to the top of the hill, and Bailey Rd. soon becomes Tumalo Reservoir Road. Follow it 3.7 miles. Just before the road bends sharply to the right and goes over a bridge, turn left into the dirt parking area. There's a sign here indicating the spot is a school bus turnaround.

Elevation: 3,500 feet

Campsites: None

Facilities: Parking for 15-20 trailers. Stock water during irrigation season.

Permits: None

Season: Nearly year-round

Lydia on Shadow and Teresa on Jane,
exploring the forest roads of Skyline Forest.

Getting to Skyline Forest

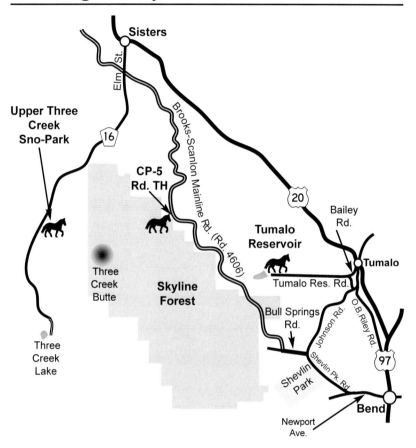

Skyline Forest Trails

Trail	Difficulty	Elevation	Round Trip
Bull Spring Loop	Easy	3,500-3,800	7 miles
Central Skyline	Easy	3,600-4,100	Varies
Skyline Gorge Loop	Moderate	3,500-4,000	11 miles
Snag Spring	Easy	3,500-4,050	10 miles
Three Creek Butte	Moderate	4,500-5,550	11.5 miles
Tumalo Reservoir	Easy	3,500-3,600	Varies

Bull Spring Loop

Trailhead: Start at the parking area at the end of Tumalo Reservoir Road

Length: 7 miles round trip

Elevation: 3,500 to 3,800 feet

Difficulty: Easy

Footing: Suitable for barefoot horses

Season: Nearly year-round

Permits: None

Facilities: Plenty of trailer parking. Stock water is available on the trail.

Highlights: This is nearly everyone's favorite ride at Skyline Forest. It's an easy jaunt, mostly on single-track trails, and much of the ride is beside pretty little Bull Creek. Of the many ways you can get to Bull Spring, this route is probably the easiest to follow.

The Ride: From the parking area at the end of Tumalo Reservoir Road, head south and ride across the bridge over the irrigation canal.

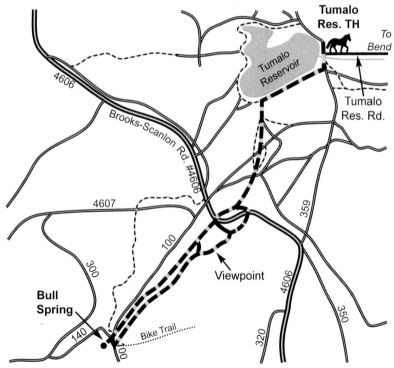

Turn right and ride down the hill toward the reservoir. As you ride along the southern edge of the reservoir, you'll see a large sagebrush-covered field on your left. At the end of the sagebrush field, about 0.7 mile from the trailhead, veer left and pick up the trail that runs up the hill. At the top of the hill, take the trail heading south, ignoring the less-distinct trails that go off to either side. This trail will take you to the Brooks-Scanlon Road (Road 4606) about 1.2 miles from the reservoir. Cross Road 4606 and pick up the trail again on the other side. The trail now runs beside Bull Creek, which is dry by the time it reaches this area. But notice all the aspen here--the creek is flowing underground. In another 1.3 miles you'll reach Bull Spring, a great spot for a picnic. To make a loop back, retrace your steps to Road 100, the dirt road you crossed as you entered the Bull Spring area. Turn right on it, cross Bull Creek, and almost immediately make a hard left (a bike trail also veers gently left here) onto the trail back along the south side of the creek. In 1.1 mile the trail splits. If you go left you'll loop back to the trail you rode in on. If you go right, you'll ride up onto the rimrock and have some nice mountain views. In 0.4 mile the trail splits again. The left trail returns you to the Brooks-Scanlon Road where you originally crossed it, and the right trail crosses the Brooks-Scanlon road farther east. If you choose the latter route, just veer left at any trail junction after crossing Road 4606 and you'll soon be back on the trail you rode out on.

Near Bull Spring, Veronica takes
Harmony to the creek for a drink.

Central Skyline

Trailhead:	Start at the intersection of Road 4606 and Road CP-5
Length:	Varies by route taken
Elevation:	3,600 to 4,100 feet
Difficulty:	Easy, but a Sisters Ranger District map and a GPS may come in handy for finding your way
Footing:	Suitable for barefoot horses
Season:	Nearly year-round
Permits:	None
Facilities:	This isn't actually a trailhead, just a spot wide enough to turn a couple of trailers around and park. No stock water on the trail.

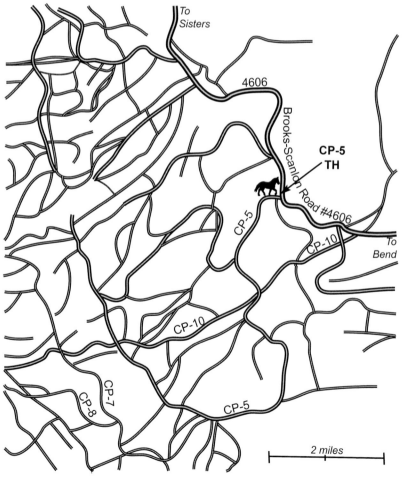

*Whitney and Debbie chat as they ride Dixie and Cowboy along
a forest road in the central Skyline Forest.*

Highlights: There are no real "destinations" in the central portion of
Skyline Forest -- no creeks or springs or impressive viewpoints. But
there are miles and miles of forest roads to ride and plenty of hills and
valleys to explore. This area was once owned by Crown Pacific Part-
ners, a timber company that logged portions of what is now known as
Skyline Forest, so you'll be riding on old logging roads. (The major
road names start with "CP" for Crown Pacific.) The only drawback to
riding here is that it's a 9-mile drive on a gravel road to get to the trailhead.

Finding the CP-5 Trailhead: From Bend, take Newport Avenue west
for 1.1 mile, then at the 3rd traffic circle veer right on Shevlin Park Rd.
Drive 3.1 miles, passing the entrance to Shevlin Park, and turn left on
Bull Springs Road. In 0.5 mile, turn right on a gravel road, just before
the entrance to Taylor Northwest. You're now on Road 4606. Follow
it for 9 miles, then turn around and park at Road CP-5.

The Ride: From your parking spot at the intersection of Road 4606
and CP-5, you can create a variety of loops using the logging roads in
the area. The "CP" roads are very lightly graveled, but the other roads
are all just dirt two-tracks. Have fun exploring!

Skyline Gorge Loop

Trailhead: Start at the parking area at the end of Tumalo Reservoir Road

Length: 11 miles round trip

Elevation: 3,500 to 4,000 feet

Difficulty: Moderate -- easy riding, but navigation skills, a Sisters Ranger District map, and a GPS will come in handy

Footing: Suitable for barefoot horses

Season: Nearly year-round

Permits: None

Facilities: Plenty of trailer parking. Stock water is available on the trail.

Highlights: Skyline Gorge is an amazing destination that highlights the powerful impact of erosion. For many years the old Columbia Southern Canal (now dry) brought water from Tumalo Creek to Tumalo Reservoir. In the Gorge section the old canal goes from 3 feet deep to about 75 feet deep in the course of a few hundred yards. And just downstream from the Gorge are the remains of the historic Pine Tree Mill.

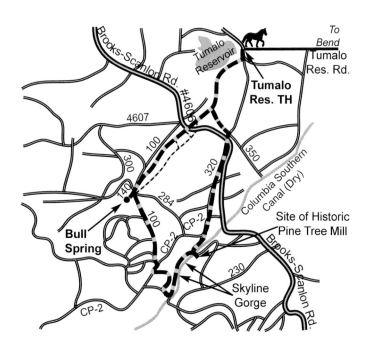

The old Columbia-Southern canal carved a surprisingly deep gorge not far from the historic Pine Tree Mill.

The Ride: Follow the directions to Bull Spring on the Bull Spring ride pages.   After watering your horse near the spring, turn right on Road 100, the dirt road you crossed as you entered the Bull Spring area. Follow it for 1.2 miles, until it reaches a T-intersection with Road CP-2. (Look for the road sign on a tree across the road.) Turn right on Road CP-2 and ride 0.1 mile, then turn on the first dirt road that goes off to the left. When it T-bones another road after 0.5 mile, turn left and continue 0.1 mile to the old Columbia Southern canal (now dry). Turn left and follow the single track trail that runs beside the canal. In 0.7 mile you'll reach the Skyline Gorge segment of the canal, where erosion formed a deep ravine. About 0.2 mile after the gorge ends, the trail enters a more open area, with a big grassy depression across the canal. This is the site of the old Pine Tree Mill, and the grassy depression was the mill's log pond. Continue riding beside the canal to see the remains of the mill's foundations, burner, and other equipment. After about 0.1 mile, loop back to the mill pond area and turn right on a dirt road that will take you to Road CP-2. Turn right on Road CP-2 and follow it 0.3 mile to where it dog-legs to the right, and veer left on dirt Road 320 (unsigned). After 1.2 miles Road 320 reaches the gravel Brooks-Scanlon Road. Cross the Brooks-Scanlon Road and in 200 feet turn left at the next junction. Follow this road 0.6 mile and it will intersect with the single-track trail you took from the reservoir. Veer right and follow the trail back to the trailhead.

Snag Spring

Trailhead: Start at the parking area at the end of Tumalo Reservoir Road

Length: 10 miles round trip

Elevation: 3,500 to 4,050 feet

Difficulty: Easy

Footing: Suitable for barefoot horses

Season: Nearly year-round

Permits: None

Facilities: Plenty of trailer parking. Stock water is available on the trail.

Highlights: Once you're familiar with the trail to Bull Spring, you may start wondering what else is nearby. It turns out there's another spring about a mile farther up the drainage. Snag Spring seeps rather than flows, and the wild flowers around it in early summer are lovely.

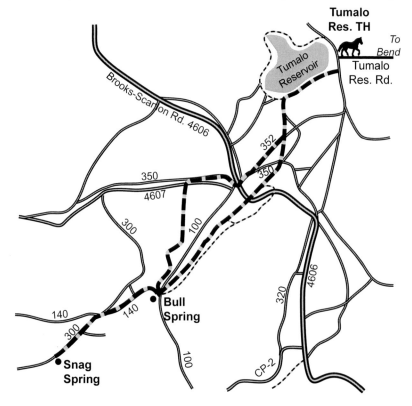

It can be a mosquito nursery in spring, though, so be sure to spray yourself and your horse.

The Ride: Take your favorite route to Bull Spring. (See the Bull Spring Loop pages for more information.) Once you've arrived at Bull Spring, pick up the dirt road that departs on the north side of the spring area. This is Road 140. It will take you around a knoll, and in 0.2 mile a road goes off to the right. Stay straight, and the road you are on will soon become a single-track. In 0.4 mile you'll reach Road 300. Turn left on Road 300 and follow it for 0.6 mile, ignoring the road that goes off to the left in 0.4 mile. Just before you reach Snag Spring you'll encounter dense aspen thickets on both sides of the road. Go past them and tie your horses, then explore on foot the fragile area around the spring's trickling stream and tiny pond. The surrounding vegetation is very thick and green. The spring is on the left side of the road, though it obviously seeps underground on both sides of the road. Return to Bull Spring. You can make a loop back to the trailhead by picking up the single-track that begins about 50 feet east of where Road 140 enters the Bull Spring area. Follow the trail 2 miles to where it reaches the wide gravel Road 4606, cross the road, and bushwhack 200 feet straight ahead to Road 350 and turn right on it. In another 0.2 mile, veer left on Road 352 and continue 0.4 mile, then turn left on the single-track trail that will take you back to the trailhead.

Veronica rides Harmony through the aspens near Snag Spring.

Three Creek Butte

Trailhead: Start at the Upper Three Creek Nordic Parking area

Length: 11.5 miles round trip

Elevation: 4,500 to 5,550 feet

Difficulty: Moderate -- easy riding, but navigation skills, a Sisters Ranger District map, and a GPS will come in handy

Footing: Hoof protection recommended

Season: May through October

Permits: Northwest Forest Pass required

Facilities: Parking for many trailers. Stock water is available on the trail.

Highlights: Forest roads take you to Three Creek Butte, where from the summit you'll have a 360-degree view of the Three Sisters, Broken Top, Tam McArthur Rim, Bend, Redmond, Sisters, and all the outlying buttes. On a clear day you can even see Mt. Hood.

Finding the Upper Three Creek Sno-Park: From Sisters, drive south on Elm Street, which becomes Three Creek Road and Road 16. Drive 11 miles and turn left into the Upper Three Creek Sno-Park.

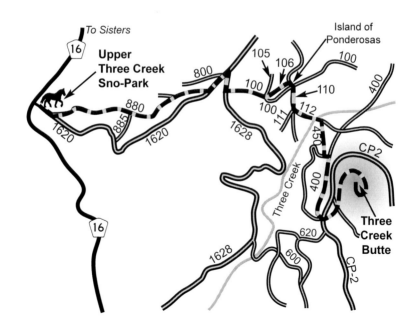

The Ride: At the south end of the parking area, turn left on paved Road 1620. In 0.2 mile the pavement ends. Immediately veer left on Road 880. Follow it 1.7 miles and veer left on Road 1620, a red cinder road. Continue 0.2 mile and turn right on Road 1628, also a red cinder road. In 0.2 mile, turn left on Road 100. After 0.4 mile, Road 100 veers to the right. Stay to the left and you'll be on Road 106. In 0.3 mile you'll reach a Y-junction with an island of Ponderosas in the middle. Turn right, and in a short distance you'll come to another junction. Take the road on the right, Road 110, and in 0.2 mile turn left on Road 112. Follow it 0.3 mile. As you approach Three Creek, a road goes to the right and appears to cross the creek. Don't follow it. Stay to the left for another 100 yards, then veer right on an indistinct trail to reach a much better crossing spot. Cross Three Creek, and in 200 yards turn right at the first dirt road, Road 450. Ride uphill 0.4 mile, jog to the left a short distance, then turn right on Road 400. Follow it uphill 0.6 mile, cross gravel Road CP-2 (marked with a small wooden sign on a tree to your right) and ride straight ahead 0.2 mile on an unsigned road toward Three Creek Butte. Take the gravel road that climbs the left side of the butte. It winds all the way around the butte, offering nice views along the way and stupendous views from the summit. To return to the trailhead, retrace your steps.

Gerry and Don with their mules Oliver and Elmer on the summit of Three Creek Butte. Middle and North Sister are behind them.

Tumalo Reservoir

Trailhead: Start at the parking area at the end of Tumalo Reservoir Road

Length: Varies by route taken

Elevation: 3,500 to 3,600 feet

Difficulty: Easy

Footing: Suitable for barefoot horses

Season: Nearly year-round

Permits: None

Facilities: Plenty of trailer parking Stock water is available near the reservoir during irrigation season.

Highlights: Most of the riding near Tumalo Reservoir isn't actually on Skyline Forest, which is located on the west side of the Brooks-Scanlon Road. But since Skyline Forest and the area around the reservoir share the same trailhead we're including the reservoir-area trails in this chapter.

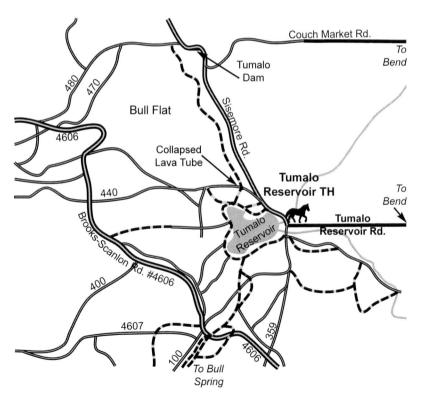

You can often ride at the Reservoir in the winter,
when the views of the snow-capped mountains are splendid.

The Ride: From the parking lot at the end of Tumalo Reservoir Road, you can ride south or west to get to forested trails, or north to get to the open sage-covered Bull Flat. If you ride out onto Bull Flat, you'll be in the area that was originally supposed to be filled with water by Tumalo Reservoir. Look to the north end of the flat to see the dam that was built in the early 1900s. When they began filling the reservoir, however, the weight of the stored water collapsed an underlying lava tube and most of the water drained away. Reportedly, you could hear the sucking sound for miles. You can see the collapsed lava tube on the north side of Road 440, near the east end of the flat. If you ride into the forest to the south of the trailhead or on the northwest side of Bull Flat you'll find plenty of dirt roads and single-track trails to explore. So saddle up and go explore the pleasant, easy riding around Tumalo Reservoir.

When you're young and you fall off a horse, you may break something. When you're my age and you fall off, you splatter.

Roy Rogers

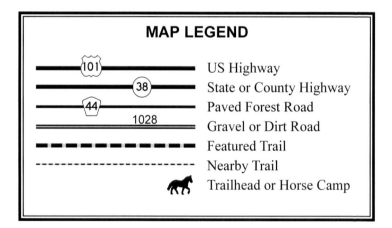

MAP LEGEND

101	US Highway
38	State or County Highway
44	Paved Forest Road
1028	Gravel or Dirt Road
▬ ▬ ▬ ▬ ▬	Featured Trail
- - - - - - - - - -	Nearby Trail
🐎	Trailhead or Horse Camp

Swamp Wells/ Horse Butte
Swamp Wells Horse Camp
Deschutes National Forest

The Swamp Wells/Horse Butte trail system is huge, with well over 70 miles of trails. Horse Butte trailhead is located on the southeast edge of Bend, and Swamp Wells Horse Camp is about 14 miles south. Three trails run from Horse Butte to Swamp Wells, and one of these trails continues from Swamp Wells to connect with the trail network at Newberry Crater. Tie trails connect these long north-south trails, creating several 7-12 mile loops, all marked with gray diamonds. You can start your rides at Horse Butte trailhead, Swamp Wells Horse Camp, Boyd Cave, the junction of Roads 9710 and 9735, or near Bessie Butte. Most of the trails are forested with ponderosa and lodge-

pole pine, and the gently rolling terrain is dotted with volcanic cinder buttes, basalt outcroppings, and lava caves. The lower-elevation trails near Bend are accessible nearly year round. This fascinating area is worth exploring, especially in the shoulder seasons when the high-elevation trails are inaccessible.

Diana and Mo check out the gaping mouth of Charcoal Cave.

Getting to the Trailheads

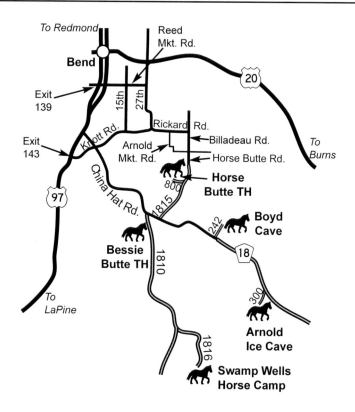

Swamp Wells/Horse Butte Trails

Trail	Difficulty	Elevation	Round Trip
Arnold Ice Cave Loop	Moderate	4,200-4,800	11.5 miles
Bessie Butte	Moderate	4,000-4,800	7 miles
Coyote Trail Loop	Moderate	4,300-5,000	8 miles
Fuzztail Butte Loop	Moderate	5,300-5,750	4.5 miles
Kelsey Butte	Moderate	4,200-5,000	12-18 miles
Lava Cast Forest	Moderate	5,400-5,800	16 miles
Newberry Crater	Moderate	5,700-7,600	11.5-21 miles
Skeleton Cave Loop	Easy	3,900-4,300	11.5 miles
Swamp Wells/Arnold Lp.	Moderate	4,500-5,750	13 miles
Swamp Wells/Coyote Lp.	Moderate	4,800-5,500	13 miles

Swamp Wells Horse Camp

Directions: From Bend, drive south on Hwy. 97 and take Exit 143 (Baker Rd./Knott Rd.) Turn left on Knott Road and continue 1.4 miles. Turn right on China Hat Road and go 4.6 miles, then turn right on Road 1810. After 5.7 miles, turn left on Road 1816 and follow the signs 2.7 miles to the horse camp.

Elevation: 5,400 feet

Campsites: 5 sites, each with 4-horse metal corrals. All sites are level, gravelled, and back-in. Two sites have room for two vehicles. There are no gates on the corrals.

Facilities: Swamp Wells has a vault toilet, manure bin, stock water from a small guzzler in spring and early summer, and a handicapped-accessible mounting ramp. All sites have fire pits and picnic tables. No potable water. The day-use area holds 10+ trailers. Contact the Forest Service to determine stock water availability.

Permits: None

Season: May through October

Contact: Bend/Ft. Rock Ranger District: 541-383-5300, www.fs.usda.gov/ centraloregon, then click on "Recreation," "Horse Riding and Camping"

Kenna sets up camp at Swamp Wells
while Gator snoozes in the corral.

Arnold Ice Cave Loop

Trailhead: Start at Boyd Cave parking area
Length: 11.5 miles round trip
Elevation: 4,200 to 4,800 feet
Difficulty: Moderate
Footing: Hoof protection recommended
Season: Early spring through late fall
Permits: None
Facilities: Parking for 4-5 trailers at Boyd Cave parking area. No stock water on the trail.

Highlights: This loop trail takes you to Arnold Ice Cave (which contains ice year round) and Charcoal Cave. There are interesting rock outcroppings along the way, and you can make a nice loop using forest roads to connect to the Coyote Trail for the return leg. The entire route is marked with gray diamonds.

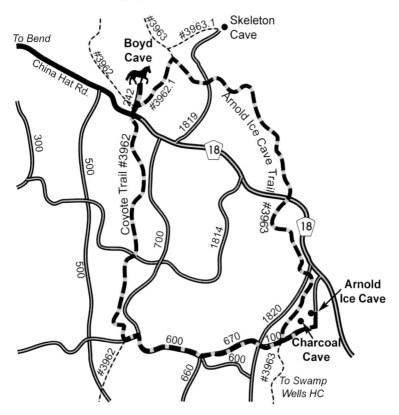

Finding Boyd Cave Parking Area: From Bend, drive south on Hwy. 97 and take Exit 143 (Baker Rd./Knott Rd.) Turn left on Knott Road and drive 1.3 miles. Turn right on China Hat Road and continue 8.2 miles, then turn left on Road 242. The parking loop at Boyd Cave is in 0.2 mile.

The Ride: Ride on Road 242 back toward China Hat Road. Just before you reach China Hat Road, turn left on Trail #3962.1 and follow it 0.9 mile to the junction with the Arnold Ice Cave Trail #3963. Turn right toward Swamp Wells Horse Camp. In 2.5 miles the trail crosses China Hat Road, and 1.2 miles after that it crosses Road 1820, a red cinder road. Continue 0.7 mile to the signed junction of Trail #3963 and Road 100. Turn left on Road 100 and ride 0.5 mile, past Charcoal Cave to Arnold Ice Cave. Once you've checked out the caves and nearby collapsed lava tubes, return to the junction and follow Road 100 to red cinder Road 1820, where you'll see boulders across the entrance to the dirt road you're on. Cross Road 1820 and pick up Road 670 directly across it. Ride 0.9 mile, following the gray diamonds, and veer right on Road 600. The road climbs a rocky ridge (be sure to look behind you at the vistas), then descends to an area where trees were planted in rows after a fire. About 1.1 miles after turning onto Road 600, the wire fence you've been riding beside makes a corner. Turn left here, and in 0.1 mile turn right on Coyote Trail #3962. Follow Trail #3962 for 3 miles back to Boyd Cave.

Linda and Beamer peer down into Arnold Ice Cave while on an early spring ride.

Bessie Butte

Trailhead: Start at the Horse Butte trailhead

Length: 7 miles round trip

Elevation: 4,000 to 4,800 feet

Difficulty: Moderate (steep climb to top of butte)

Footing: Suitable for barefoot horses

Season: Early spring through late fall

Permits: None

Facilities: Parking for 6-8 trailers at Horse Butte trailhead. No stock water on the trail.

Highlights: This ride travels through pretty Ponderosa forest, then through a burned area, then steeply uphill 500 feet to the top of Bessie Butte. The 360-degree panorama from the summit is fabulous.

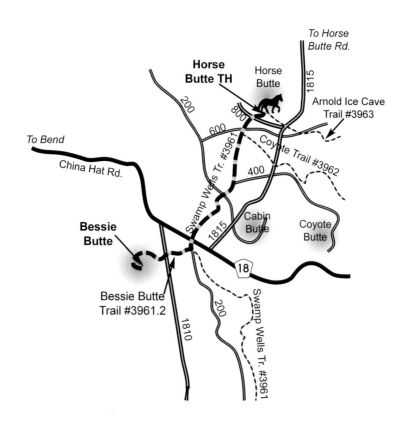

Debbie on Cowboy, Lydia on Shadow, and Teresa on Kodie,
enjoying the 360-degree view from the top of Bessie Butte.

Finding Horse Butte Trailhead: From Bend, drive south on Hwy. 97 and take Exit 139 at Reed Market Road. Turn left and follow Reed Market Road 2.3 miles. Turn right on 27th St., and in 2 miles turn left on Rickard Road. Continue 1.8 miles and turn right on Billadeau Rd. After 1 mile Billadeau becomes Horse Butte Rd., and after another mile it turns to gravel and becomes Road 1815. Drive 0.5 mile farther, then turn right on Road 800 and continue 0.3 mile to the trailhead.

The Ride: Pick up the Swamp Wells Trail #3961 on the south side of the parking area. In 0.5 mile you'll reach a junction with the Coyote Trail #3962. Stay to the right and continue 1.8 miles to paved China Hat Road. Cross it, and in about 100 feet turn right on the Bessie Butte Trail #3961.2. You will shortly enter an area burned in 2003's 18 Fire, which was named after the Forest Service's road number for China Hat Road. In 0.4 mile you'll cross gravel Road 1810 and begin climbing the butte. The 18 Fire killed a lot of trees, but it certainly opened up some impressive vistas from the flanks of Bessie Butte. The trail gains 500 feet in 0.7 mile, but the expansive views from the summit are worth the climb.

Coyote Trail Loop

Trailhead: Start at the Boyd Cave parking area
Length: 8 miles round trip
Elevation: 4,300 to 5,000 feet
Difficulty: Moderate
Footing: Hoof protection recommended
Season: Early spring through late fall
Permits: None
Facilities: Parking for 3-5 trailers. No stock water on the trail.

Highlights: This pleasant trail is rideable almost year-round. Most of the route is forested, but there are a couple of spots where you'll find nice views to the east. The trail can be very dusty in summer.

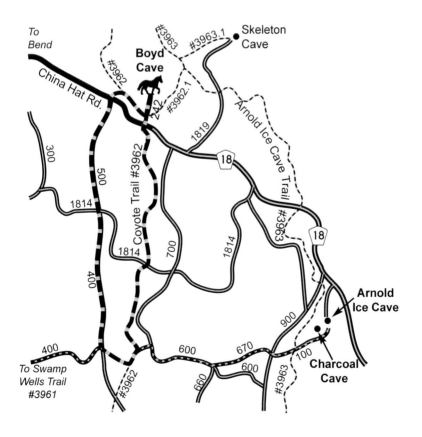

Debbie on Cowboy, Whitney on Dixie, and Connie on Diamond,
enjoying a beautiful day on the Coyote Loop Trail.

Finding Boyd Cave Parking Area: From Bend, drive south on Hwy. 97 and take Exit 143 (Baker Rd./Knott Rd.) Turn left on Knott Road and drive 1.3 miles. Turn right on China Hat Road and continue 8.2 miles, then turn left on Road 242. The parking loop at Boyd Cave is in 0.2 miles.

The Ride: Ride south on Road 242, cross China Hat Road, and pick up the Coyote Trail #3962. The trail starts out on a dirt road, then veers left and becomes a single-track. About 1.8 mile after crossing China Hat Road, the trail crosses dirt Road 1814 and continues straight ahead. In another 1.2 miles the tie trail that leads toward Arnold Ice Cave goes off to the left. Stay to the right and continue 0.3 mile to the junction with the tie trail that goes right toward the Swamp Wells Trail #3961. Turn right and ride 0.5 mile to dirt Road 400, then turn right again and follow Road 400 for 3.7 miles back to China Hat Road. (It becomes Road 500 on the north side of Road 1814.) Cross China Hat and ride cross-country to Trail #3962, then turn right and follow the trail back to the parking area.

Fuzztail Butte Loop

Trailhead: Start at Swamp Wells Horse Camp

Length: 4.5 miles round trip

Elevation: 5,300 to 5,750 feet

Difficulty: Moderate, but the trail to the summit of Fuzztail Butte is steep, rocky, and somewhat overgrown

Footing: Hoof protection recommended

Season: Late spring through fall

Permits: None

Facilities: Toilet, manure bin, plenty of trailer parking, and stock water through early summer at the horse camp. No stock water on the trail.

Highlights: This is a short, pleasant loop trail that features a side trip to the top of Fuzztail Butte. The Fuzztail Butte trail is quite steep,

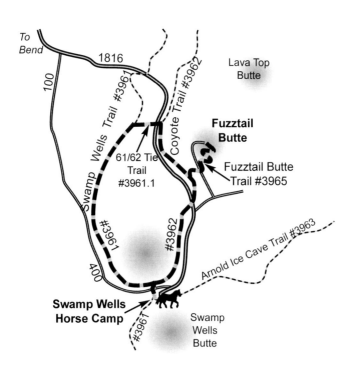

gaining 300 feet of elevation in 0.5 mile, but riders who persevere will be rewarded with a 360-degree view from the summit.

The Ride: At the horse camp, pick up the trail that runs behind the corrals and follow it north (to the right if you are standing in the campground road facing your campsite). At the junction in 0.2 mile, veer right on the Coyote Trail #3962. In 0.6 mile the trail crosses Road 1816, and 0.2 mile later the Fuzztail Butte Trail #3965 goes to the right. Follow it, and in 0.2 mile it crosses the road to the top of the butte. You can either turn left on the road and take it to the top (easier), or stay on the trail and take the switchbacks (more challenging). After enjoying the tremendous views, return to the Coyote Trail #3962 and turn right. In 0.6 mile you'll reach the 61/62 Tie Trail #3961.1, which will take you to the Swamp Wells Trail. Turn left here, and in 0.2 mile turn left on the Swamp Wells Trail #3961. Follow it 1.8 miles back to the horse camp.

Lydia and Shadow take in the view
from the summit of Fuzztail Butte.

Kelsey Butte

Trailhead: Start at Horse Butte trailhead or at an unofficial dirt turnout on the left side of China Hat Road 0.1 mile before Road 1810

Length: 12 miles round trip from the unofficial parking spot, or 18 miles round trip from Horse Butte trailhead

Elevation: 4,200 to 5,000 feet

Difficulty: Moderate

Footing: Suitable for barefoot horses

Season: Early spring through late fall

Permits: None

Facilities: Parking for 2-3 trailers at the unofficial dirt turnout, or for 6-8 trailers at Horse Butte trailhead. No stock water on the trail.

Highlights: Be sure to ride this trail on a clear day, because the 180-degree views from the flank of Kelsey Butte are panoramic. You'll see

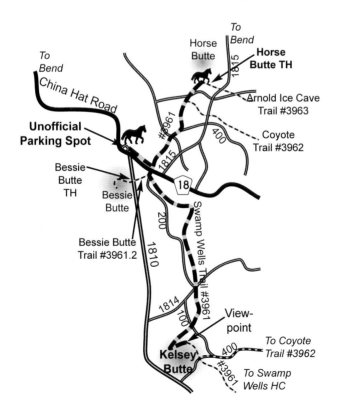

all of the Cascades from Mt. Hood through Broken Top, plus views to the north and east. The open ponderosa forest on the way to the butte is very pretty.

Finding the Unofficial Parking Spot: From Bend, drive south on Hwy. 97 and take Exit 143 (Baker Rd./Knott Rd.) Turn left on Knott Road and continue 1.4 miles. Turn right on China Hat Road and go 4.5 miles. Turn left into a dirt pullout that encircles 3 ponderosas on the left side of China Hat Road, about 0.1 mile before you reach Road 1810.

The Ride: <u>From Horse Butte trailhead</u>, follow the directions on the pages for the Bessie Butte ride, but don't turn right on the Bessie Butte Trail #3961.2 after crossing China Hat Road. <u>From the unofficial parking spot</u>, ride cross-country beside China Hat Road for 0.5 mile, then turn right on the Swamp Wells Trail #3961. The trail crosses China Hat Road and almost immediately comes to the junction with the Bessie Butte Trail. <u>All</u>, stay to the left on the Swamp Wells Trail. For the next 5 miles the trail winds through open forest and gently rolling terrain, then it begins climbing Kelsey Butte through young ponderosas that were planted in rows after a forest fire. The trail then angles up the flank of Kelsey Butte, taking you above the tree line and providing expansive views. Enjoy the sights, then retrace your steps to return to the trailhead.

Gillian rides Allegro on the flank of Kelsey Butte.
The Cascades are arrayed across the horizon behind them.

Lava Cast Forest

Trailhead: Start at Swamp Wells Horse Camp

Length: 16 miles round trip

Elevation: 5,400 to 5,800 feet

Difficulty: Moderate -- easy riding, but navigation skills, a Ft. Rock Ranger District map, and a GPS will be helpful

Footing: Hoof protection recommended

Season: Late spring through fall

Permits: None

Facilities: Toilet, manure bin, plenty of trailer parking, and stock water through early summer at the horse camp.   No stock water on the trail.

Highlights: On a late spring camping trip to Swamp Wells, we discovered that we couldn't ride very far south on Trail #61 (toward North Paulina Peak) because of low-elevation snow. Instead we rode forest roads westward to Lava Cast Forest to see the "casts" made when molten lava flowing from Newberry Crater encased the trees that were standing at the time. The route goes through interesting forest and past huge lava flows and cinder buttes. Once you arrive at Lava Cast Forest, tie your horse in the trees and take the short and fascinating hike to see the lava casts.

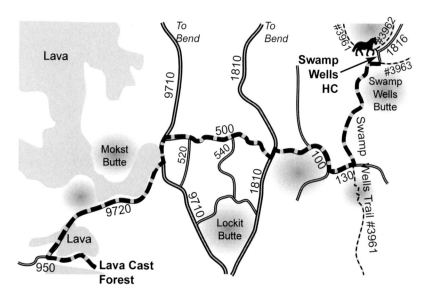

The Ride: On the southeast edge of the horse camp, pick up Swamp Wells Trail #3961 southbound (toward North Paulina Peak). Ride it 1.7 miles to Road 130 (the first forest road you come to), and turn right. Follow Road 130, which is quite rocky, for 0.4 mile. At the base of an unnamed butte it comes to a T-intersection with Road 100. Turn right and follow Road 100 as it circles the butte. After 1.0 mile, turn left on gray-cinder Road 1810. In 0.1 mile, turn right on dirt Road 500, which is clearly signed. Follow it 1.2 miles, enjoying the occasional views of the Cascades, and turn left on gray cinder Road 9710. Follow it only 0.3 mile and turn right on the well-signed dirt Road 9720. After a short distance you'll encounter a large lava flow on your right, then later you'll come to another lava flow on your left. Continue 2.2 miles along Road 9720 to the junction with a well-traveled red cinder road that has a sign directing you to Lava Cast Forest. Turn left here and follow Road 950 (which can be pretty busy on weekends) for 0.7 mile to the parking area for Lava Cast Forest. Tie your horses in the trees and take the 1-mile walk through the impressive Lava Cast Forest, then mount up and retrace your steps back to the horse camp.

Lydia rides Shadow along a large lava flow beside Road 9720,
on the way to the Lava Cast Forest.

Newberry Crater

Trailhead: Start at Swamp Wells Horse Camp or at the junction of Roads 9710 and 9735

Length: 21 miles round trip from Swamp Wells Horse Camp, or 11.5 miles round trip from the Road 9710 / 9735 junction

Elevation: 5,700 to 7,600 feet from Swamp Wells, or 6,000 to 7,600 feet from the Road 9710 / 9735 junction

Difficulty: Moderate

Footing: Hoof protection recommended

Season: Summer through fall

Permits: None

Facilities: Toilet, manure bin, plenty of trailer parking, and stock water through early summer at the horse camp. Parking for one trailer at the 9710 / 9735 junction. No stock water on the trail.

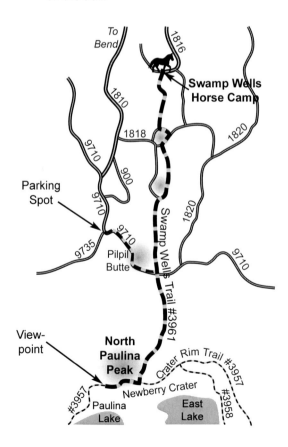

Highlights: This delightful trail goes through mostly-lodgepole forest, over and around cinder buttes, and past a lava flow to the Crater Rim Trail at Newberry Crater. The trail is very lightly used because it is so long, but you can drive part of the way there and still enjoy the most scenic parts of the trail.

Finding the Road 9710 / 9735 Parking Spot: From Bend, drive south on Hwy. 97. Take Exit 143 (Baker Rd./Knott Rd.) and turn left on Knott Road. In 1.4 miles, turn right on China Hat Road. Continue 4.6 miles, then turn right on Road 1810. When the road ends in 10.9 miles, turn left on Road 9710. In 1.4 miles, Road 9735 comes in on the right. Turn around here and park beside the road.

The Ride: From Swamp Wells Horse Camp, on the southeast side of camp, pick up the Swamp Wells Trail #3961. In 2.6 miles you'll ride around a cinder butte, crossing cinder Road 1818. About 1.5 miles later you'll skirt another cinder butte, and 2.6 miles after that you'll reach dirt Road 9710. From the Road 9710 / 9735 junction, ride eastward on Road 9710 for 2.2 miles and turn right on the Swamp Wells Trail #3961 at the sign. All: In 4.5 miles the trail goes through a cinder canyon, crosses a pumice plain and runs along a lava flow, and 1.3 miles after that it comes out at the Crater Rim Trail #3957 at Newberry Crater. To reach an excellent viewpoint, turn right on the Crater Rim Trail and ride 0.5 mile farther.

Mona rides Roi along the trail to the rim of Newberry Crater.

Skeleton Cave Loop

Trailhead: Start at Horse Butte trailhead
Length: 11.5 miles round trip
Elevation: 3,900 to 4,300 feet
Difficulty: Easy
Footing: Suitable for barefoot horses
Season: Nearly year-round
Permits: None
Facilities: Parking for 6-8 trailers at Horse Butte trailhead. No stock water on the trail.

Highlights: This is an easy, low-elevation loop ride that goes through Ponderosa forest, past several large cinder buttes, and across broad expanses of grass and rabbitbrush punctuated with the charred remains of trees torched by the Skeleton Fire in 1996. Wildflowers can be plentiful in spring. This trail is popular with mountain bike riders.

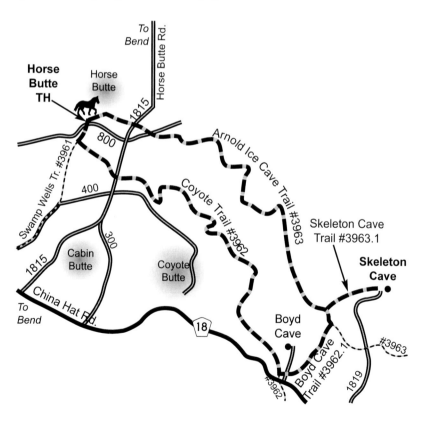

Finding Horse Butte Trailhead: From Bend, drive south on Hwy. 97 and take Exit 139 at Reed Market Road. Turn left and follow Reed Market Road 2.3 miles. Turn right on 27th St., and in 2 miles turn left on Rickard Road. Continue 1.8 miles and turn right on Billadeau Rd. After 1 mile Billadeau becomes Horse Butte Rd., and after another mile it turns to gravel and becomes Road 1815. Drive 0.5 mile farther, then turn right on Road 800 and continue 0.3 mile to the trailhead.

The Ride: Pick up Arnold Ice Cave Trail #3963 on the east side of the parking area. In the first mile, several user-created trails depart from Trail #3963, so follow the gray diamonds that mark all of the trails in the Swamp Wells system. After 4.3 miles you'll reach a junction where the trail crosses a dirt road and the Skeleton Cave Trail #3963.1 goes off at a hard left. Follow Trail #3963.1 and in 0.7 mile you'll reach Skeleton Cave, situated in a grove of large pines. This is a nice lunch spot. Note that Skeleton Cave is closed to the public to protect the cave from vandalism and to protect the habitat for the bats that hibernate here. Follow Trail #3963.1 back to Trail #3963 and turn left, then in 0.1 mile turn right on Boyd Cave Trail #3962.1. Follow it 0.8 mile, then veer right on the Coyote Trail #3962. Continue 4.2 miles and turn right on the Swamp Wells Trail #3961. In 0.5 mile you'll arrive back at the trailhead.

*Whitney on Dixie and Debbie on Split,
gazing into the mouth of Skeleton Cave.*

Swamp Wells/Arnold Cave Loop

Trailhead: Start at Swamp Wells Horse Camp or at the Arnold Ice Cave parking area

Length: 13 miles round trip

Elevation: 4,500 to 5,750 feet

Difficulty: Moderate

Footing: Suitable for barefoot horses

Season: Late spring through fall

Permits: None

Facilities: Toilet, manure bin, plenty of trailer parking, and stock water through early summer at the horse camp. Parking for 2-3 trailers at Arnold Ice Cave, depending on the number of hiker cars there. No stock water on the trail.

Highlights: This delightful forest trail meanders between Swamp Wells and Arnold Ice Cave, using dirt roads to connect Trails #3963 and #3962 to make a loop.

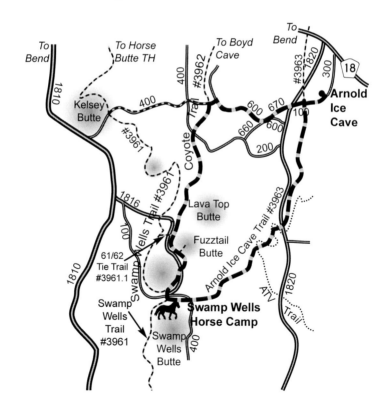

Lydia rides Shadow along the Arnold Ice Cave Trail between Swamp Wells and Arnold Ice Cave.

Finding Arnold Ice Cave Parking Area: Head south of Bend on Hwy. 97. Take Exit 143 (Baker Rd./Knott Rd.) Turn left on Knott Road and drive 1.3 miles. Turn right on China Hat Road (Road 18) and continue 11.5 miles, then turn right on Road 300. The parking area is at the end of the road in 0.5 mile.

The Ride: From Swamp Wells, pick up the Arnold Ice Cave Trail #3963 on the southeast edge of the horse camp. In 3.2 miles you'll cross Road 1820 next to a cattle guard and go through a fence. In this general area you'll cross an ATV trail several times, and you'll notice a previously-burned area to the right that is now covered with young ponderosas. After 2.7 more miles you'll reach the signed junction with Road 100. Turn right to reach Arnold Ice Cave in 0.5 mile. From Arnold Ice Cave, ride up the hill between the two collapsed lava tubes next to the parking area and follow the gray diamonds on the trees to Arnold Ice Cave Trail #3963. All, head west on dirt Road 100 and in 0.2 mile you'll reach a junction. Turn right toward the boulders that are blocking the road, go between them, and cross red-cinder Road 1820. Jog slightly left and pick up dirt Road 670, which goes straight ahead. Follow the gray diamonds on the trees, and in about 0.2 mile veer right on Road 600. In another 1.6 miles you'll notice that the trees have been planted in rows. There is a fence on your left, and in 0.3 miles the fence ends. Turn left on the dirt road just past the end of the fence and follow it 0.2 mile, then turn left on the Coyote Trail #3962. In 3 miles you'll pass the 61/62 Tie Trail #3961.1, then the Fuzztail Butte Trail #3965, and 0.8 mile later you'll arrive at Swamp Wells. If you started at Arnold Ice Cave, follow the directions above to return to the parking area.

Swamp Wells/Coyote Loop

Trailhead: Start at Swamp Wells Horse Camp

Length: 13 miles round trip

Elevation: 4,800 to 5,500 feet

Difficulty: Moderate

Footing: Suitable for barefoot horses

Season: Late spring through fall

Permits: None

Facilities: Toilet, manure bin, plenty of trailer parking, and stock water through early summer at the horse camp. No stock water on the trail.

Highlights: This pleasant loop trail showcases interesting basalt outcroppings and open ponderosa and lodgepole forest.

The Ride: From Swamp Wells Horse Camp, pick up the trail that runs behind the corrals and follow it north (to the right if you are standing

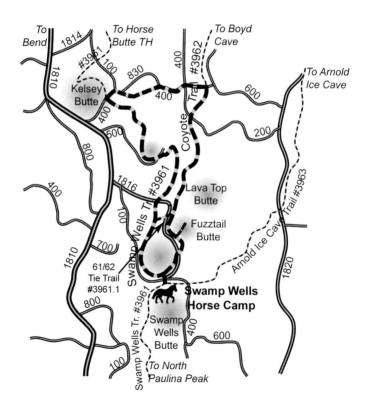

in the campground road facing your campsite). At the junction in 0.2 mile, veer right on the Coyote Trail #3962. In 0.6 mile the trail crosses Road 1816, and 0.2 mile later the Fuzztail Butte Trail #3965 goes to the right. Stay to the left, and in 0.7 mile the 61/62 Tie Trail #3961.1 goes off to the left. In another 2.2 miles, you'll go through a gate in a fence, and 0.5 mile after that you'll reach the double track Road 400. Turn left at the sign toward Swamp Wells Trail #3961, and stay on Road 400 (marked with gray diamonds) for 2.3 miles. (Watch out-- Road 400 makes a couple of 90-degree turns when it meets other roads.) After an uphill stretch you'll reach the base of Kelsey Butte, and Road 400 makes a 90-degree turn to the left. Go left and in about 0.1 mile the Swamp Wells Trail #3961 crosses Road 400. Turn left on Trail #3961 and follow it 1.7 miles to the flank of an unnamed butte. As you circle the butte you'll see a trail that crosses Trail #3961 and appears to head toward the top of the butte. This isn't actually a trail, it's the boundary of a cutting area. Stay on Trail #3961 and in 1.5 miles you'll ride through an interesting grotto that lies between two rock outcroppings. About 0.5 mile after that you'll cross red cinder Road 1816 and in 0.6 mile the 61/62 Tie Trail goes off to the left. Then you'll begin to circle the butte just north of the horse camp, and in 1.8 miles you'll arrive back at the horse camp.

Mark and Janice ride Sonny and Baron through an interesting grotto on the South Coyote/Swamp Wells Loop.

There are only two emotions that belong in the saddle; one is a sense of humor and the other is patience.

John Lyons

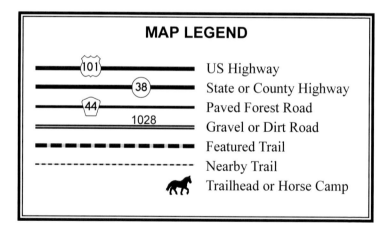

Three Creek
Three Creek Meadow Horse Camp
Deschutes National Forest

If you want to ride in a beautiful area with great views, pretty creeks, lush meadows, and plentiful wildflowers, then the Three Creek area is the place for you. Whether you want to camp or take a day ride, your base of operations will be Three Creek Meadow Horse Camp. From there, you can ride to Tam McArthur Rim, Three Creek Lake, Park Meadow, and Golden Lake and see spectacular scenery framed by the Three Sisters and Broken Top.

Note: The area's lakes, meadow, and horse camp take their names from nearby Three Creek. There aren't three creeks, there is only one creek, and its name is Three Creek. Got it?

Tam McArthur Rim towers above the Three Creek Meadow area.

Getting to the Three Creek Area

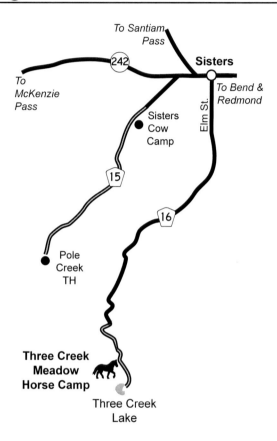

Three Creek Area Trails

Trail	Difficulty	Elevation	Round Trip
Golden Lake	Moderate	6,000-6,850	15.5 miles
Park Meadow	Moderate	6,000-6,850	12 miles
Tam McArthur Rim	Moderate	6,400-7,750	16.5 miles
Three Creek Lake Loop	Moderate	6,350-6,700	4 miles

Three Creek Meadow Horse Camp

Directions: In Sisters, turn south on Elm Street, which becomes Three Creek Road/Road 16. Drive 15 miles to the campground. Skip the first entrance, which leads to the people-only camping sites. Instead, drive 0.2 mile farther and turn right into the campground's equestrian entrance. The day-use parking area is in 0.1 mile and the horse camp is in 0.2 mile. For large trailers, the campground loop on the right is easier than the loop on the left.

Elevation: 6,350 feet

Campsites: 9 sites allow horses and have 4-horse log corrals. Most sites are back-in. While the parking is tight, most sites have room for 2 vehicles. All sites have fire pits and picnic tables.

Facilities: Vault toilet, manure bin, garbage cans, day-use parking area. Stock water but no potable water.

Permits: Camping fee. No fee for day-use parking.

Season: Summer through fall

Contact: Sisters Ranger District: 541-549-7700, www.fs.usda.gov/centraloregon, then click on "Recreation," "Horse Riding and Camping." Concessionaire: 541-338-7869, www.hoodoo.com, then click on "Campgrounds," "Horse Camping," "Three Creek Horse Camp."

All of the Three Creek Meadow sites have 4-horse corrals.

Golden Lake

Trailhead: Start at Three Creek Meadow Horse Camp

Length: 15.5 miles round trip

Elevation: 6,000 to 6,850 feet

Difficulty: Moderate -- creek crossings, navigation skill needed

Footing: Hoof protection recommended

Season: Summer through fall

Permits: Camping fee. No fee for day-use parking.

Facilities: Toilet, stock water, and manure bin at the horse camp. Parking for 4-5 trailers in the day-use area. Stock water is available on the trail.

Highlights: The spur trail to Golden Lake isn't an official trail so there is no sign marking the way, but with some navigation skills you can find the trail to this beautiful spot. Please keep your horse out of the lake, as it is used by backpackers for drinking water.

The Ride: Follow the directions to Park Meadow later in this chapter. Where the Park Meadow Trail #4075 intersects the Green Lakes

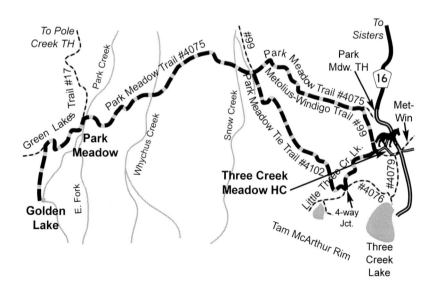

Trail #17 in Park Meadow, veer left (south) toward Green Lakes. The trail heads up along a ridge. After 0.8 mile you'll reach an unmarked trail that goes off to the left. Follow this trail, and in 0.9 mile you'll reach Golden Lake. The middle of the lake is blue, but the perimeter is a beautiful golden color. The lake is situated in a cirque, with Broken Top on one side and South Sister on the other. The best place to water your horse is downstream from the lake's outlet.

Riders head to Golden Lake, with Broken Top soaring above them.

Everybody had their cameras out on this ride. That's South Sister in the background.

Park Meadow

Trailhead: Start at Three Creek Meadow Horse Camp

Length: 12 miles round trip

Elevation: 6,000 to 6,850 feet

Difficulty: Moderate -- creek crossings

Footing: Hoof protection recommended

Season: Summer through fall

Permits: Camping fee. No fee for day-use parking.

Facilities: Toilet, stock water, and manure bin at the horse camp. Parking for 4-5 trailers in the day-use area. Stock water is available on the trail.

Highlights: Park Meadow is a lush green meadow nestled on the north side of Broken Top and South Sister. This trail travels through dense forest, along streams, and across meadows. Wildflowers abound, and the mountain views are splendid. Several creek crossings provide opportunities to water your horses. If you want to extend the ride you can continue on to Green Lakes (see below) or to Golden Lake.

The Ride: There are two ways to reach the Park Meadow Trail from Three Creek Meadow Campground. We suggest this semi-loop route:

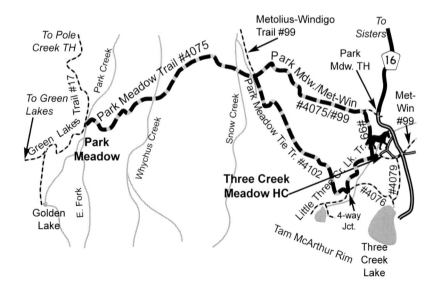

Veronica rides Harmony across Park Meadow,
with South Sister in the background.

Pick up the trail between campsites 12 and 13. In 100 yards, veer right on the Metolius-Windigo Trail #99, which is marked with yellow diamonds and wooden signs with horseshoes on them. In 0.7 mile, the Met-Win Trail veers left onto the Park Meadow Trail #4075. For the next 1.8 miles, the two trails are combined, then the Met-Win splits off to the right. Stay left on the Park Meadow Trail and continue 3 miles to reach Park Meadow. To return, ride the Park Meadow Trail for 3 miles, then at the junction where the Met-Win Trail goes to the left, turn right on the Park Meadow Tie Trail #4102. As the trail gains elevation, be sure to look behind you at the mountain views. Ride 2.4 miles, and when you reach the 4-way junction, turn left on the Little Three Creek Lake Trail to return to the horse camp.

Green Lakes Extension: If you aren't ready to head home after enjoying Park Meadow, you can continue another 3 miles (one way) on the Green Lakes Trail #17 to the spectacular Green Lakes on the southern side of Broken Top and South Sister. The elevation gain is about 900 feet from Park Meadow to the pass, and then the trail descends 600 feet to the lakes. The trail passes between Broken Top and South Sister, which loom so close you'll feel like you could reach out and touch them.

Tam McArthur Rim

Trailhead: Start at Three Creek Meadow Horse Camp
Length: 16.5 miles round trip
Elevation: 6,400 to 7,750 feet
Difficulty: Moderate
Footing: Hoof protection recommended
Season: Summer through fall
Permits: Camping fee. No fee for day-use parking.
Facilities: Toilet, stock water, and manure bin at the horse camp. Parking for 4-5 trailers in the day-use area. Stock water is available on the trail in season.

Highlights: Horseback riders and hikers have historically shared a short, steep, rocky, and crowded trail to Tam McArthur Rim. A couple of years ago the Forest Service created a new trail for horses, a route that is easier and safer although it's quite a bit longer than the

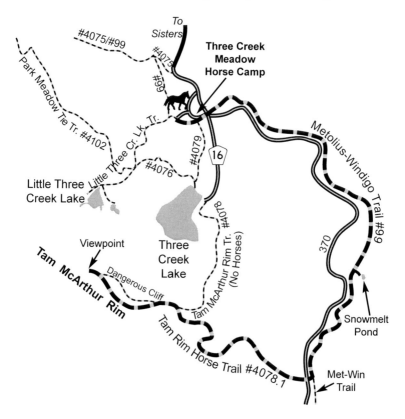

Whitney rides Dixie along the rim trail, taking in the great view.

hiker trail. The views from the rim are breathtaking. You can see the lakes 1,000 feet below, plus Broken Top, the Three Sisters, Mt. Washington, Three Fingered Jack, Mt. Jefferson, and Mt. Hood. Stunning!

The Ride: Pick up the trail between campsites 12 and 13 and ride about 200 feet. Just before the trail sign at the edge of the meadow, turn left on the Metolius-Windigo Trail #99. In 0.3 mile the trail passes the day-use parking area and runs for about 0.1 mile down the road that is the equestrian entrance into the campground. Ride across Road 16 and continue on the Met-Win Trail for 3.2 miles. You'll see a rock cairn on the left side of the trail. Turn left here and ride down the hill and through the trees to a small seasonal pond (we dubbed it "Snowmelt Pond"), the only possible source of stock water along the trail. After watering your horse, return to the Met-Win Trail and ride 1.4 miles farther to the junction with the Tam Rim Horse Trail #4078.1. Turn right on the horse trail, which crosses Road 370 and then follows an old and very eroded forest road for 2.1 miles. Where the tie trail intersects with the Tam Rim hiker trail (#4078), turn left and ride 1.1 miles to the summit. Near the top, the trail splits in several places, allowing access to the edge of the rim and the 1,000-foot sheer drop to the lakes below. We suggest tying your horses and walking to the rim to enjoy the panorama.

Three Creek Lake Loop

Trailhead: Start at Three Creek Meadow Horse Camp
Length: 4 miles round trip
Elevation: 6,350 to 6,700 feet
Difficulty: Moderate
Footing: Hoof protection recommended
Season: Summer through fall
Permits: Camping fee. No fee for day-use parking.
Facilities: Toilet, stock water, and manure bin at the horse camp. Parking for 4-5 trailers in the day-use area. Stock water is available on the trail.

Highlights: This ride features creeks, wildflowers, meadows, lakes, and forest. The terrain is quite varied, and the footing is good except for a couple of rocky spots. You'll pass both Three Creek Lake and Little Three Creek Lake nestled at the base of Tam McArthur Rim.

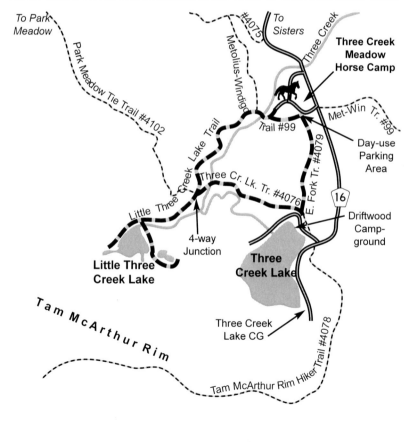

Wildflowers grow in abundance along the creeks, and several stream crossings provide opportunities to water the horses.

The Ride: Pick up the trail between campsites 12 and 13 and ride about 200 feet. Just before the trail sign at the edge of the meadow, turn left on the Metolius-Windigo Trail. In 0.2 mile you'll reach the day-use parking area at the other end of the campground. Veer right on the East Fork Trail #4079. Ride it for 0.6 mile and it will T-bone the Three Creek Lake Trail #4076 near Driftwood Campground. Horses are not allowed in the lake or on the beach of Three Creek Lake, so enjoy the view of the lake and Tam McArthur Rim from the trail, then turn right toward Little Three Creek Lake. In 0.9 mile you'll come to a 4-way junction. Turn left toward Little Three Creek Lake, and in 0.5 mile you'll reach it. The trail to the right along Little Three Creek Lake continues 0.2 mile before ending in a rocky area. The trail to the left goes over to another small lake and ends on the far side of it. To return to Three Creek Meadow, retrace your steps to the 4-way junction, and this time go straight on the Little Three Creek Lake Trail. In 0.8 mile you'll be back at the horse camp.

Jane gazes at Tam McArthur Rim across Little Three Creek Lake.

Grooming: the process by which the dirt on the horse is transferred to the groom.

Anonymous

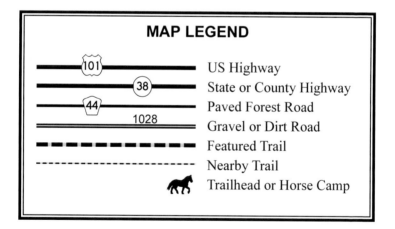

Trout Creek Butte
Whispering Pine Horse Camp

Deschutes National Forest

It's possible that you've never heard of Trout Creek Butte, but if you live in or you've traveled to Central Oregon, you've almost certainly seen it. When you're in the town of Sisters and you look up toward the Three Sisters, that low butte between you and the mountains is Trout Creek Butte. Whispering Pine Horse Camp, situated at the base of the butte, provides very nice accommodations for overnighters and is a good starting point for day riders as well. There aren't any "official" trails that lead out of the horse camp, but a network of forest roads can take you to the official forest service trails and on to fabulous destinations like Scott Pass, the Matthieu Lakes, and Trout Creek Butte. You can even ride to Sisters Cow Camp from here.

Pat and Ellen ride Secret and Tucker
on a forest road near Whispering Pine Horse Camp.

Getting to Trout Creek Butte Area

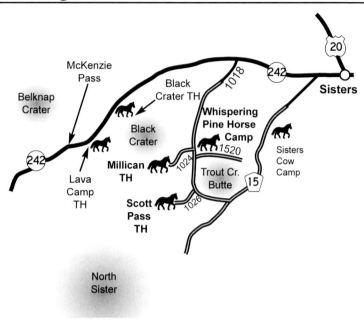

*Pat relaxes in her hammock at Whispering Pine
with dogs Nina and Taz; her horse Secret looks on.*

Whispering Pine Horse Camp

Directions: From Sisters, take Hwy. 242 (McKenzie Hwy.) west for 6 miles, turn left on Road 1018, drive 4 miles and turn left on Road 1520. The campground is on the left in 0.1 mile. All road junctions are well signed.

Elevation: 4,400 feet

Campsites: 9 sites, each with a 4-horse log corral. All sites have room for 2 vehicles. One site has pull-through parking and the rest are back-in. All sites have fire pits and picnic tables.

Facilities: Vault toilet, manure bin, garbage cans. No drinking water, but stock water is available from Trout Creek, which runs along the west side of the horse camp. There is no day-use parking at Whispering Pine, but day riders can drive through the campground to turn around and then park on the side of Road 1520.

Permits: Camping fee

Season: Summer through fall

Contact: Sisters Ranger District: 541-549-7700, www.fs.usda.gov/centraloregon, then click on "Recreation," "Horse Riding and Camping." Concessionaire: 541-338-7869, www.hoodoo.com, then click on "Campgrounds," "Horse Camping," "Whispering Pine."

Trout Creek Butte Area Trails

Trail	Difficulty	Elevation	Round Trip
Scott Pass/Matthieu Lks.	Moderate	4,400-6,100	16 miles
Sisters Cow Camp	Moderate	3,400-4,500	11 miles
Trout Creek Butte	Easy	4,400-5,550	10 miles
Trout Creek Loop	Moderate	4,400-5,300	9 miles

Scott Pass/Matthieu Lakes

Trailhead: Start at Whispering Pine Horse Camp

Length: 16 miles round trip

Elevation: 4,400 to 6,100 feet

Difficulty: Moderate

Footing: Hoof protection recommended

Season: Summer through fall

Permits: Camping fee for the horse camp. No fee to park beside Road 1520.

Facilities: Toilet and manure bin at the horse camp, stock water in the nearby creek. Stock water is available on the trail.

Highlights: This ride goes through dense forest, along a huge lava flow, over Scott Pass, and past the picturesque Matthieu Lakes. Scott Pass offers expansive views of lava flows and cinder cones. Many lodgepoles in the area have been killed by pine beetles, but the forest is regenerating.

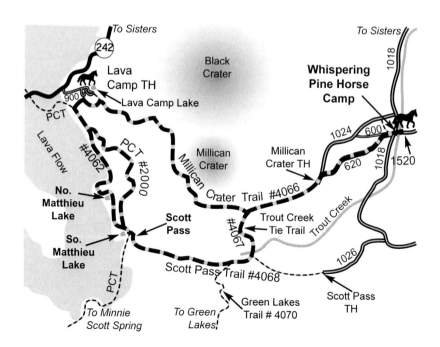

The Ride: From Whispering Pine Horse Camp, ride west on Road 1520, cross Road 1018, and pick up the single-track trail that leads up the hill. At the top of the hill take Road 600, the dirt road straight ahead of you, and in 0.2 mile turn left on Road 620. Follow it 1.4 miles, then veer left on red-cinder Road 1024 and ride a short distance to reach the Millican Crater trailhead. Continue on the Millican Crater Trail #4066 for 1.1 mile and turn left on the Trout Creek Tie Trail #4067 toward Scott Pass. In 1.0 mile turn right on the Scott Pass Trail #4068, toward Green Lakes and the PCT. After 0.4 mile, the Green Lakes Trail #4070 goes off to the left. Stay right and continue 1.8 miles to Scott Pass, with its impressive views. After a short distance the trail intersects with the Pacific Crest Trail #2000. Turn right on the PCT and continue to South Matthieu Lake, which offers a good view of North Sister. From here you can either stay on the PCT or detour left on Trail #4062 to North Matthieu Lake. Since the detour adds no distance and runs along an interesting lava flow, we recommend taking it. The trail rejoins the PCT in 2 miles. In another 0.7 mile turn right on the Millican Crater Trail #4066 and follow it 4.6 miles to the Millican Crater trailhead. From here, retrace the first leg of your route to return to Whispering Pine.

Lydia and Shadow take a breather on Scott Pass. An immense lava flow dotted with patches of snow is behind them.

Sisters Cow Camp

Trailhead: Start at Whispering Pine Horse Camp

Length: 11 miles round trip

Elevation: 3,400 to 4,500 feet

Difficulty: Moderate -- easy riding, but navigation skills, a Sisters Ranger District map, and a GPS will come in handy

Footing: Hoof protection recommended

Season: Summer through fall

Permits: Camping fee for the horse camp. No fee to park beside Road 1520.

Facilities: Toilet and manure bin at the horse camp, stock water in the nearby creek. Stock water is also available in summer at Sisters Cow Camp.

Highlights: This is a fun road ride that takes you through an area burned by the Black Crater fire in 2006, so you'll have great views of the Cascades, Black Butte, and Sisters. Most of the route is on dirt roads in beautiful ponderosa forest. (Please note that while we show road numbers in the text and on the map, some of the roads don't have road number signs on them.)

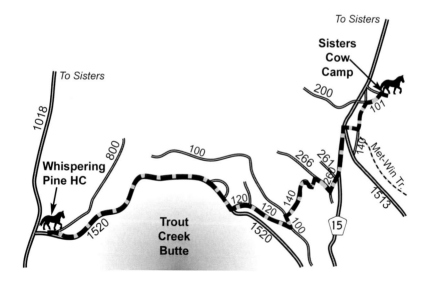

The Ride: From Whispering Pine Horse Camp, ride east on red cinder Road 1520 for 2.5 miles. This section of road goes around the north flank of Trout Creek Butte and through an area burned by the Black Crater fire, so it offers good views. After leaving the burned area, turn left on the 3rd dirt road you come to. There is a rock cairn beside this road, Road 120, but it isn't signed. From here on, it's a steady downhill grade until you get close to Cow Camp. Follow Road 120 for 0.2 mile, and at the next junction veer right, which will keep you on Road 120. In another 0.7 mile, turn left on Road 100, which is signed. In 0.2 mile, veer right on Road 140. Continue downhill for 0.7 mile, then turn right on Road 266. It will lead you to Road 260 in 0.3 mile. Turn left on Road 260, and in 0.2 mile you'll reach gray gravel Road 15. Turn left and ride beside Road 15 for 0.5 mile. At the junction of Roads 15 and 1513 (another gray gravel road), turn right and ride cross-country through the trees for 0.1 mile, then turn left when you come to a dirt road. (Be sure to mark this spot so you can find it again for your return trip.) Turn left here and follow the yellow diamonds of the Metolius-Windigo Trail for 0.5 mile along Roads 140 and 101 to reach Sisters Cow Camp.

Donna on Taffy and Pat on Tucker,
enjoying the vistas along Road 1520.

Trout Creek Butte

Trailhead:	Start at Whispering Pine Horse Camp
Length:	10 miles round trip
Elevation:	4,400 to 5,550 feet
Difficulty:	Easy
Footing:	Hoof protection suggested
Season:	Summer through fall
Permits:	Camping fee for the horse camp. No fee to park beside Road 1520.
Facilities:	Toilet and manure bin at the horse camp, stock water in the nearby creek. No stock water on the trail.

Highlights: There are a couple of user-created trails that climb steeply to the summit of Trout Creek Butte, but this road ride is easier, safer, and much more scenic. About 2 miles into the ride the trail goes through an old clear cut, providing a great view of North Sister, Black

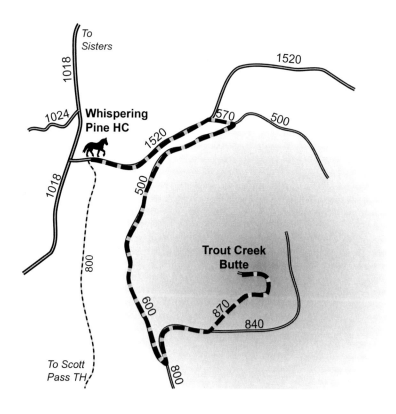

Susan, Sharon, Darcy, and Pat ride down from the summit of Trout Creek Butte. North Sister is in the background.

A group of Oregon Equestrian Trails riders pose for a group photo at the top of Trout Creek Butte.

Crater, Three Fingered Jack, and Mt. Jefferson. As you round Trout Creek Butte, Middle and South Sister, Broken Top, Tam McArthur Rim, and Whychus Creek Falls will come into view. The summit is tree covered so you won't have a view from the top, but the vistas you'll see on the way up more than make up for that.

The Ride: Ride east on Road 1520, the road that runs past the horse camp. After 1 mile, turn right on Road 570. In 0.2 mile, turn right on the overgrown Road 500, which soon becomes Road 600. After 2.3 miles, turn left on red-cinder Road 800 and follow it for 0.5 mile, then turn left on Road 870 and continue 1 mile to arrive at the summit.

Trout Creek Loop

Trailhead: Start at Whispering Pine Horse Camp

Length: 9 miles round trip

Elevation: 4,400 to 5,300 feet

Difficulty: Moderate

Footing: Hoof protection recommended

Season: Summer through fall

Permits: Camping fee for the horse camp. No fee to park beside Road 1520.

Facilities: Toilet and manure bin at the horse camp, stock water in the nearby creek. Stock water is available on the trail.

Highlights: This is a relatively easy ride through mostly-lodgepole forest. The first and last legs of the loop are on old forest roads that take you to/from the Scott Pass and Millican Crater trailheads. From there you can pick up the official forest service trails that make up the

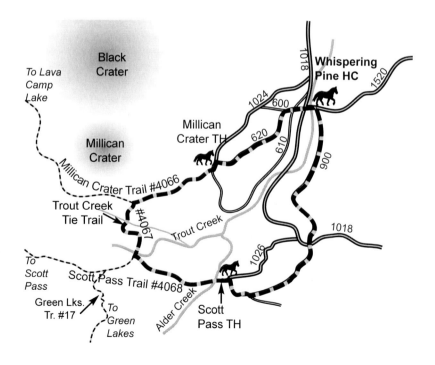

middle segment of this loop. The first leg of the trail offers tree-filtered views of North Sister and Black Crater.

The Ride: The trail begins where Road 900 intersects with Road 1520, just past the entrance to the horse camp. Or you can pick up the connector trail that runs behind the campground's manure bin. Either way, the first 3 miles of the loop run along the old Road 900. After 2.1 miles you'll cross gravel Road 1018, and a mile after that Road 900 runs into another dirt road. Turn right, and in 0.6 mile it will take you to red-cinder Road 1026. Turn left and in 0.1 mile you'll arrive at the Scott Pass trailhead. Fill out a wilderness permit and pick up the Scott Pass Trail #4068. In 1.2 miles you'll reach the junction with the Trout Creek Tie Trail #4067. Turn right toward Lava Camp Lake and immediately cross Trout Creek. About 0.4 mile after that you'll cross another arm of Trout Creek, and 0.5 mile later you'll reach the Millican Crater Trail #4066. Turn right and in 1.1 mile you'll arrive at the Millican Crater trailhead. Turn left on red cinder Road 1024 and ride 0.2 mile, then turn right on an old forest road, Road 620, which is blocked with large rocks to keep motorized vehicles out. Follow it 1.2 miles, and when it intersects with dirt Road 600, go to the right. In 0.2 mile you'll cross dirt Road 610, go straight ahead, and ride down a steep hill to Road 1018. Cross it and ride along Road 1520 for 0.2 mile to return to the horse camp.

*Debbie rides Cowboy across Alder Creek
on the Scott Pass Trail segment of the Trout Creek Loop.*

No one can teach riding so well as a horse

C. S. Lewis

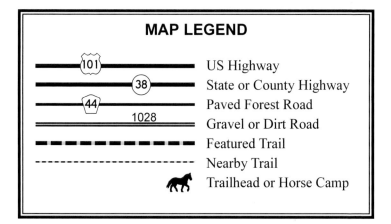

Western Ochocos
Dry Creek Horse Camp

Ochoco National Forest

Located just east of Prineville, the western Ochocos are lower in elevation, farther east, and less rugged than the Cascades. You can ride here in late spring, long before the high Cascades are accessible. The trails in this area wind through beautiful ponderosa forest to fascinating geologic formations or to mountaintops with breathtaking vistas. Dry Creek Horse Camp, the only horse camp in the area, is a nice, quiet spot at the edge of the Mill Creek Wilderness. From the horse camp you can explore several trails and the surrounding forest roads. And since the horse camp is only 2.5 miles from a paved road, it's a breeze to trailer from the horse camp to your favorite rides nearby.

One of many panoramic views from the Lookout Mountain Trail.

Getting to Western Ochocos

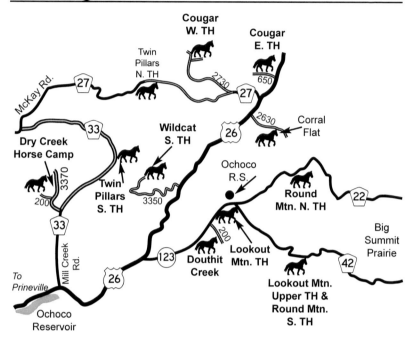

Western Ochoco Trails

Trail	Difficulty	Elevation	Round Trip
Brennan Palisades	Moderate	3,350-3,900	5-7 miles
Cougar Creek	Challenging	3,400-4,900	7-16 miles
Douthit Creek	Moderate	3,900-5,600	Varies
Giddy Up Go Loop	Challenging	3,900-5,100	11 miles
Independent Mine Loop	Moderate	5,400-7,000	7-10 miles
Lookout Mountain	Challenging	4,000-7,000	16 miles
Round Mountain North	Challenging	5,400-6,800	9 miles
Round Mountain South	Moderate	5,400-6,800	10 miles
Twin Pillars	Moderate	3,800-5,400	12.5-17 miles
Wildcat	Challenging	5,400-5,700	17 miles

Dry Creek Horse Camp

Directions: From Prineville, take Hwy. 26 east about 8 miles, and just past the 28-mile marker, turn left on Mill Creek Road (Forest Road 33). Continue for 5 miles, then turn left on Road 3370 at the Forest Service kiosk, just before the pavement ends. Drive 2.5 miles and veer left on Road 200 (unsigned) to reach the camp.

Elevation: 3,900 feet

Campsites: Six sites. Two have 4-horse corrals and 4 have 2-horse corrals. All sites are back-in and several have room for 2 vehicles. Some parking areas are not very level.

Facilities: Vault toilet, manure pit. All sites have fire pits and picnic tables. Stock water is available from nearby Dry Creek, but there is no drinking water.

Permits: None

Season: Summer through fall

Contact: Ochoco National Forest: 541-416-6500, www.fs.usda.gov/centraloregon, then click on "Recreation," "Horse Riding and Camping"

Dry Creek Horse Camp

Brennan Palisades

Trailhead: Start at Dry Creek Horse Camp

Length: 5 miles round trip to Brennan Palisades, or 7 miles round trip to the old homestead

Elevation: 3,350 to 3,900 feet

Difficulty: Moderate -- trail is easy except for small creek crossings and the downed logs you may encounter on this unofficial trail

Footing: Hoof protection recommended

Season: Late spring through fall

Permits: None

Facilities: Parking for 2-3 rigs at the horse camp.   Stock water is available on the trail.

Highlights: This trail runs through a beautiful riparian area beside Dry Creek, taking you to the impressive and quite unexpected Bren-

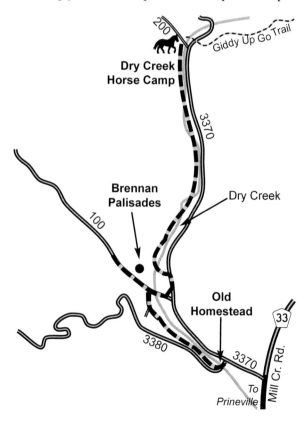

nan Palisades. If you like you can continue on to the site of an abandoned homestead.

The Ride: Pick up the trail on the right just outside the entrance to Dry Creek Horse Camp. Follow it for 1.6 miles until you come to a fence line. Veer left and follow the fence around to Road 3370, then continue along Road 3370 for 0.1 mile, following the fence to Road 100. Turn right on Road 100 and continue about 0.5 mile to Brennan Palisades, a surprising geologic formation complete with reddish cliffs, spires, and columns. You can almost see faces and primitive figures in the rocks. The palisades extend for about 0.2 mile along Road 100. To continue on to the old homestead, retrace your steps along Road 100 for 0.4 mile and turn right on an unnumbered forest road. When the road forks after a short distance, stay to the left and the road will soon become a single-track trail that will take you to Road 3380. You'll see an old barn on your left. If you'd like an up-close look at what remains of the old homestead, tie your horses and walk across the cattle guard and the bridge. Retrace your steps to return to the horse camp.

This is but a small segment of the Brennan Palisades.

Cougar Creek

Trailhead: Start at the Cougar East or Cougar West trailheads, or at the quarry just off Road 2730

Length: 16 miles round trip between the trailheads, or 9 miles round trip from the quarry to the west trailhead, or 7 miles round trip from the quarry to the east trailhead

Elevation: 3,400 to 4,900 feet from the quarry to the west trailhead, or 4,200 to 4,900 from the quarry to the east trailhead

Difficulty: Challenging, with some traverses on steep inclines

Footing: Hoof protection recommended

Season: Late spring through fall

Permits: None

Facilities: Parking for 2-3 trailers at the east trailhead, plenty of parking at the west trailhead and the quarry. Stock water is available on the trail.

Highlights: You can access this trail from trailheads on the east or west ends, or from the quarry on the flank of Cougar Butte. The trail west of the quarry follows a historic pack trail that was used from 1915 to 1922. It is more rugged and steep than the trail east of the quarry. It is also traverses some very rocky and exposed slopes, and has more

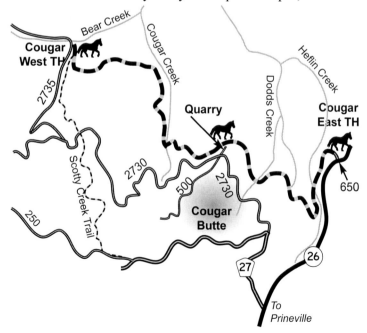

Connie rides Diamond across a steep ridge on the western part of the Cougar Creek Trail.

elevation gain and loss. Both segments cross pretty creeks and offer good vistas to the north. The trail is well marked with yellow or white diamonds and rock cairns.

Finding the Cougar Trailheads: Cougar East Trailhead: Take Hwy. 26 east from Prineville for 27 miles (2 miles past the Ochoco Divide). At the 52-mile marker, turn left on Road 650 and continue 0.1 mile to the trailhead. Turn around in the grassy area beside Road 650. Cougar West Trailhead: Take Hwy. 26 east from Prineville for 25 miles and turn left on Road 27, which is 0.4 mile past the Bandit Springs rest stop. Go 1.3 miles and turn right on Road 2730. Continue 6.5 miles, turn right on Road 2735, and drive 1.5 miles to the trailhead. Quarry: Follow the directions toward the Cougar West trailhead above, but after driving 1.7 miles on Road 2730, turn right into the quarry.

The Ride: From the east trailhead, the first mile is on an old dirt road that heads downhill almost parallel to the highway. There is a confusing junction about 1.5 miles from the trailhead where a sign indicates that the trail you came on and the trail straight ahead are the Cougar Creek Trail. It looks like you should continue straight, but instead turn right at the sign and continue following the trail marked with yellow diamonds. The trail crosses a meadow, climbs a ridge to the quarry, and then heads down to the west trailhead along a historic pack trail. This section of the trail drops down to Cougar Creek, traverses the steep ridge above Cougar Creek, then crosses very rocky, exposed slopes and descends steeply to the west trailhead.

Douthit Creek

Trailhead: Start at the Douthit Creek primitive camp
Length: Multiple rides are possible
Elevation: 3,900 to 5,600 feet
Difficulty: Moderate -- easy riding, but navigation skills, a Prineville Ranger District map, and a GPS may come in handy
Footing: Hoof protection recommended
Season: Late spring through fall
Permits: None
Facilities: Parking for many rigs. Stock water is available on the trail.

Highlights: There isn't an official trailhead at Douthit Creek, but you'll find plenty of places to ride near this pleasant primitive camping spot. Enjoy the area's lightly-traveled dirt roads, follow a trail, or strike off cross-country. The terrain around Douthit Creek is beautiful and varied. The area is home to several herds of wild horses, so keep an eye out and you may spot some.

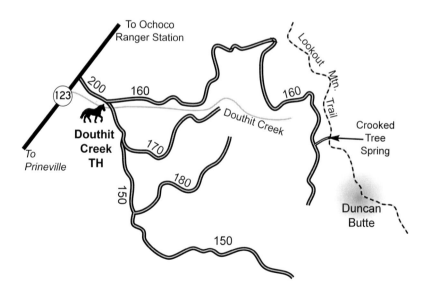

Finding the Douthit Creek Trailhead: Take Hwy. 26 east from Prineville for 15 miles, and between the 34- and 35-mile markers turn right on Hwy. 123 toward the Ochoco Ranger Station. Drive 6 miles and turn right on Road 200. After 0.4 mile, Road 160 splits off to the left and Road 200 becomes Road 150. Continue right on Road 150 for 0.1 mile to reach the camping/parking area.

The Ride: From the Douthit Creek primitive camping area you can do several road rides, link up with the trail to the summit of Lookout Mountain, follow other unofficial trails in the area, or head off on your own through the forests and meadows that blanket the gentle hillsides. Several bands of wild horses live here. If you want to see them, watch for large manure piles. (The horses use them to mark their territory.) When you find a pile with fresh manure on top, ride the surrounding forest and meadows looking for hoofprints. Chances are good some wild horses will be nearby. If you camp at Douthit Creek, there is even a chance that wild horses will come right into camp to check you out.

A bachelor band of wild horses trots
through a sunny meadow near Douthit Creek.

Giddy Up Go Loop

Trailhead: Start at Dry Creek Horse Camp
Length: 11 miles round trip
Elevation: 3,900 to 5,100 feet
Difficulty: Challenging -- trail overgrown and not maintained, rocky, with significant elevation gain. Navigation skills, a Prineville Ranger District map, and a GPS are needed.
Footing: Hoof protection recommended
Season: Late spring through fall
Permits: None
Facilities: Toilet, manure bin, and stock water at the horse camp. Stock water is available on the trail.

Highlights: How well-developed is your sense of adventure? If you're pretty high up on the I-Like-A-Challenge scale, then this trail is for you. If this trail were well maintained (or even if only the route signs were maintained) it would be a fine ride. It passes a couple of

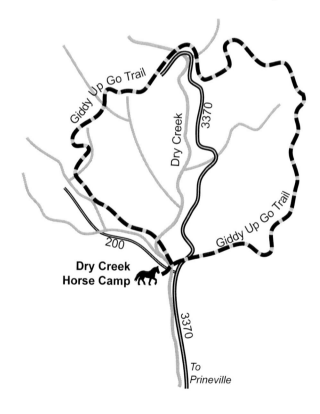

derelict cabins, goes through beautiful forest and meadows, and runs over ridges offering views of the Ochocos, including Lookout Mountain and Steins Pillar. However, the trail apparently hasn't been maintained for years. It is quite overgrown and at times a real challenge to follow, despite the occasional yellow wooden diamonds marking the trail. We recommend riding it with a GPS in hand, so you can make your way back to the horse camp via a forest road if you happen to miss one of the turns.

The Ride: The trail departs across Road 200 from the horse camp. It crosses Dry Creek and climbs fairly consistently on a single-track trail for the first 3.5 miles, gaining about 1,200 feet. In this section the trail has been partially obliterated by a logging operation, so at times you'll be navigating from one yellow diamond to the next. The trail then heads gradually downward, at times following a single-track trail and at other times following forest roads. Although we had a GPS and a map, at least 20% of the time we could not follow the official trail and ended up bushwhacking. With a little help from our GPS we were able to navigate through the obscured sections and make it back safe and sound to the horse camp. Be sure to allow extra time for circling around in the woods, searching for the next yellow diamond trail marker.

Linda and Beamer enjoy the view along the Giddy Up Go Trail.

Independent Mine Loop

Trailhead: Start at Lookout Mountain Upper Trailhead
Length: 7 to 10 miles round trip
Elevation: 5,400 to 7,000 feet
Difficulty: Moderate
Footing: Hoof protection recommended
Season: Summer through fall
Permits: None
Facilities: Parking for several trailers. Stock water is available on the trail.

Highlights: Three trails lead to the summit of Lookout Mountain, creating several options for making a loop. The trails run through dense forest at lower elevations and flower-filled mountain meadows near the top. On a clear day the views from the mountaintop are breath-

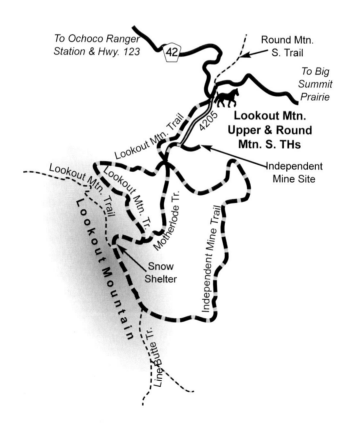

taking. A short detour to the historic Independent Mine site is worthwhile.

Finding Lookout Mountain Upper Trailhead: Take Hwy. 26 east from Prineville for 15 miles, and between the 34- and 35-mile markers turn right on Hwy. 123 toward the Ochoco Ranger Station. Drive 8.5 miles, turn right on Road 42, continue 6.5 miles, and turn right to enter the trailer parking area just off the highway.

The Ride: The Lookout Mountain Trail departs near the kiosk at the entrance to the trailer parking area. It parallels Road 4205, and after a mile it leads to a car parking area and the Motherlode Mine/Independent Mine trailhead. Then it continues westward to the top of Lookout Mountain. From the car parking area to the summit, the Lookout Mountain Trail is 3 miles, the Motherlode Mine Trail is 1.5 miles, and the Independent Mine Trail is 4 miles. You'll see evidence of mining activity along all three trails. When you return from your ride, if you'd like a close-up view of the abandoned buildings at the main Independent Mine site, don't take the trail back to the trailhead. Instead, ride down Road 4205 and turn east at the sign about 1/3 of the way between the car parking and trailer parking areas.

You can see evidence of mining activity, including mine buildings and an entrance to an old mine shaft, along the trail.

Lookout Mountain

Trailhead: Start at the Lookout Mountain trailhead

Length: 16 miles round trip

Elevation: 4,000 to 7,000 feet

Difficulty: Challenging -- trail is long and very rocky in places, with big elevation gain and one steep drop-off beside the trail

Footing: Hoof protection recommended

Season: Summer through fall

Permits: None

Facilities: Parking for 2-3 trailers. Stock water is available on the trail.

Highlights: On a clear day, the summit of Lookout Mountain offers panoramic views of the Cascades, Big Summit Prairie, and the surrounding Ochocos. Wildflowers bloom in profusion in late spring and early summer, and wild horses inhabit the surrounding area.

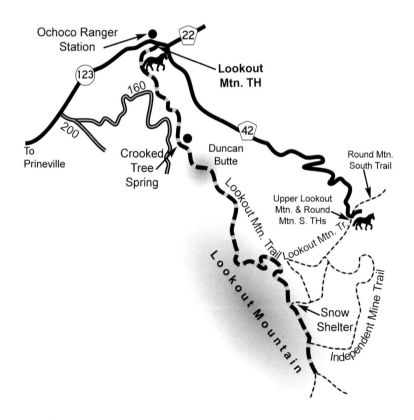

Lydia on Shadow and Connie on Moose,
enjoying the views from the summit of Lookout Mountain.

Finding the Lookout Mountain Trailhead: Take Hwy. 26 east from Prineville for 15 miles, and between the 34- and 35-mile markers turn right on Hwy. 123 toward Walton Lake. Drive 8.3 miles. Just past the Ochoco Ranger Station, park on the right shoulder of the road, next to the trailhead sign.

The Ride: The trail climbs steeply for the first mile, then settles into a more moderate but steady ascent to the broad, flat summit of Lookout Mountain. Most of the ride is through beautiful ponderosa forest. Crooked Tree Spring is 2.5 miles from the trailhead, just to the right of the trail. About 3 miles after the spring, the trail makes a series of switchbacks through hanging meadows loaded with wildflowers in season. Near the end of the switchback section you'll pass an interesting rock pile, and 0.5 mile later the trail comes up a ridge and makes a switchback at the edge of a steep drop-off. Fortunately, this breathtaking moment is over almost before it has begun. Very shortly you'll arrive at the tabletop summit and can enjoy the sweeping views. For a fun 13-mile variation on this ride, you can drop a trailer at the Lookout Mountain Upper trailhead (see the Independent Mine pages), drive another trailer the 6.5 miles back to the Lookout Mountain trailhead, then ride the Lookout Mountain Trail up and the Independent Mine trail down to retrieve the dropped trailer.

Round Mountain North

Trailhead: Start at the Round Mountain North trailhead
Length: 9 miles round trip
Elevation: 5,400 to 6,800 feet
Difficulty: Challenging -- rocky and steep in some places
Footing: Hoof protection recommended
Season: Summer through fall
Permits: None
Facilities: Parking for 5-6 trailers. Stock water is available on the trail.

Highlights: The trail leads through open forest, grassy meadows, and a flower-filled mountain meadow. The summit of Round Mountain is the highest point around, and you can see for miles in every direction.

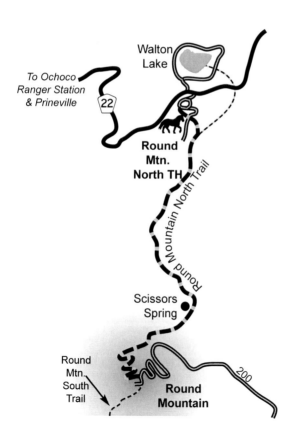

Connie rides Moose through a flower-filled meadow near the summit of Round Mountain.

Finding the Round Mountain North Trailhead: Take Hwy. 26 east from Prineville for 15 miles, and between the 34- and 35-mile markers turn right on Hwy. 123 toward Walton Lake. Continue 8.5 miles. Shortly after passing the Ochoco Ranger Station, turn left on Road 22. Go 6.7 miles, and just past the road to Walton Lake campground turn right at the sign to the Round Mountain trailhead. Drive to the loop trailhead in 0.2 mile. Park on the side of the loop.

The Ride: The first part of the trail goes through the forest and over a low, rocky ridge. After 2.5 miles you will reach a large meadow and Scissors Spring, where you can water your horses in the livestock troughs. Shortly after the spring you'll begin the switchbacks that traverse the forest and mountain meadows to reach the top of Round Mountain. The views from the mountaintop are vast, with Big Summit Prairie to the southeast, Lookout Mountain to the west, and rows of hills marching off in all directions. On a clear day you can see the Three Sisters and Mt. Jefferson. Note that downed logs can be an issue on this trail, so check with the forest service to be sure the trail has been logged out. If the trail hasn't been cleared, be prepared to step over and bushwhack around downed logs.

Round Mountain South

Trailhead: Start at the Round Mountain South trailhead
Length: 10 miles round trip
Elevation: 5,400 to 6,800 feet
Difficulty: Moderate -- rocky trail, and a few steep stretches
Footing: Hoof protection recommended
Season: Summer through fall
Permits: None
Facilities: Parking for 5-6 trailers. Stock water is available on the trail through early summer only.

Highlights: This trail to the summit of Round Mountain is slightly longer but not as steep as the North Round Mountain Trail. It has fewer mountain meadows to enjoy, but offers more shade. The views from the summit are impressive.

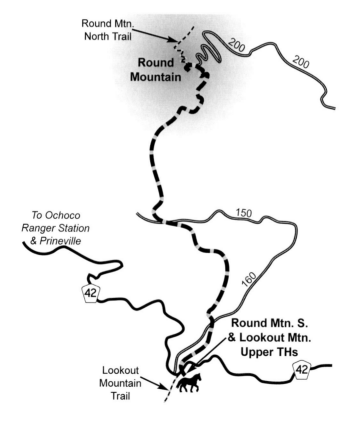

Finding the Round Mountain South Trailhead: Take Hwy. 26 east from Prineville for 15 miles and turn right on Hwy. 123 toward Walton Lake. In 8.5 miles, just after passing the Ochoco Ranger Station, veer right on Road 42. Drive 6.2 miles farther, then turn right into the trailhead for the Round Mountain South and Lookout Mountain Upper Trails.

The Ride: The trail departs from the north side of the parking area. In 0.3 mile it crosses Road 42, travels over a low ridge for the next 1.7 miles, then steadily climbs to the summit of Round Mountain in the last 3 miles. Most of the ride goes through ponderosa or hemlock and fir forest, so the route is fairly shady. However, the last 0.5 mile to the top runs through steep open meadows of corn lilies and other wildflowers. At various points on the ride up you'll enjoy views of Big Summit Prairie on the right and Lookout Mountain on the left. On a clear day you can see almost forever from the summit.

Mona and Roi take a breather at the summit of Round Mountain, with Lookout Mountain in the background.

Along the trail you'll have a good view of Big Summit Prairie.

Twin Pillars

Trailhead: Start at either the Twin Pillars South or Twin Pillars North trailhead

Length: From the south trailhead, it is 7.5 miles round trip to where you can first see the Twin Pillars, or 12.5 miles round trip to the base of the pillars, or 17 miles round trip for the entire trail

Elevation: 3,800 to 5,400 feet

Difficulty: Moderate

Footing: Hoof protection recommended

Season: Late spring through fall

Permits: None

Facilities: Parking for 3-4 rigs at each trailhead. Stock water is available on the trail.

Highlights: From the south trailhead, the first 3.5 miles of the trail run along the beautiful East Fork of Mill Creek. The creekside ripar-

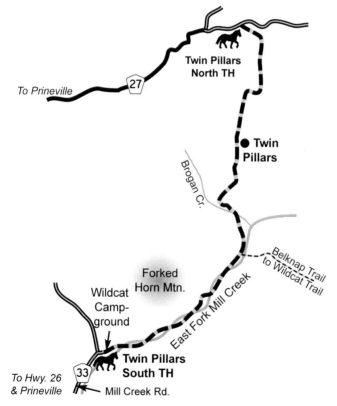

The Twin Pillars

ian vegetation contrasts sharply with the more arid ponderosa forest on the adjacent slopes. Then the trail leaves the creek and heads uphill into an area marked by hundreds of acres of dead trees from the Hash Rock Fire in 2000. The Twin Pillars rise impressively from the top of a ridge. These plugs are all that remain of an eroded volcano that was active some 44 million years ago. Be sure to call the Forest Service before you ride to make sure the trail has been logged out, since fallen trees in the burned area can make the trail impassible.

Finding the Twin Pillars Trailhead: Twin Pillars South Trailhead: Take Hwy. 26 east from Prineville about 8 miles, and just past the 28-mile marker turn left on Mill Creek Road (Road 33). Drive 9.5 miles to Wildcat Campground. The trailhead parking is to the right just before you enter the campground. Twin Pillars North Trailhead: From Prineville, go north on Main St., which turns into McKay Creek Rd. (Road 27). Follow it 14 miles to the trailhead.

The Ride: The trail departs from the north edge of the Twin Pillars South parking area and follows the East Fork of Mill Creek for about 3.5 miles, with frequent creek crossings. The trail then climbs steeply for 2.7 miles through badly burned ponderosa forest to the Twin Pillars. From there it continues 2.3 miles to end at Bingham Spring on Forest Road 27.

The Twin Pillars Trail near Mill Creek.

Wildcat

Trailhead: Start at the Wildcat South trailhead
Length: 17 miles round trip
Elevation: 5,400 to 5,700 feet
Difficulty: Challenging -- the trail traverses some steep hillsides
Footing: Hoof protection recommended
Season: Late spring through fall
Permits: None
Facilities: Parking for 2-3 trailers. Toilets and stock water at the trailhead at White Rock Campground. Stock water is only available on the trail at the far northern end.

Highlights: This trail runs along the east side of a ridge that runs between White Rock Campground and Whistler Spring, traversing several very steep hillsides in the second half of the ride. Along the way

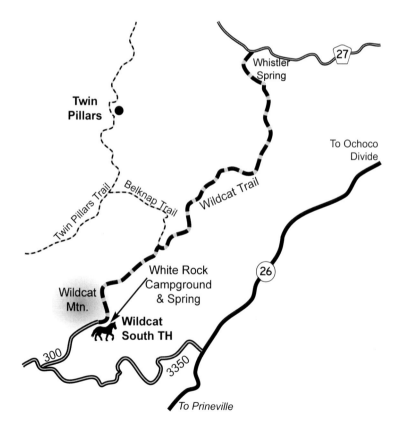

you'll have views of Round Mountain and Lookout Mountain to the east and Twin Pillars, Mt. Jefferson, and the Three Sisters to the west.

Finding the Wildcat South Trailhead: Take Hwy. 26 northeast from Prineville about 22 miles. Turn left on Road 3350 and continue 5.4 miles up a steep and winding gravel road. Turn right on Road 300 and drive 1.5 miles to White Rock Campground and the trailhead. Park near the spring at the rear of the campground.

The Ride: Most of the trail runs through beautiful ponderosa and fir forest, but some of it was badly burned in the Hash Rock Fire in 2000. While the fire killed a lot of trees, it also opened up some views you wouldn't have otherwise had. It's interesting to see how the forest is regenerating. After 2.4 miles, the Belknap Trail that connects with the Twin Pillars Trail goes off to the left. The northern half of the trail has several very steep traverses. The trail ends on Road 27 near Whistler Spring.

Linda and Beamer gait along the Wildcat Trail.

Happy trails to you, until we meet again.

Dale Evans Rogers